REVELATION'S RHAPSODY

ROBERT A. LOWERY

REVELATION'S RHAPSODY

Listening to the Lyrics of the Lamb

HOW TO READ THE BOOK OF REVELATION

COLLEGE PRESS PUBLISHING COMPANY · JOPLIN, MISSOURI

Printed and bound in the United States of America

Cover design by Mark A. Cole

Cover photo by Jamie Simkins

Library of Congress Cataloging-in-Publication Data

Lowery, Robert, 1948-

Revelation's rhapsody : listening to the lyrics of the lamb : how to read the book or Revelation / by Robert Lowery.
p. cm.

Includes bibliographical references.
ISBN 0-89900-946-8 (hardback)
1. Bible. N.T. Revelation--Criticism, interpretation, etc. I. Title.
BS2825.52.L69 2006
228 '.06--dc22 2006019350

Rhapsody . . .

A musical composition of irregular form having an improvisatory character . . .
A free style instrumental piece characterized by dramatic changes in mood . . .
A free fantasia—an instrumental composition in which a composer yields to his imagination in regard to form and organization of the composition . . .

Rhapsodic . . .

Ecstatic . . . Thrilled . . . Exhilarated . . . Enthusiastic . . .
Excited . . . Elated . . . Overjoyed . . . Ravished . . .
Overcome . . . Transported . . . In heaven . . .
In seventh heaven . . . On cloud nine . . . Walking on air . . .
In orbit . . . Intoxicated . . . Delirious . . . Beaming . . .
Bouncing with joy . . . Blissful . . .
Joyful

"Even on earth, who that sings or plays well on an instrument knows not the joy of waking music? Merely to listen often-times moves to tears, to light-heartedness, to longings, to feelings one would not or could not utter. What will it be in heaven to be singer, musician, listener, to be one voice in a harmony, yet as individually listened to, approved, commended. . . . Heaven is revealed to earth as the homeland of music."

— Christina Rossetti

Dedication

This book is written in memory of my mother, Adrene Lowery (1921–1992), who was the first to read Scripture to me. I pray that this work will honor her admonition to me that I should teach and write in such a way that everyone could understand God's Word better.

This book is written in honor of my family. My wife Marilyn has provided encouragement throughout the project. My ministry at home and abroad would be impossible without her faithful support. My daughter and son and their spouses, Joe and Rachel Mollet and Brian and Sarah Lowery, have prayed for me and encouraged me while I worked on the book. My prayer is that my two granddaughters, Carissa and Jocelyn Mollet, will someday follow Jesus the Lamb and learn to sing his lyrics.

All books by Christians should ultimately be dedicated to the glory of God. This one is no exception.

Phil. 1:3-7

I thank my God every time I remember you. In all my prayers for all of you, I always pray with joy because of your partnership in the gospel from the first day until now, being confident of this, that he who began a good work in you will carry it on to completion until the day of Christ Jesus.

It is right for me to feel this way about all of you, since I have you in my heart; for . . . all of you share in God's grace with me.

ACKNOWLEDGEMENTS

I want to acknowledge the rich contributions my brothers and sisters in Christ made in the writing of my book.

First, to the countless congregations around the United States and in Eastern Europe who have invited me to teach and preach the book of Revelation, thank you.

Second, to the numerous students of Lincoln Christian Seminary (Lincoln, Illinois) and the TCM International Institute (Heiligenkreuz, Austria) who have taken my class on the book of Revelation and have challenged me to think and drink deeply from John's writing, thank you.

Third, to two students who reviewed the initial outline and content of my book with me in June, 2005, at Haus Edelweiss in Heiligenkreuz, Austria—Ivan Ivanov of Bulgaria and Janos Lehotay-Kery of Hungary—thank you.

Fourth, to the fifteen students who read an early draft of the book and spent a week with me in October, 2005, discussing the content—Tom Byford, Mike Cahill, Sam Draper, Rod Godley, Ann Hastings, Dee Kinman, Matt Martin, Brent McCrory, Doug Phillips, Andrew Ramey, Greg Robbins, Paul Stroup, Bryce Wiley, Heath Williams, and Shane Wood—your candor and critiques made the book a better one.

Fifth, to students of the Word—Gene Appel, Craig Blomberg, Paul Boatman, Jim Boudouris, Ken Cooper, Tom Ewald, Dinelle Frankland, Tom and Stephenie Graham, Gary Hall, J.K. Jones, Ronnie Jones, Brian Lowery, David McFadden,

Jim and Debbie Poer, Jeff Snell, Bob Szoke, Tom Tanner, Tony Twist, and Marilyn Lowery—individuals who took time out of very busy schedules to read and critique one or more drafts, thank you. In addition to these individuals, Gerry and Joan Baldwin read the very first draft and made helpful editorial and formatting suggestions.

Three individuals need to be mentioned in a special way. Ann Hastings read several of the drafts and her expertise in editing proved invaluable. She pulled no punches; the red ink flowed from her pen. Shane Wood has been my research assistant par excellence and provided many helpful insights from the beginning to the end of the project. He went the second mile. Carmen Trenton graciously gave hundreds of hours reading, discussing, and editing the work. She balanced grace and truth as she pressed me time and again for greater clarity, and every paragraph benefited from her scrutiny.

To Richard and Judith Rowe who provided me a retreat center by allowing me to stay at their cabin on Lake Michigan, thank you. It was in that peaceful setting that the first draft of the book was written in six days, August 28–September 2, 2005.

To my son, Brian, one of the most gifted thinkers, preachers, and teachers I have ever had the privilege to teach, thank you. It was on a trip to Madison, Wisconsin, to see a Bob Dylan concert in the Fall of 1999 that you planted the seed for this book. You respectfully rebuked me for not doing more writing on Revelation and dismantled my excuses one by one. That conversation set the project in motion.

To the administration of Lincoln Christian Seminary, thank you for the sabbatical time so that I could research, reflect, and write. Especially supportive were President Keith Ray, Vice President of Academics Tom Tanner, Seminary Associate Dean, Paul Boatman, and Becky Boggs, my administrative assistant.

To the staff of College Press and Logos Bible Software, thank you for supporting and promoting the project.

TABLE OF CONTENTS

PROLOGUE

AN INVITATION TO LISTEN TO THE LYRICS OF THE LAMB

Out of his mouth came a sharp double-edged sword. . . . The one who sat there had the appearance of jasper and carnelian. . . . Then I saw a Lamb looking as if it had been slain, standing. . . . There before me was a pale horse. . . . The locusts looked like horses prepared for battle. . . . The great dragon was hurled down. . . . And I saw a beast coming out of the sea. . . . Let him calculate the number of the beast, for it is man's number. His number is 666. . . . Armageddon. . . . Fallen! Fallen is Babylon the Great! . . . Then I saw a great white throne. . . . Come, I will show you the bride, the wife of the Lamb. . . .
(Rev. 1:16; 4:3; 5:6; 6:8; 9:7; 12:9; 13:1, 18; 16:16; 18:2; 20:11; 21:9)

Have you ever begun to read the book of Revelation only to be defeated by a swirling set of bewildering images: winged creatures, beasts, trumpets, bowls, the number 666? If so, then my book is for you. I have written out of *compassion* for those who have tried to read, understand, and apply the book and who have abandoned hope of ever understanding it.

Are you ever puzzled at the way some authors, preachers, and teachers use the book to predict the future, all the way from interpreting the most recent events in the Middle East to pinpointing the date of Christ's return? Then my book is for you. I write out of *concern* because we live in an era when many disciples of Jesus are obsessed with using Revelation to know and control the future.

Do you believe that Revelation has nothing to do with your life as a follower of Jesus? Then my book of guidelines for interpreting John's message is for you. I write out of *conviction* that Revelation's message needs to be heard and obeyed by God's people.

Lamb of God, who takes away
the sins of the world,
Have mercy on us.
Lamb of God, who takes away
the sins of the world,
Grant us peace.

Agnus Dei (Lamb of God)
Seventh century

Over the years, I have met people from all walks of life who are troubled by Revelation. Church members along with college and seminary students have confessed to being baffled by Revelation's mysterious language. Seasoned preachers, and not a few professors, have disclosed to me that they are puzzled by the work. It is often perceived to be a favorite book of weird people or individuals who have too much time on their hands. Perhaps you have blushed because of comments made by those who promote embarrassingly sensationalistic and inevitably incorrect interpretations, rooted in motives not always noble.

My writing this book stems from years of personal study and teaching the Bible in the context of Christian community. I did not compose it in some ivory tower divorced from believers and from conditions in our world. Instead, I offer here insights I have presented in congregations, conferences, conventions, colleges, and seminaries, at home and abroad. I want Christians to replace the word "mysterious" with "meaningful" when they study the book. As a student and teacher of Scripture, I have tried to take seriously the counsel of Ernst Käsemann:

> It would do us good to read and re-read the Revelation of John. . . . Patmos is not an idyllic haven of rest for retired scholars who look back on a hard-working life of piety and integrity. . . . For over there on the mainland world history is moving, and the churches are spent and either do not see it or try to come to terms with it. They praise Christ as the Lord of heaven, and do not hear him saying to them: 'The world and all that is in it is mine.' . . . Christianity has to take notice of earthly things if it is to be worthy of its call to heavenly things.[1]

PROLOGUE

On one occasion, one of my colleagues asked me a perceptive question: "Bob, what tone will your book have?" Let me share my response. First, in dealing with how to read a book that so many people view as unapproachable, I told him that I wanted this book to be a friendly one. Even though I hope my work reflects solid scholarship, I want it to appeal to people from all backgrounds, from individuals in congregations who love God's Word and desire to understand it better, to preachers who desire to pass on the whole counsel of God, to professors who are equipping students to be faithful interpreters, and to the curious who wonder whether God speaks to them through the apostle John, the author of Revelation.

In the long run, I believe the approach laid out in this book makes Revelation much easier to understand. My guidelines will probably not lead you to the sensationalistic interpretations that other methods produce: end-times hysteria, date-setting craze, rapture fever, Antichrist obsession, and "666" mania. And yet from another perspective, I believe my approach will lead to Revelation becoming even more sensational, though in a surprising way. How? It will challenge you, motivate you, excite you to go deeper into the book. Indeed, the deeper you go into the book, the deeper will be your understanding, and you will become a better disciple of Jesus in light of the future God has revealed for his people.

My regret is that those of us who have approached Revelation the way I recommend have not been passionate or urgent enough in relating a different way to read and apply it. When you begin applying the guidelines of my book in your own study, you will see that you have questions to answer: What view of the future will influence how you live now? What kind of Jesus do you want to follow? What kind of follower of Jesus do you want to be?

Often the work of Bible scholars is too far removed from the needs of the local congregation. In light of this concern, the book avoids, wherever possible, the technical jargon often associated with academic study.[2] I want Christians from a diversity of backgrounds to read this book. It is often anecdotal in style as well. This is the case, in part, because I have presented the material to audiences in a variety of settings. Moreover, because I have had the opportunity to teach in other cultures, my understanding has been enriched significantly. In particular, as I have taught throughout Eastern Europe, students have raised issues and questions that drive me time and again to apply the universal message of Revelation today. I have tried to balance this desire to apply the book today with an appreciation for how the original audience would have understood it.

I want my book to be readable a gift to the church at home and abroad. As John wrote a circular letter for Christians with diverse backgrounds (Rev. 1:9, 11), so I desire this book to be a circular one, speaking to students of Scripture throughout the world who have a variety of levels of understanding and skills. This is not a book for "idiots";[3] it is one for those who are devoted to God and who are willing to dig deeply to correctly handle the Word of truth recorded by John.

I gave a second response to my colleague. Even though I want to provide a book that is approachable for a variety of audiences, I do not want it to be argumentative in tone. I want the book to be conciliatory. The subject of Christ's final return in general, and the book of Revelation in particular, causes considerable controversy, to say the least. Sides are drawn up, and a censorious spirit often develops. One's orthodoxy is either suspect or confirmed. I suggest a way to read Revelation that finds its roots deep in the history of the church and is viewed as a valid approach by many contemporary scholars who accept the trustworthiness of Scripture. And yet I am afraid it is an approach that is not known by many.

Naturally, then, my conclusions will come into conflict with others, and my interpretive approach will not be accepted by all. But I want to be as clear and accurate as possible while avoiding a combative attitude and approach. I have deliberately made the effort to be restrained and respectful. Above all, I want the book to advance the dialogue on the best way to read Revelation.

Therefore, I hope that three of the designations often associated with the apostle and author John will also be associated with my effort. First, I write as a *pastor*. My desire is to shepherd God's people in reading Revelation. I want disciples of Jesus to see how John's message can help them on their journey to their eternal home where they will dwell with God.

Revelations's message needs to be heard and obeyed.

Second, I write as a *preacher* who wants to help people see the good news about Jesus (for those who embrace the gospel) and the bad news (for those who reject or abandon the good news) found in John's work. The message of the book needs to be heard in the twenty-first century just as much as it did in the first century, if not more.

Third, I write as a *professor* who respects the prophetic spirit of the book. Revelation is prophetic in both character and intention. John the prophet viewed his task as presenting the Word and will of God to the people of God in a particular place at a particular time. It is a prophetic work that still speaks today. John was given the opportunity to penetrate to the eternal issues behind the crises of his day and our day as well. Like his Old Testament predecessors, John reminded the recipients of God's blessings. At the same time, he also revealed to God's people their duties to be carried out in challenging times. And he reassured them that God's purposes would indeed be fulfilled.

As a professor who is both a pastor and a preacher, I want the message of Revelation to get into the heads and hearts of followers of Christ. Why? So that it may be lived out by those who live in hostile or seductive cultures.

God willing, this book is the first volume of a proposed three-volume series. A second book is to be a commentary based on the interpretive principles found in this book. Its goal will be to make known in contemporary language, metaphors, and illustrations the message of the book of

Revelation. It will not be a verse-by-verse treatment but an examination and explanation of the symbolism in each chapter, moving back and forth between the symbols' meanings for John's readers and possible meanings for us today. A final volume is to focus on issues such as setting a date for Christ's return or other events, the millennium, antichrist, rapture, the mark of the beast, Armageddon, and more.

To receive maximum benefit as you read the following chapters, I encourage you to read Scriptures cited and endnotes as well. I know that often we skip over them, but we do so at great risk. Reading the verses will help you check out the accuracy of my conclusions in light of God's Word. You will notice that I include additional material in endnotes as well. Even though you could read my book without consulting the notes, you will find they serve a variety of functions. Sometimes I use notes to simply document quotations, express my indebtedness to an author, or provide further support for a particular point being presented. Other times I use notes to direct you to additional studies. I also use them to make observations or raise questions for you to pursue on your own.

As I worked on my book, I always tried to keep in mind the wise counsel my mother penned in a Bible she gave to me in 1969:

> *My Dear Son,*
> *It is my prayer that you will always follow the teachings of this book. May it always remind you that through the years he is the greatest teacher and the most educated person who ever lived, yet his teachings were simple enough that everyone could understand them.*
> *My son, use your wisdom to win others to him. May God grant you the power to continue to serve him all your life. An education is very important but most important is the education of others for Christ.*
> *Let your education be a tool for Christ and not a tool for man.*

My prayer for you as you read this book is that it may help you bring glory to the Lamb by following him even more closely.

CHAPTER 1

THE OVERTURE:

MY STRATEGY

Critics are much madder than poets. . . . And though St. John the Evangelist saw many strange monsters in his vision, he saw no creature so wild as one of his own commentators.[1]

Composed in 1908 by G.K. Chesterton, this statement still speaks to the embarrassing way John's visions are used even in our day, nearly 100 years later. Far too often interpreters of the visions are like crystal-ball polishers, explaining what John saw and heard in light of their current events. As another commentator on Revelation, I desire to offer a more sane strategy for interpreting the book.

When we open this last book of the Bible, we experience a collision of sounds, smells, and sights. The book both strikes and soothes our senses. We see the promiscuity of a whore and her lovers and the wedding celebration of a bride and bridegroom (17:1-6; 19:6-9). We smell rotting carcasses and sweet incense (19:19-21; 8:3-4). We hear wailing and rejoicing (18:11-20; 19:1-8). We taste bitter waters now, and we desire to be refreshed by springs of living water someday (8:10-11; 7:17). We feel the winds of judgment blowing and the gentle breeze of the Spirit speaking to God's people (7:1; 2:7). Despite the comforting scenes, we are tempted to close the book and think: Never again should we open this book and read. John may have seen and heard, but we do not desire to do either. Or if we wish to read and study it, we are frustrated because we do not know how.

No wonder many Christians never make it past the first three chapters, if even that far. On the one hand, there are

Revelations is as relevant as any other work found in Scripture.

students who divorce the book from its original setting and adopt a self-centered approach, believing the book speaks only to the so-called "end-time" generation, often meaning their own generation. On the other hand, there are some who want to limit its message exclusively to Christians in the first century.

I argue that Revelation is a book for all generations until Christ returns. We are called to study it properly so that we find God's timeless words of encouragement and exhortation. It is as relevant as any other work found in Scripture. We are called to meditate upon it because it is as inspired as Romans or Psalms. The book beckons us to look at it because its profound message applies to all Christians. We live in a world wherein we are called to be witnesses to the Christ revealed in Revelation, the one who was, and is, and is to come. And as in John's day, many in the world reject the church's call to repent and follow Jesus and even violently resist God's witnesses. Church history reveals that God's servants seem to be either always living on the edge of compromise or living under the shadow of efforts to destroy the church. Indeed, it is a book that will be relevant until Christ comes a final time.

Chesterton's assessment reminds us of the importance of all Christians being the best Bible critics possible. Please do not be alarmed at such a call. The designation "critic" does not mean something negative. A critic is someone who engages in analysis and evaluation. Such a person knows that probing leads to a deeper appreciation of what has been communicated. A movie critic evaluates films; an art critic appraises paintings; and a music critic analyzes compositions or the performers. Bible critics are those who attempt to examine Scripture, using the best principles and methods so that God's voice is clearly heard. Scripture challenges all disciples of Jesus to do their best in studying it (2 Tim. 2:15). We can be guilty of adding to, or taking away from, the message of Revelation if we are poor students of the message given to John (Rev. 22:18-19).

When I was a teenager I took a class on music appreciation. The teacher taught us how to listen to various kinds of music to appreciate the richness and variety of the compositions. Likewise, we must listen to Scripture correctly to comprehend the beauty and the power of the Lamb's composition. Repeatedly in Revelation, the Spirit calls upon us to hear and evaluate what God is saying: "He who has an ear, let him hear what the Spirit says to the churches" (2:7, 11, 17, 29; 3:6, 13, 22; see also 1:3; 13:9, 18; 22:9). In the exhortation of one Bible scholar, we are called upon to listen to the symphony of Scripture.[2]

Accordingly, my book is written with the conviction that Revelation is a fitting piece ending God's symphony. Indeed, it is a reminder that God's Word is not an unfinished symphony. As Genesis is a fitting prelude, introducing the dominant themes found throughout Scripture (e.g., creation, sin, the promise of a redeemer, covenant, and so forth), so Revelation brings us to a fitting finale where there is no longer any curse. If we are to listen to the "symphony of Scripture," we must listen to the whole symphony, including Revelation.

In music the overture is the orchestral introduction to a musical dramatic work. It hints of music to come, be it in a musical or an opera. This chapter serves as an introductory movement for the ones to follow. It is divided into three parts that set out my task for the book: a mission, a metaphor, and a method.

A Mission

For more than forty years, I have been teaching and preaching Scripture. As a seminary professor, I determined long ago that I would not be primarily a lecturer but an equipper. In my classes I have not stood before students and lectured on particular New Testament writings, emphasizing only my own interpretation of a passage. Instead, I have attempted to equip students with interpretive guidelines, both general ones relevant for all books and special ones that apply to a book's style. Once I have presented them, I assign each student a passage to study, and, following weeks of disciplined study, the student then shares conclusions with the entire class. Of course, I encourage the students to use the best resources available,[3] drawing from the contributions God's people have made over the centuries. When they complete a class, I want them to have the ability to study on their own. I teach with this conviction: The deeper we probe Scripture and reflect upon it, the more powerfully it will speak to our lives.

I modify the classroom approach when teaching in churches. On those occasions I am not hesitant to share my insights concerning a passage's original meaning and its message for us today. Above all, I attempt to share the principles I use so that people can study on their own once I depart. If time permits, we apply the guidelines by actually studying select passages.

Similarly, in the chapters to follow, I will apply the guidelines, usually moving from the more easily interpreted passages to the more challenging ones. I have wrestled with the question of how broad or how deep to go in illustrating the principles. Nevertheless, I hope that the examples I provide are helpful and will serve as a guide for you to do your own study of Revelation. I suggest that once you have done your own initial study it would be valuable to interact with published contributions of other students of Scripture who have devoted years of their lives to mining the riches of God's Word.

Whether in the seminary classroom or in a congregational setting, I am on a pilgrimage to be a better student of Scripture, and I invite others to join me. I am committed to teaching people how to read the Bible responsibly. People find great delight when they are given the guidelines and encouraged to use the best tools, and they commit themselves to better Bible study. This book attempts to capture what I have offered on Revelation over the years so that it can be used as a handbook by others who want to join me on this journey to understand better the heart and mind of Christ. I invite you to study with me. We will be stretched no doubt, but the blessings will be rich.

THE OVERTURE: MY STRATEGY

It is not surprising to me that when I teach Revelation in either an academic or local church environment there is either incredible interest or disdainful disinterest. Even though both extremes are unhealthy, I appreciate the sentiments of both camps. I readily admit that I had a troubled relationship with Revelation for years because I was exposed to two radical positions.

God's word is not an unfinished symphony.

On the one hand, some taught me that most of the book was written only for the first-century recipients and had nothing to say to us today. (However, they said, chapters 1–3 contained some nuggets worth examining!) Thus Revelation is reduced to being exclusively a history of the earliest Christians. I wondered: If this is true, should I bother?

On the other hand, some of my teachers argued that most of the book (especially chapters 4–22) was written only for believers living in the days immediately preceding the final coming of Christ.[4] This perspective holds that John has given us a detailed blueprint of the events leading up to Christ's coming. Proponents of this approach suggest that all we have to do is to determine how the events occurring in our lifetime fit in with John's visions. Where we are on the prophetic timetable is the dominant concern. When exposed to this approach I asked: If so, what relevance did Revelation have for John and his fellow disciples?

For years, then, I believed that to understand and apply Revelation's message you either needed knowledge of the first-century events involving the church and the Roman Empire that could be found in ancient history books or of contemporary culture gleaned from news headlines. One approach consigned Revelation to the past, while the other used it to tell us the future. The book either meant virtually nothing to me or everything to me. The former approach was all about the past and events beyond our control, and I found it unexciting. I was drawn to the latter approach if any at all. Why? Because if Revelation tells us in detail about our

The deeper we probe Scripture and reflect upon it, the more powerfully it will speak to our lives.

future, my future, then it appeals to our desire to have such knowledge, so we are tempted to think we can be in control. Ultimately, however, because of these approaches taken by some of my early teachers, I found the book unappealing. I avoided reading and studying it. Talking with other believers, I knew I was not alone. So for nearly a decade I virtually ignored the book.

Then in the early 1970s, more than seven years into my formal biblical-theological training, I took a course on John's writings and then another course on Revelation in particular. I began to develop a passion for the book. I realized that I had not been taught how to read and study the work properly. I repented of my neglect and began to reflect on the value of the revelation given to John. Accordingly, my relationship with the book has matured over the years until it ceased being a courtship and took its place alongside other books of Scripture where I hear the Bridegroom speaking to his Bride. I deeply love this book, and I am committed to honoring it as a priceless portion of God's revelation.

I have desired to respect it by teaching followers of Jesus how to read Revelation so that they can find both comfort and challenge in its teaching. My book reflects a slow process of formation, something like the way a moving stream shapes the rocks over the long passage of time. My thoughts have been sharpened by my teachers, students I have taught, conversations I have had with both believers and nonbelievers, and countless books and articles I have read. Even though the journey is not yet complete (How anyone can claim to be an expert on any portion of Scripture, let alone Revelation, is beyond me!), I hope the guidelines will aid Christians who desire to be blessed by hearing and obeying Revelation.

A Metaphor

I have decided to use the metaphor or "image" of music to connect the chapters. Of all the arts, music seems to be the most universal. Even though I do not read music and have never played an instrument, I love music. We live in an *iPod* or *MP3* world where we can listen to any kind of music, anytime and anywhere. I believe God has created us so that we are attuned to listen to this earthly-heavenly form of communication since heaven's communication often finds one of its best expressions in music. To pair music, especially singing, and Revelation is natural because the book is filled with songs. In Revelation we do not have the musical score, but we possess the poetic lyrics.

Please note the subtitle to my book: *Listening to the Lyrics of the Lamb*. The "Lyrics of the Lamb" essentially paraphrases John's opening to his book, "The revelation of Jesus Christ." The revelation was given in both visions and words, which John wrote down for the people. Webster's Dictionary defines "lyrics" as "the words of a song."[5] I am using the term "lyrics" as a synonym for John's words. I use the term "Lamb" the way John did, to mean Jesus.[6] So, "the lyrics of the Lamb" are the words given to John *by* Jesus *about* Jesus.

Listening means more than hearing; it requires an obedient response to Jesus' revelation. "Listening to the lyrics of the Lamb," then, is a call to hear and obey the truths given *by* Jesus and *about* Jesus. John reveals, unveils, and discloses these truths through vivid and colorful poetic imagery. J.B. Phillips reflects on John's poetry when he writes:

> The effect of the language of this book is most powerful. The crowns, the thrones, the gold, the jewels, the colours, the trumpets, the violence of action and the impact of incredible numbers and awe-inspiring size—all these images stir that threshold of the brain where monsters lurk and supernatural glories blaze. John is stirring with a kind of surrealistic artistry the vastnesses of our unconscious minds. The book is probably an impossibility of the pictorial illustrator, but the figures created in the mind are vivid and powerful enough to transport us to another spiritual dimension.[7]

From one perspective, then, there is mystery in both music and John's message. In that mystery there takes place a piercing of the heart and mind, provoking the emotions, and preparing the whole person to hear Jesus' lyrics. Phillips observes that "the poetic impact of the book carries us away to a realm where the pedestrian rules of grammar no longer apply—we are dealing with celestial poetry and not with earthly prose. To be literal-minded and studiously analytical in such a work is to kill its poetic truth. Dissection is not infrequently the death of beauty."[8]

The pages of Scripture overflow with heavenly song, poetry put to music.[9] God's people sing hymns, choruses, and doxologies. They celebrate, they mourn, they praise. Quite often the songs found in Scripture help people make sense of God and his ways, the world in which we live, and what it means to be human. They even help us understand Scripture.

We find singing in the first book of the Bible (Gen. 31:27), as well as the last where songs are sprinkled throughout (Rev. 4:8, 11; 5:9-10, 12-14; 7:10, 12, 15-17; 11:17-18; 12:10-12; 14:2-3; 15:3-4; 16:5-7; 19:1-3, 6-8).[10] In between, we see music and singing associated with birth and death (Luke 1:46ff. and Jer. 48:36), war and peace (Isa. 30:32 and Isa. 27:2), and people and creation (Ps. 98:4-6 and Job 38:7; Pss. 65:12-13; 96:12; 98:7-8). Music is found in times of exile (Ps. 137:2-4) and restoration (Isa. 24:14; 49:13), and in seasons of joy (Pss. 149, 150) and sadness (2 Sam. 3:32-34; 2 Chr. 35:25; Ezek. 32:16; Luke 7:32). New songs (Pss. 33:3; 40:3; 96:1; 144:9; Isa. 42:10; Rev. 5:9; 14:3) take their place alongside familiar songs. Music is even used to symbolize the sin of rebellion against God (Amos 5:23-24; 6:4-6; see also Isa. 5:11-12) or the intimacy between a man and a woman (Song of Songs).

The notions of giftedness and inspiration are tied to music (1 Chr. 15:22; 25:7; 2 Chr. 34:12; Ps. 33:3). David is perhaps the preeminent musician; he is Israel's anointed and inspired composer and performer (2 Sam. 23:1). But above all other singers is the divine One, God himself. He writes the songs individuals sing (Ps. 40:3) as well as those sung by nations (Deut. 31:19) and about nations (Jer. 48:36; Zeph. 3:17).

In the end, God is the ultimate origin and object of all sacred music found in Scripture and of all music sung by God's people through the centuries. Indeed, in Israel's greatest events, we hear music praising God—the Exodus (Exod. 15), conquering the Canaanites (Judges 5), recapturing the Ark of the Covenant (2 Sam. 6:5, 14-15; 1 Chr. 15:16), dedicating the temple (Neh. 12:27-43), crowning the king (2 Chr. 23:13), and a return from exile (Isa. 12:5). And of course, most prevalent of all, music was used in corporate worship (Pss. 147:1; 149:1; 150:1-5), as well as in personal worship (Pss. 13:6; 27:5-6; 71:20-23).

Listening requires an obedient response to Jesus' revelation.

As to music in the New Testament, we find singing in the Gospels (Matt. 26:30), Acts (16:25), and the letters (Rom. 15:9; 1 Cor. 14:14-15, 26; Eph. 5:19; Col. 3:16). Revelation's music focuses on God's power at work in creating and in judging his creation, as well as God's redeeming acts through Jesus Christ (Rev. 4:8, 11; 5:8; 14:2; 15:2). We read of trumpets (1:10; 4:1; 8:2, 6, 13; 9:14) and harps (5:8; 14:2; 15:2). We hear angelic (5:11-13; 11:15-18) and heavenly choirs (4:11; 5:9-10; 15:3-4) sing God's praises. As the saints in the Old Testament sang their old songs, likewise the saints in Revelation sing the new ones (5:12-13; 7:12; 14:3; 15:3).

Thus, throughout biblical history and beyond, God's people have loved music. They sang and celebrated God's words and acts of grace and glory, as well as his justice and judgment. God's people sang alone and in the presence of others. They celebrated by singing in beautiful temples and in prison cells. They carried their songs into the streets of the city and into the deserts. They brought their music to barren islands like Patmos or to cities and villages of rich provinces like Asia Minor. God's pilgrims sang while dwelling in the Promised Land as well as in foreign lands.

"How can we sing the songs of the Lord while in a foreign land?" asks the Psalmist about God's people who lived in

Babylon (Ps. 137:4). No doubt John and his brothers and sisters in Christ would have asked the same as they lived in the shadow of a reborn Babylon, the Roman Empire. As twenty-first-century people of God, if we have eyes to see and ears to hear, we know that there are still followers of Jesus who also live in Babylon. Revelation helps us find where we are in our relationship with God and the world in which we live, either a people seduced or suppressed or a people serving faithfully and fearlessly.

Scripture's songs and their theology speak to the chaos and confusion of the world in which we live. John wishes to address the issue: Is there any guidance for disciples of Jesus who live in hostile and seductive times? What lyrics does God desire us to hear? What lyrics are we to sing? If we are to hear in a perceptive way and if we are to sing truth in a world that is often hostile to gospel witness because it is committed to worshiping idols of destruction, we must know how to interpret what God has revealed in John's writing. Or to continue with the metaphor, how are we to hear Revelation's music and understand its songs? How does a reading of it influence our singing?

A Method

If we make an effort to read Revelation, we may at various points think that we have picked up a demented copy of the *National Geographic* magazine filled with grotesque creatures—a slaughtered Lamb, bleeding yet standing; a dragon sweeping stars out of the sky with its lethal tail; a beast with seven heads and ten horns; and a lamb who shepherds. Or we may think we have been surfing the television with our remote control and have come upon a weather channel chillingly revealing a world gone amok with severe lightning and thunderstorms, horrific hundred-pound hailstones and raging seas, sinking islands and melting mountains, and fierce tsunami-like conditions, with cities collapsing in the twinkling of an eye. Or we may feel that reading the book is like picking up a box containing a 5,000-piece jigsaw puzzle and trying to assemble the puzzle when we have no picture on the front of the box to show what we are trying to piece together. Or we may conclude that we have been handed a graduate-level higher mathematics book with incomprehensible numbers and equations involving threes, fours, tens and multiples of ten, and twelves and multiples of twelve, and "time, times and half a time." Or perhaps upon reading through the book—if we even make it to the end—we conclude that it reads like a poorly directed film whose director and editor did not know where and how to end the movie. Simply put, Revelation can appear to be out of focus when compared with other writings in the Bible.

Yet reflect with me on a scene from the book of Acts. It is the story involving Philip the evangelist instructing the Ethiopian eunuch (Acts 8:26-40). On his journey to Jerusalem to worship God, the eunuch has been reading Isaiah 53 and fails to understand its message. The Spirit instructs Philip to go and teach the government official. Philip joins the eunuch in the chariot and Bible study commences when the evangelist asks his fellow traveler if he understands what he has been reading. It is a study that ends with the official being baptized and becoming a follower of Christ. One lesson we can learn from this story is that studying the Bible should lead us closer to Jesus.

In the past when you have attempted to study Revelation, did you ever wish that someone could have sat down beside you and asked: "Do you understand what you are reading?" You may well have responded: "How can I unless someone explains it to me?" (Acts 8:30-31). The word that is translated "explain" can also be rendered "guide." I hope this book will serve as a guide. I desire to provide guidelines for responsibly interpreting Revelation. But they only set the parameters. As Bible students we need to observe how others study Scripture, and we must practice studying Scripture. By understanding Revelation better, we will know and serve Jesus better. I invite you to study with me as I use numerous examples drawn from both the Old and New Testaments.

What I am referring to is hermeneutics, the science and art of understanding and interpreting Scripture. Or put another

Quite often the songs found in Scripture help people make sense of God and his ways.

way, the word refers to those principles we must follow to interpret correctly what the book meant to the original recipients so we may know what it means for us today. I am convinced that confusion usually occurs due to faulty biblical hermeneutics. This is especially the case with Revelation. Regrettably, it appears that often the principles one follows when studying other biblical books are abandoned when one comes to the Bible's last entry. False interpretations are the result. I believe that Scripture is trustworthy and true. The same cannot be said about our interpretation of God's Word.

I am also referring to exegesis. "Exegesis" comes from the Greek, meaning "to lead" or "to draw out." To do exegesis means we draw out the meaning of, or explain, passages in Scripture. We do this by studying the grammar, the meaning of words, the form and structure, the historical and biblical contexts, and so forth. The goal is to determine what the authors communicated to the original recipients. Such exegetical work is foundational, and only when it is completed should we attempt to determine what Scripture means to us today.

What is the relationship between hermeneutics and exegesis? Hermeneutics is concerned with principles we follow when we interpret Scripture. Some key principles include: (1) interpreting Scripture by Scripture; (2) interpreting the obscure by the clear rather than vice-versa; and (3) interpreting a book of the Bible in light of its style. Exegesis, on the other hand, is the practice of studying Scripture, the steps one follows. Hermeneutical principles inform and drive exegesis.

When put into practice, hermeneutics and exegesis demand that we follow a somewhat scientific set of steps based on fundamental principles. However, interpreting Scripture is also a learned art. We are more than willing to agree that successful musicians, artists, teachers, carpenters, and homemakers must learn both the art and science of their professions. Likewise, Bible students need to learn how to successfully combine both the scientific and the artistic in their craft. I suggest adhering to the following interpretive guidelines: (1) Knowing—students need to know key hermeneutical principles and exegetical steps, (2) Observing—students need to observe the way others study Scripture, and (3) Doing—students need to study Scripture on their own. Only when students perform all three of these steps are they in the position to apply the results to their own lives—the ultimate goal of hermeneutics. They must live their hermeneutics in belief and behavior.

How, then, do we listen to the lyrics of the Lamb? How do we read the book of Revelation? Answer: We are able to listen to the lyrics only when we tune our ears to hearing John's unique composition on its own terms. How do we hear his composition with an ear tuned to particular elements of his composition? By listening to the elements described below. If we don't adhere to these fundamentals, then we will not hear what the Lamb wants us to hear. The music becomes distorted. We become out of tune with the message. We don't hear and we don't understand. Accordingly, I set before you six essential elements we must take note of as we listen to the lyrics, the lyrics given by the Lamb about the Lamb, as recorded by John.

I pray that these foundational elements will lead you to a correct interpretation of John's marvelous writing. They assume what I said earlier and what I believe to be fundamental to responsible interpretation of Scripture: We first seek to understand what the book meant for its original recipients before we can see its significance for us today.

But with Revelation, often the "meant-ness" of the book is either overemphasized to the neglect of any contemporary application or it is virtually ignored. The result is that today's interpreters, readers, and critics often impose improbable interpretations based primarily on what is going on in our world today. As I explore with you John's culture and his use of symbols, I cite examples from Revelation and show how its message resonates with other books of Scripture. We may begin to reevaluate notions of Revelation's perceived strangeness when we realize that it has much in common with other books in Scripture.

While I present six seemingly discrete elements, I need to stress that there is no nice, neat compartmentalization. We cannot be sensitive to one without interacting with one or more of the others. For example, we cannot appreciate the significance of a book's style without placing it in a historical setting. Or the symbols cannot be understood without understanding their origins in the Old Testament. Applying the principles is not like putting together a new toy. For example, when you begin to assemble a new toy, you should follow the instructions step-by-step as laid out by the designer. Hermeneutics is not a sequential enterprise. Instead the interplay between the elements means that you will move back and forth in order to reach proper interpretation. We are reminded that not only is the practice of good hermeneutics a science, it is also an art. You must reflect on the interconnectedness of these elements. With this in mind, then, let me give a preview of the six elements we must study for proper interpretation of Revelation.

Listening to the Lyrics: The Scriptural Stage (Chapter 2). In chapter 2, I discuss the scriptural stage of the book. Specifically, we need to place the last book of the Bible in the larger context of the other sixty-five books. John's message does not contradict the larger revelation from God but rather it complements it, although in some unique ways. In particular I focus on the notion of what it means to live between God's redemptive actions rooted in the first and final comings of Christ.

Listening to the Lyrics: The Storied Setting[11] (Chapter 3). What is the story behind the book? This is the question that is answered in chapter three. Each book of the Bible must have meant something to the original audience. A real author addressed real people in real cities. The word "storied" is used in the sense of having an interesting history, and the story of John and the disciples at the end of the first century is just that, interesting. As we build a bridge to our world, we find we must be sensitive to John's first-century world. I show that Revelation was written to a people who faced one of two, if not both, threats: (1) the danger of opposition and persecution and (2) the peril of seduction by a culture to the point where Christians were compromising their beliefs and behavior.

What lyrics does God desire us to hear?

Listening to the Lyrics: The Style (Chapter 4). Chapter four deals with misunderstandings that take place when we fail to be sensitive to the style of a biblical work. If we do not understand what kind of book we are studying, then we will ask the wrong questions, and its meaning will likely elude us. We will explore the importance of John's combining three genres—the prophetic, the apocalyptic, and the epistle (letter)—with special focus on how this unique combination guides us in asking the right questions of the text.

Listening to the Lyrics: The Sources (Chapter 5). A major reason Christians fail to understand Revelation is that they are unaware of the way the Old Testament permeates John's work. Chesterton's "wild commentators" exist to this day, in part because they do not respect the way John uses these Old Testament writings to communicate the revelation. These commentators take the Old Testament writings out of their original contexts and interpret them in light of contemporary events. Chapter five demonstrates that John uses language and imagery that were thoroughly familiar to his fellow disciples. We see how John adopts and adapts scores of Old Testament passages in order to communicate what he saw and heard.

Listening to the Lyrics: The Symbolism (Chapter 6). Should Revelation be interpreted literally or symbolically? This topic provokes much discussion and debate, and we examine it in chapter six. Ultimately, the question is not one of either-or. It is obvious that the various genres in Scripture (law, history, poetry, prophecy, gospel, letter, and so forth) can express truth in literal and nonliteral ways. All biblical authors use metaphors. The issue is to interpret each book naturally in light of its dominant genre as well as its subgenres. Since John's work is clearly a Christian prophetic-apocalyptic work, we should expect significant use of symbolism. Indeed, each chapter in Revelation contains symbolism.

Listening to the Lyrics: The Structure (Chapter 7). Every book of the Bible has structure. Sometimes the way a book is organized is clear, sometimes not. It may be relatively simple or very complex. Revelation is a complex work. Nevertheless, I believe that we can understand John's organization, both the whole and the parts, even though we may not be able to tie up all the loose ends. Chapter seven shows that John creatively uses the strategies of repetition and recapitulation in order to drive home what he has seen and heard.

Summarizing, I have emphasized in this chapter that the disciple's life with respect to Scripture is a life of hermeneutics: We are called to live a life of carefully reading, painstakingly interpreting, prayerfully meditating, passionately obeying, and faithfully proclaiming Scripture. I close this chapter with two additional guidelines, seldom found in textbooks on hermeneutics.

First, we must honor the principle of humility. We not only study Scripture, but we must submit to Scripture. In the final analysis, Scripture is the subject, and we are the object. God speaks, we listen and obey.[12] We must strive to approach God's Written Word with the willingness to allow God to impose his agenda on us so we can hear his Word and, therefore, live faithfully in his world. This is painful at times because of our arrogance. Some people are so puffed up when they study Scripture that they are rarely hindered or humbled by the difficulties and complexities of a book like Revelation. Their approach confirms the truth of another observation by Chesterton: "The simplification of anything is always sensational."[13] Unfortunately, some approaches to Revelation, especially the ones that lead to date-setting and interpreting the book only in terms of our day, lead to sensationalism. It is a luridness that is based on a simplistic, yet flawed, reading of the book.

Second, the principle of honesty needs to be kept in the forefront. Integrity demands that we change our beliefs as well as our behavior when a better understanding of Scripture demands it. As a student of the Bible, I have had some of my long-held views challenged, and I have had to reject some cherished interpretations. I have done my best to resist the temptation to impose a system on Scripture. Truly, Scripture should shape any theological system we hold. It takes courage to acknowledge when we have been wrong in our interpretation of the Bible. But that courage is a part of what it means to know that the disciple's life is a life of hermeneutics.

As I conclude this chapter, I want to remind you that you do not need to be a college or seminary graduate or Bible scholar to understand Revelation. You need to be a disciple of Jesus who has three characteristics: (1) a desire to know God's Word, (2) a willingness to learn and use sound principles, and (3) a passion to come humbly to the text, fervently desiring to hear God speak.

If we want to listen to God's music as recorded in Scripture, we need to be taught how to listen. Just as important, we must desire to listen to heaven's music on its terms, not ours.

CHAPTER
2

LISTENING TO THE LYRICS: THE SCRIPTURAL STAGE

Does John's Revelation sound a discordant note when compared with the other biblical works? Is he out of tune with the other sixty-five books and their teachings about God and his people? Is he marching to the beat of a different drummer? Some would argue that John's voice ought to be heard above all others. The songs he sings and the instruments he plays ought to dominate those sung and played by others. His solo, so to speak, is the most important one in the symphony of Scripture; his work provides the key to understanding the entire Bible.

In Umberto Eco's novel, *The Name of the Rose,* two monks living in fourteenth-century Italy are investigating the murders of seven other monks associated with a wealthy abbey. In this philosophical whodunit and tale of books, censorship, and religious tension, English Brother William of Baskerville must uncover the abbey's dark secrets in order to solve the murders. William and his assistant, Adso, hold the following exchange as they seek to find the murderer: Adso inquires: "I asked him why he thought the key to the sequence of crimes lay in the book of Revelation. He looked at me, amazed: 'The book of John offers the key to everything.'"[1]

Even though Brother William's point of view is a dominant one in certain parts of the church, there are other viewpoints.[2] It is well known that Martin Luther dismissed the book's importance because he did not find Christ in it. Neither he nor John Calvin wrote commentaries on Revelation. Another perspective is that Revelation is certainly not as important as other books found in Scripture; not much is missed if it is not preached or taught.[3]

Be still, my soul!
Thy God doth undertake
To guide the future
as He has the past.
Thy hope, thy confidence
let nothing shake;
All now mysterious
shall be bright at last.
Be still, my soul!
The waves and winds still know
His voice who ruled them
while He dwelt below.

"Be Still, My Soul"
Katharina A. Von Schlegel
1752

The goal of this chapter is to show how John's contribution enriches the message of Scripture without impoverishing the other books or elevating it above all other books. Revelation complements the other biblical authors who write about Christ's final coming. To continue the music metaphor introduced earlier, John occupies a key chair in the orchestra that plays the symphony of God's Word. Indeed, the decision made by early Christians to place it as the last book of Scripture is fitting. The whole Bible with its emphasis on creation, covenant, Christ, church, and other themes reaches its crescendo in the final book's message about the consummation (i.e., Christ's final coming and the end of the world). Scripture closes with what it means to live as God's people in a hostile and seductive world, between Christ's first and final comings, while anticipating a new heaven and a new earth free from the presence of evil and the curse of sin.

When we study a book of the Bible, or even a specific passage, it is necessary to see how the book or passage fits with the rest of Scripture. This task is called canonical exegesis. Earlier, we defined exegesis as drawing out the meaning of a biblical text and explaining it. "Canon" refers to the list of books viewed as Scripture. Therefore, canonical exegesis seeks to determine the contribution a passage or book makes to the whole of Scripture. In other words, we seek to see the connectedness between Bible books or between a passage and the rest of Scripture.

We usually make connections between the individual

books of the Bible without giving much thought. For example, we readily connect 1 and 2 Samuel or 1 and 2 Thessalonians. We link the books of the Pentateuch (Genesis through Deuteronomy) or the prophetic books associated with particular periods in Israel's history, such as the eighth-century B.C. prophets Hosea, Amos, Micah, and Isaiah. We do this with Matthew, Mark, and Luke when we identify them as the "synoptic gospels" ("synoptic" means "to have a common view" with regard to their telling the story of Jesus) or with the writings of Paul that are called the prison epistles (Ephesians, Philippians, Colossians, and Philemon). These examples emphasize canonical exegesis on what may be called a micro level. What we need to do, of course, is see how all of the writings fit in with God's revelation as a whole, that is, the macro level. For example, how do the books of the New Testament fit in with those associated with the Old?

How do we apply the notion of canonical exegesis to Revelation? Does it stand apart from the rest of the Bible, either to be ignored or to be used as the lens through which we read all other Scripture? I believe that neither position is ultimately valid. Instead, we should focus on how the five documents associated with John are connected and then ask how Revelation, in particular, is linked with the rest of Scripture.[4] John's works can be viewed from the following perspective. The Gospel of John is a book about faith, the letters (or epistles) of John are about love, and the book of Revelation is about hope—the confident certainty that God will judge and reward or punish.

But what about Revelation's connection with the other documents found in Scripture, especially the New Testament? If John received Revelation at the end of the first century,[5] how does it fit in with the other biblical writings? If John is the last of the apostles to contribute to the New Testament, and if he is an old man at that, is he a doddering old prophet who hums a tune that no one could have understood then, let alone comprehend today?

I believe that John's message fits in with the larger biblical message—that God desires and acts to bring people back into proper relationship with him through Christ—even though its literary style may jar some of us. John's book has a unique style that affects the way he communicates God's message, but that makes it no less authoritative.

How, then, does Revelation fit in with the rest of Scripture? For sake of space, I want to focus in particular on John's connection with three themes in the New Testament: "the last days" (and synonyms such as "last times"), "eschatology," and the relationship between "the already and the not yet." When properly defined, these ideas can help us see how John's message fits in with other biblical authors. But there is danger in using these expressions. For example, there is risk in using the phrase "the last days" because it is frequently used in a narrow way, at least on a popular level. Also there is peril in using the word "eschatology" because its meaning is often vague, and even when it is defined, it is usually used in a restricted way, on both popular and scholarly levels.

The Last Days

Many refer to "the last days" as a period immediately before the final coming of Christ or the so-called millennial (one-thousand-year) reign of Christ (Rev. 20:4ff.). Through the centuries, countless Christians have felt they were living in the last days: They expected Christ to return in their lifetime.[6] This can be healthy if Christians do not get caught up in date-setting but live with a sense of expectancy that Christ can come anytime. Truly, his final coming is possible any day, impossible no day.

Unfortunately, however, we often hear today that we are the generation living right before Christ comes to establish an earthly kingdom. Many times I hear preachers say we are the end-time generation or we are living in the last days. No doubt, other believers in previous generations felt the same way. But is this the language we should be using? I think not.

When we look at the use of the phrase in the New Testament, we must conclude that we have been living in "the last days" since the first coming of Christ. By using a concordance of the Bible,[7] we can see that there are several places where the notion of "the last days" or "the last times" is used only in this sense (Acts 2:17; 1 Tim. 4:1; 2 Tim. 3:1; Heb. 1:2; James 5:3; 1 Pet. 1:20; 2 Pet. 3:3; 1 John 2:18; Jude 18). Except for 1 Pet. 1:5 where the phrase "the last time" (note the singular "time") refers to the final scene of this age, the phrase "the last days" is *never* used to speak of the time immediately preceding an appearance of Christ. The "last days" or "the last times" are leading up to the time of the Final Judgment. That event is described in a number of ways: the end of the age (Matt. 13:39, 40, 49; 24:3; 28:20), the end (Matt. 10:22;[8] 1 Cor. 1:8; 10:11; 15:24; Heb. 3:14; 6:11; 1 Pet. 4:7; Rev. 2:26), the day (Matt. 25:13), the day of the Lord (1 Cor. 1:8; 5:5; 2 Cor. 1:14; Phil. 2:16; 1 Thess. 5:2), the day of God (2 Pet. 3:12), the great day (Acts 2:20; Jude 6; Rev. 6:17), the day of wrath (Rom. 2:5; Rev. 6:16-17), the day of judgment (Matt. 10:15; 11:22, 24; 2 Pet. 2:9; 3:7; 1 John 4:17), the day of redemption (Eph. 4:30), and the last day (John 6:39, 40, 44, 54; 11:24).

Of the Father's love begotten
Ere the world began to be,
He is Alpha and Omega,
He the source, the ending He,
Of the things that are,
that have been,
And that future years shall see,
Evermore and evermore.

"Of the Father's Love Begotten"
Fourth century

Let me highlight three individuals who stress that Christians in the first century lived in "the last days." First, consider Peter's sermon following the ascension of Christ. On the day of Pentecost, upon the giving of the Holy Spirit, Peter announced to the crowds that the display of the work of the Spirit was to be fulfilled in "the last days" (Acts 2:17), a reference to Joel 2:28ff. Nearly thirty years later he describes the same period as "the last times" (1 Pet. 1:20; see also 1:5; 2 Pet. 3:3). In other words, be it 30 years or 2,000 years later, we are still living in the last days.

Second, in Paul's thinking, humanity is heading toward "the end" (1 Cor. 1:8). But the time between Christ's first coming and the end is a period designated "the latter times" or "the last days" (1 Tim. 4:1; 2 Tim. 3:1).

We have been living in "the last days" since the first coming of Christ.

Third, the unknown author of Hebrews places himself in the last days. In Hebrews 9:27-28 he refers to Christ's first coming, summed up in the reference to his sacrificial death (9:27), along with Christ's appearing "a second time." This is the only place in the Bible where the adjective "second" is used with Christ's final coming. At Christ's final coming, he will "bring salvation to those who are waiting for him" (9:28). This fits in with the opening verses of the document where the author refers to God's past spokespersons, the prophets (Heb. 1:1). He then writes that God has spoken decisively in Jesus: "but in these last days he has spoken to us by his Son, whom he appointed heir of all things, and through whom he made the universe" (1:2).

I am regularly asked if I believe that we are living in the last days. I answer with a decisive "Yes! We have been living in the last days for nearly two thousand years." There is usually an acknowledgement ("Well, yes!") followed by another inquiry: "But do you believe that we are living in the *very* last days?" My response? The Bible does not provide an answer to that question because it does not use such language, and it would be presumptuous of me to answer a question the Bible does not pretend to answer. Besides, I do not want to outdo Christ (Matt. 24:36)!

So, even though many refer to "the last days" as a period immediately before the final coming of Christ, the witness of New Testament Scripture is that we are living in it now, have been for two thousand years, and will be until Christ returns. Events associated with "the last days" cannot, therefore, be narrowly ascribed to the period just before the return of Christ. We must view Revelation's contribution in light of this, namely that the book was written to challenge and comfort Christians no matter how long "the last days" last.

Eschatology

The use of the term "eschatology" frequently creates confusion because of a failure to define it clearly. How are we to understand a word that did not enter our vocabulary until 1844?[9] Even though the term never appears in Scripture, it is frequently used by scholars to describe the events associated with Christ's final coming, ironically like the phrase "the last days."

The term comes from two Greek words, *eschatos* which means "last" and *logos* which means "word," "teaching," or "study." Eschatology, then, is the teaching concerning "the last things" or "the study of the last things." Defining what constitutes "the last things," however, can be quite slippery. Sometimes the word is used in a narrow sense to refer to death, judgment, heaven, and hell. Others use it in a broader sense, saying that it also includes the nature of the Kingdom of God, especially as it relates to the history of the world, the coming of Christ,[10] the end of time, and the surrounding events like the Final Judgment. In theology books, the topic of eschatology is usually covered at the very end, after all other major doctrines have been discussed.[11]

Similarly, many who focus their study on the book of Revelation evaluate its eschatology from a narrow perspective. For example, some demonstrate a misconception when they argue that most of the book deals with the events immediately preceding a coming of Christ to reign on the earth for one thousand years.

But I believe the topic of eschatology should not be defined so narrowly. The last days and eschatology can be used to help us place Revelation in the larger context of Scripture. I suggest that together these terms deal with God's acts of redemption, especially those associated with the first and final comings of Christ and everything that happens between these two momentous events. In other words, the concepts should not be used in a narrow way to refer either to events immediately preceding an earthly reign of Christ or to the Final Judgment. Ultimately, "eschatology" has to do not with "the last things" but with the person of Jesus Christ, who is the First and the Last (Rev. 1:17). In the following chapters, I discuss how the book of Revelation fulfills one of its greatest purposes: to help the first-century Christians, and all Christians through the subsequent centuries, live responsible lives between Christ's first and final comings.[12]

The Already and the Not Yet

I must develop the concept in the title of this section gradually. This will permit us to see how John's writing fits in with the rest of the New Testament. An analogy first offered by a theologian decades ago is helpful. Oscar Cullmann argued that God has revealed himself in history through a series of redemptive acts. For the Old Testament believer, the midpoint of history lay in the future, but for the New-Testament-era disciples and succeeding ones, this midpoint now lies in the past.[13] The first coming of Jesus is the great midpoint of history; it lies behind us.

Cullmann's analogy is a stirring one because he compares the position of the disciple of Jesus with that of a person living between D-Day (June 1944) and V-Day (Spring 1945) during World War II. D-Day was when the allied troops invaded Europe and began to push the German army back to Germany, while V-Day was when they actually claimed victory:

> The decisive battle in a war may already have occurred in a relatively early stage of the war, and yet the war still continues. Although the decisive effect of that battle is perhaps not recognized by all, it nevertheless already means victory. But the war must still be carried on for an undefined time, until "Victory Day." Precisely this is the situation of which the New Testament is conscious, as a result of the recognition of the new division of time; the revelation consists precisely in the fact of the proclamation that that event on the cross, together with the resurrection which followed, was the already concluded decisive battle.[14]

Scripture clearly teaches this perspective: Christ has already won the victory (1 Cor. 15:1ff.; Eph. 1:15ff.; Col. 2:15; and Heb. 2:14ff.). The crucial battle has been fought and won in the incarnation and the resurrection. The cease-fire is yet future. Jesus' followers continue to fight against the principalities and powers (Eph. 6:10ff.) until he comes again to bring about the final end of the war. We do not know how long the warfare will continue. As we battle the forces of evil, we also witness in the shadow of Christ's victory on the cross and his ultimate victory to be achieved at the final coming. We fight with the conviction that someday all weapons will be placed at the feet of Jesus. This concept should encourage all believers. It can also exhort all to be faithful to Jesus and his cause.

There is an additional emphasis offered by Cullmann that can help us understand the nature of the Christian life and the place of Revelation in scriptural context. He believes that we live in the overlap of two ages, this present age and the age to come. We already live in the new age, and yet we do not fully live in the new age since Christ's final coming has not yet occurred. He writes:

> The *new element* in the New Testament is not eschatology, but what I call the *tension* between the decisive 'already fulfilled' and the 'not yet completed,' between present and future. The whole theology of the New Testament, including Jesus' preaching, is qualified by this tension.[15]

D-Day is past; V-Day is in the future. Meanwhile, we who follow Christ live "between the times." We know that Christ is Victor and Deliverer now, but we also know that there is more to come. This fits in with the definition of "eschatology" and a proper understanding of "the last days." The biblical notion of eschatology embraces both an "inaugurated" emphasis (we are already in the Kingdom and enjoy blessings as disciples of Jesus) and a "future" accent (we await future events like the final coming, the resurrection, the Final Judgment, the new heaven and new earth, and so forth).

I am reminded of the cartoon depicting a person walking

Jesus came, the heavn's adoring,
Came with peace
from realms on high,
Jesus came for man's redemption,
Lowly came on earth to die;
Alleluia! Alleluia!
Came in deep humility,
Came in deep humility.
Jesus comes
on clouds triumphant
When the heavens
shall pass away;

Jesus comes again in glory,
Let us then our homage pay;
Alleluia! Alleluia!
Till the dawn of endless day,
Till the dawn of endless day.

Jesus Came, the Heavens Adoring
Godfrey Thring
1864

around the city, carrying a sign that reads "The End is Near!" According to Scripture, there should be three characters carrying signs. Their messages would communicate Scripture's testimony: The End has come! The End is near! The End has not come! We live confidently with this tension between what we already enjoy and what we do not yet possess, all with the sense of expectancy that the end is always near.[16]

This notion of living between the times is developed in the writings of the nine authors associated with the New Testament. Actually there is not a New Testament writer, John aside for the moment, who does not speak about what it means to live between Christ's first and final comings (e.g., Matt. 28:16-20; Mark 13:32-36; Acts 17:30-31; Titus 2:11-15; Heb. 10:19-25; James 2:1; 5:8; 1 Pet. 1:13-25; Jude 3, 14-16, 18, 21).

Consider some specific themes in which this already and not yet tension is found. Christians are already in the Kingdom, and yet they await the coming of the Kingdom in its totality (Col. 1:13-14; Rev. 11:15). Already we experience God's presence through the indwelling of the Holy Spirit, but we await the complete presence of God (Eph. 1:13-14; Rev. 21:3). Already we worship, but we know that someday there will be perfect worship (Rom. 12:1; Rev. 22:3-5). Already we have fellowship with God and one another, but the perfect fellowship is yet to come (1 John 1:5-7; Rev. 21:1–22:6). Already we experience peace, joy, and love, but these will be perfect some day (Gal. 5:22-23; Rev. 22:3). Already we have experienced a resurrection, but we await a future one (Rom. 6:1-10; Rev. 20:4-6, 11-15). Already we participate in a special meal with Christ, but we await the wedding supper of the Lamb (1 Cor. 11:23-26; Rev. 19:9).

We find this theme in the writings of John as well. The tension between the now and the not yet is found in such passages as John 6:39, 40, 44, 54; 11:24; 12:48 and in 1 John 1:2; 2:18, 22, 28; 3:2-3. We already have eternal life, but we await the total fulfillment of eternal life (John 6:26ff.; 11:25; 12:23ff.; 14:1ff.). We already receive blessings because we belong to Christ, but we anticipate even richer blessings at his coming.

In Revelation, John writes about the victory that Christ has won in the past (1:5, 18; 5:5-7, 9-10; 12:1-4, 7-12), as well as the final victory at the final coming (1:7; 6:12-17; 7:1-17; 11:15-19; 16:15-21; 19:1-21; 20:7-15; 22:7, 12, 20).[17] Reflect on the following examples in the next few paragraphs.

In Revelation 1:5-8 there is a clear reference to Christ's first coming (v. 5 announces that he is the one who is "the faithful witness, the firstborn from the dead, and the ruler of the kings of the earth" and the one who "has freed us from our sins"). There is also mention of Christ's final coming in 1:7 ("Look, he is coming with the clouds, and every eye will see him"). Wedged between the references to the past and the future is a call to Christians to realize that now they are part of the Kingdom and now they are priests who belong to God (1:6).[18]

Further, consider the structure of the messages to the seven churches in chapters 2 and 3. The descriptions of Christ found at the beginning of each communication draw from the vision in 1:12ff., one that is rooted in the first coming of Christ and all that he accomplished when he lived on earth, along with the ongoing consequences of his death, burial, resurrection, and ascension. Each message ends with a promise concerning the future where final victory and blessing will be experienced. Between the two comings, the followers of Jesus are called upon to overcome such temptations as doctrinal error, immorality, idolatry, and complacency and such pressures as rejection and persecution. The term translated "to the one who overcomes" has a military background[19] and connects nicely with Cullmann's analogy of D-Day, V-Day.

Finally, we can ponder this scheme from another vantage point. The following passages focus on the tension of living a life in the middle, that is, a life between the two comings of Christ as depicted in Revelation:

- Because of Christ's first coming, how much richer are we than the Old Testament people of God (1 Pet. 1:10-12)! Even though we enjoy blessings now because of Christ (Rev. 1:5ff.; 2:9; 3:7ff.; 5:9ff.; 12:10), there is still the "not yet." We still are not free from sin (2:4ff., 14ff., 20ff.; 3:1ff., 15ff.; 18:4), and many Christians still suffer even to the point of dying for Christ (1:9ff.; 6:9ff.; 11:1ff.; 12:11; 13:9-10; 14:13; 17:6; 20:4-6). And yet we anticipate even richer blessings (7:9ff.; 21:1ff.), looking forward to a new heaven and earth where there will be no evil or sin (20:11ff.; 21:1—22:6).
- Any signs John provides with regard to the final coming of Christ are sufficiently ambiguous to keep us living as if Christ's coming is possible any day, even if we do not know the timing (3:3; 16:15). As one reads through Revelation, it appears as if the world will grow increasingly worse (e.g., 16:16ff.; 20:7ff.), that there will be a succession of evil kingdoms in the image of Rome leading up to the end. In the meantime, the church is reminded of its responsibility to worship and witness and make war against the forces of evil as it waits for Christ to come.[20]
- In Revelation the disciple's life is one of imitating the life of Christ, a life that bears faithful witness to God (1:2, 9; 6:9; 11:7; 12:11, 17; 19:10; see also 14:4ff.) while also acknowledging that the disciple will not achieve perfection in this life. Nevertheless, there is a persistent pressing on in the pilgrimage (2:10; 17:14; 22:11). John summarizes the Christian life in terms of salvation as a past fact, a present duty, and a future hope. Because Christ has saved us (1:5b) and because someday that salvation will be complete (19:1ff.), Christians must be faithful in living out the implications of their salvation.

Just as there was still conflict between D-Day and V-Day in the final days of World War II, so there will be conflict between Christ's first and final comings. The conflict involves God and his servants and the Dragon and his servants. Accordingly, Revelation was written to help

Christians remain loyal to Christ, a notion that we will explore more fully in the chapters dealing with genre and the historical setting.

Revelation was written to help us remain loyal to Christ.

This chapter reminds us that the numerous references to Christ's final coming in Scripture are not there to satisfy our curiosity about the future or enable us to work out a detailed schedule leading up to the end of the world. After all, hasn't there been consistent failure on the part of those who have made such attempts? Then what is the main purpose of those references? The New Testament writings teach that the present and future are secure in the hands of God because of his faithfulness in the past. What more did the original recipients need to know, be it those who read Romans or those who heard Revelation? For that matter, what more do we today need to know? What matters is the certainty of God's triumph when Christ is confessed as Lord and the kingdoms of this world become the Kingdom of our Lord, rooted in the first coming of Christ. His return is certain regardless of our knowing the time of the event.

There is a common theme found in passages that speak about Christ's coming a second time. It is especially applicable to the book of Revelation: Whenever and wherever Scripture speaks about Christ's final coming, its purpose is always to challenge Christians with regard to belief and behavior or to provide comfort. As disciples, we are called to worship God as creator and redeemer and to offer faithful witness to him. When we face trials, we should be comforted by the conviction that God still reigns and that he will have the final word concerning evil. We are to live lives that reflect that God has come and that he is coming again. So whenever we come across a passage addressing the final coming of Christ, we should look for a word of comfort or a word of challenge, or perhaps a bit of both. Eugene Peterson underscores this sensitivity:

> In the Revelation we are immersed not in prediction, but eschatology: an awareness that the future is breaking in upon us. Eschatology involves the belief that the resurrection appearances of Christ are not complete. This belief permeating the Revelation makes life good, for when we are expecting a resurrection appearance we can accept our whole present and find joy not only in its joy but also in its sorrow, happiness not only in its happiness but also in its pain. We travel on through either happiness or pain because in the promises of God we see possibilities for the transient, the dying, and the dead.[21]

The Bible would be, both biblically and literarily speaking, significantly poorer without Revelation. The trumpets that are sounded and the harps that are plucked are in tune. The whole book is in accord with the whole of Scripture.

Revelation provides a grand, symphonic finale to the Bible taken as a book or as one great narrative. And it corresponds nicely to Genesis. You have "protology" (the first things)[22] and eschatology (the last things). Even though God's purposes in the beginning were defiled by sin, God will have his way. In the beginning there was the garden (Gen. 2:8), the tree of life (Gen. 2:9), and a bride and a groom (Gen. 2:21-25), and so there will be when Christ comes a final time (Rev. 22:1-5). In the beginning there was the serpent (Gen. 3:1-4, 14); in the end, the serpent will be crushed (Rev. 12:9; 20:10).

If we are truly followers of Jesus the Lamb, we must listen to the lyrics he has provided John. The Victorian poetess Christina Rossetti's last sentence in her devotional commentary on Revelation sums up the role Revelation plays as well as our responsibility: "We have heard enough when God ceases to speak; we have learned enough when we have learned to do his will."[23]

CHAPTER 3

LISTENING TO THE LYRICS: THE STORIED SETTING

Behind any piece of music there is a story. A love song is written out of an experience involving an intimate relationship, or at least the hope for one. A song of lament arises out of some personal or national tragedy. A ballad tells a tale. Likewise, the book of Revelation has a fascinating story.

On the compact disk, *Unveiled Hope*,[1] singer-songwriter Michael Card recorded a biblically based and musically interesting series of songs inspired by the book of Revelation. Card's music appeals to a wide range of musical tastes from Celtic to classical, gospel to folk. In a devotional commentary that accompanied the release of the compact disk, he wrote a letter explaining the story behind the writing of the music.[2] He acknowledged that he needed to hear Revelation in the music of John's time before he could hear the book in the music of his own time. In particular, Card wrestled with the differences between John's Gospel and Revelation and observed:

> Perhaps the initial reason for my difficulty in grasping John's Revelation was not the seeming disparity between the Apocalypse and his gospel, but the seeming disparity between the Jesus revealed in each work. In the gospel, Jesus is on the whole so gentle. In the Apocalypse, He roars. But this difference is as false and artificial as the distinction many make between the God of the Old Testament and the God of the New.
>
> John wants us to understand that they both are the same Jesus. The heartbreaking beauty of His second coming is no less aweight with His glory than His first coming. The Word

made flesh, who walked dusty roads to share the good news of the kingdom, is the same as the Rider on the war horse aflame with holiness.[3]

The backdrop for all of Revelation's songs are stories involving God and his people. They are the accounts of John and other servants of God who lived in a hostile and seductive world at the end of the first century. Jesus no longer walked the dusty roads of the land of Israel. In John's day, Jesus walked among the lampstands of seven churches located in Roman Asia Minor. What was the narrative of the church at the end of the first century? How did the stories of the individual congregations fit in with the larger story God was writing? We will see that a careful reading of the book in light of its situation challenges us to reflect on how the stories of those ancient Christian communities are similar to our own.

Yesterday before Today

Revelation did not appear in a time-space vacuum. It is not to be read first and foremost in light of our historical situation but in light of the one Christians faced at the end of the first century. The book was written by a real person to real people who identified themselves with congregations in Roman Asia. Every effort must be made to understand the culture in which the original author and recipients lived. What was going on in John's life and in the lives of the members of the churches dwelling in the seven cities in Asia Minor? Why was the book written? Was there more than one reason?

Because some are so focused on learning how the book speaks to our day, the above questions are often ignored. To do so places the Bible student in great peril. Such an approach will lead the student to ask the wrong questions of individual passages, as well as the entire book. And in asking the wrong questions, we may very well miss the point of what John communicated. Bible students know that we must seek to understand the historical setting of every other book in the Bible. Why should we not do so with Revelation? Indeed, I believe when we take the time to explore the situation in John's day, the book becomes even more exciting and encouraging to Christians living in the twenty-first century.

When we fill in the historical background of a biblical work in order to understand how it spoke to the original receivers, it is like using a film-making technique called "the green screen" (some use a "blue screen"). Anyone who has seen a special on how a movie was made is familiar with the green screen. Whenever a scene calls for a backdrop that cannot safely be shot or reproduced on location, the director will film the actors in front of a completely green background. Later, using usually computer technology, the background is filled in wherever the green appears.

Salvation to God,
who sits on the throne!
Let all cry aloud,
and honor the Son.
The praises of Jesus
the angels proclaim,
Fall down on their faces,
and worship the Lamb.

Then let us adore
and give him his right,
All glory and power,
all wisdom and might
All honor and blessing,
with angels above,
And thanks never ceasing,
and infinite love.

"Ye Servants of God"
Charles Wesley
1707-1788

Reading a book of the Bible without understanding the historical background is like watching actors perform before such a screen. Until we fill in the green, the scenes do not make any sense. When it comes to Revelation, many fill in the green with situations drawn from their own day rather than John's. When they fill in the background with their own beliefs, prejudices, behavior, and practices, they are likely to distort the author's intended meaning. Sadly, when the book is interpreted primarily in light of what is going on today, current events are read back into a first-century text. And then when the newspaper headlines fade, newer headlines are inserted in a vain attempt to give Revelation an up-to-date look and relevancy.[4]

The necessity of interpreting Revelation in light of the situation in John's day remains one of the hardest fought

Without an understanding of the historical background we distort the author's intended meaning.

battles. As Bible students, we may be tempted to take what is thought to be the easiest path. But the shortcut to application that ignores John's situation and focuses on our own day has consistently resulted in misunderstanding the book's message. Before there can be application, there needs to be investigation of what each book of the Bible meant to the original recipients. This is a fundamental principle. We do this, for example, when studying Paul's letters to the church in Corinth or Philippi, and we must do so when studying God's message to the seven churches in Asia Minor.

As we attempt to comprehend the historical setting of John and his recipients we find ourselves blessed for at least two reasons. First, Revelation itself is a key source for understanding the conditions in which it was written, for both John and his audience. It describes the situation Jesus' disciples encountered at the end of the first century, specifically their trials and temptations—past, present, and future. John's work is a very reliable guide to understanding the place the church occupied in the ancient pagan world amidst the ocean of conflicting influences threatening to overwhelm many congregations.

Second, among the resources outside of Scripture, we have access to an exchange of letters between a Roman Emperor and a provincial governor. The correspondence gives an account of events of the early years of the second century, shedding light on how Roman politicians and people in general viewed Christians.

In John's day, disciples of Jesus faced both internal and external dangers. Externally, John describes opposition Christians experienced at the hands of Jews and Romans. The internal menace concerned the temptation to compromise with culture and involved such issues as doctrinal, ethical, and spiritual problems found in the congregations. These external and internal perils are related: "For where there is tribulation without, it is important to deal with the temptations within."[5]

Persecution

The term "conflict" describes the circumstances involving Christians and Romans at the end of the first century. I am using the word to refer to a clash between two opposing forces, powers, ideologies, or kingdoms because they cannot peacefully coexist. They cannot occupy the same space at the same time without strife. As the Kingdom of God expanded, it was increasingly perceived to be a danger to the Roman Empire. The very lifestyles of Christians challenged the Roman culture, which emphasized worshiping gods, embracing materialism and hedonism, and showing loyalty to the Empire by worshiping Caesar as a god.

The opening and closing chapters of the book present in a general way the nature of the conflict. Even though John sets himself apart as a prophet who receives visions, in 1:9 he aligns himself with the recipients of the book on three levels. First, the author and audience are brothers and sisters and companions because they are in the Kingdom. Second, because they submit to God's rule, together they share the same end, experiencing persecution and opposition. Third, side by side they are called upon to demonstrate steadfastness.

John also alludes to the difficult conditions at the time of writing in Revelation 22:9 and 11. In verse 9 the angel associates himself with John, the other prophets, and with all Christians by declaring that together they are those "who keep the words of this book" (see 1:3). The teaching in verse 11 is to be understood in the context of the whole document. John is drawing a contrast between those disciples who show unyielding perseverance ("let him who does right continue to do right; and let him who is holy continue to be holy") and those who refuse to be faithful in their worship of God as well as those who never worship God and instead pledge their allegiance to Satan ("let him who does wrong continue to do wrong; let him who is vile continue to be vile"). Evil and evildoers are a part of this world, and Christians must not compromise but remain constant in their loyalty to Christ (22:14-15).

Ten thousand times ten thousand
In sparkling raiment bright,
The armies of the ransomed saints
Throng up the steeps of light:
'Tis finished, all is finished,
Their fight with death and sin:
Fling open wide the golden gates,
And let the victors in.

"Ten Thousands Times
Ten Thousand"
Henry Alford
1867

We can be more specific. Consider the Jewish opposition to the Christian movement. From its beginnings the church not only won converts among the Jews (Acts 2:41; 5:14; 9:1ff.; 14:1), but it also suffered at the hands of those Jews who rejected Jesus as the Messiah (Acts 5:17ff.; 7:57–8:3; 9:1-2; 12:1ff.; 14:4ff.; 17:1ff.; 18:5ff.; 28:17ff.; 1 Thess. 2:14ff.). Such opposition continued up to John's day, as evidenced in Revelation 2:9 and 3:8-9.[6]

In Smyrna and Philadelphia, the Jews slandered the Christians by saying they were not God's people. Perhaps they argued that only those who were associated with the Jewish synagogue belonged to God. The irony is that Jesus calls the synagogue of the Jews a "synagogue of Satan." Furthermore, Revelation 2:9 refers to the afflictions and poverty experienced by Christians in Smyrna, a possible reference to physical and economic pressures exerted by the Jews (Heb. 10:32-34).[7]

Even though we should not minimize the harm done to Christians by Jews in the first century, it was the Roman attitudes and actions toward Christians that deserve special attention. Revelation suggests that at the end of the first century, Roman toleration of Christians was fading and was being replaced by growing suspicion and vindictiveness (see also Acts 16:37ff.; 19:35ff.; and 1 Peter). The Christians in Asia Minor found themselves in a period of transition where the response of the Roman government and populace toward them was changing for the worse.[8]

Rejection and oppression came about because disciples faithful to Jesus realized they could not compromise their loyalty by pledging their allegiance to the Roman government. Faithful Christians simply could not worship the Emperor as a god, nor could they accept the Roman way of life filled with idolatry and immorality.

Let's first consider the importance of the imperial cult. The Roman imperial religion was ultimately concerned with the welfare of the state, especially maintaining unity and peace in the Empire. As long as people expressed their loyalty to the superpower by participating in the imperial cult, then diverse customs and religious beliefs and practices were tolerated.

The overwhelming majority of scholars agree that the Roman cult in which the Emperor was worshiped as a god is the background behind such passages as Revelation 13:1-18; 14:9-11; and 19:19-20.[9] It was this state religion that provided the means of securing the loyalty of the people and maintaining the unity of the Empire.

The Christian faith stood in clear opposition to the idolatrous claims of the state (along with the idolatrous and pagan lifestyle it sanctioned). John challenged the followers of Jesus to spurn the state religion since they acknowledged an authority greater than the Emperor in whom the authority of the government was incarnate. Furthermore, it is well known that the imperial cult was especially strong in Asia Minor, the region where the seven churches were attempting to live out their faith.

Written correspondence between the Roman Emperor Trajan and Pliny, the governor of the Roman province Bithynia, located north of Asia Minor, illustrates the nature of the Roman state religion and the threat it posed to Christians. What is remarkable is that the exchange of the letters took place less than twenty years after John wrote the Revelation (around A.D. 95). Trajan was Emperor A.D. 98–117 and Pliny was governor A.D. 111–112.

The two letters are reproduced here in their entirety for two reasons. First, they make for fascinating reading by shedding light on how Roman officials viewed the Christian faith. Second, many Christians have never had the opportunity to read a document outside of Revelation that helps us understand the environment just a few years after John's writing had circulated among the churches in Asia Minor.

These letters are the key records we have concerning the official policy toward the Christians in the two centuries from Nero (A.D. 54–68) to Decius (A.D. 249–251), in whose brief reign the organized imperial persecution of Christianity was begun. The correspondence highlights the political charges against Christians (e.g., disobedience of imperial officials, violation of the laws on illegal meetings, and so forth) and popular grievances against the disciples (e.g., Christians were accused of being atheists because they did not worship the gods, and they were also suspected of cannibalism, due to a misunderstanding concerning the celebration of the Lord's Supper).

The two letters reproduced here demand little comment due to their clarity. The first is Pliny asking Trajan for guidance in dealing with the trials of Christians. He writes:

> It is my practice, my lord, to refer to you all matters concerning which I am in doubt. For who can better give guidance to my hesitation or inform my ignorance? I have never participated in trials of Christians. I therefore do not know what offenses it is the practice to punish or investigate, and to what extent. And I have been not a little hesitant as to whether there should be any distinction on account of age or no difference between the very young and the more mature; whether pardon is to be granted for repentance, or, if a man has once been a Christian, it does him no good to have ceased to be one; whether the name itself, even without offenses, or only the offenses associated with the name are to be punished.
>
> Meanwhile, in the case of those who were denounced to me as Christians, I have observed the following procedure: I interrogated these as to whether they were Christians; those who confessed I interrogated a second and a third time, threatening them with punishment; those who persisted I ordered executed. For I had no doubt that, whatever the nature of their creed, stubbornness and inflexible obstinacy deserve to be punished. There were others possessed of the same folly; but because they were Roman citizens, I signed an order for them to be transferred to Rome.
>
> Soon accusations spread, as usually happens, because of the proceedings going on, and several incidents occurred. An

What was the greatest menace facing the Christians in John's day?

anonymous document was published containing the names of many persons. Those who denied that they were or had been Christians, when they invoked the gods in words dictated by me, offered prayer with incense and wine to your image, which I had ordered to be brought for this purpose together with statues of the gods, and moreover cursed Christ—none of which those who are really Christians, it is said, can be forced to do—these I thought should be discharged. Others named by the informer declared that they were Christians, but then denied it, asserting that they had been but had ceased to be, some three years before, others many years, some as much as twenty-five years. They all worshipped your image and the statues of the gods, and cursed Christ.

They asserted, however, that the sum and substance of their fault or error had been that they were accustomed to meet on a fixed day before dawn and sing responsively a hymn to Christ as to a god, and to bind themselves by oath, not to some crime, but to not commit fraud, theft, or adultery, not to falsify their trust, nor to refuse to return a trust when called upon to do so. When this was over, it was their custom to depart and to assemble again to partake of food—but ordinary and innocent food. Even this, they affirmed, they had ceased to do after my edict by which, in accordance with your instructions, I had forbidden political associations. Accordingly, I judged it all the more necessary to find out what the truth was by torturing two female slaves who were called deaconesses. But I discovered nothing else but depraved excessive superstition.

I therefore postponed the investigation and hastened to consult you. For the matter seemed to me to warrant consulting you, especially because of the number involved. For many persons of every age, every rank, and also of both sexes are and will be endangered. For the contagion of this superstition

> has spread not only to the cities but also to the villages and farms. But it seems possible to check and cure it. It is certainly quite clear that the temples, which had been almost deserted, have begun to be frequented, that the established religious rites, long neglected, are being resumed, and that from everywhere sacrificial animals are coming, for which until now very few purchases could be found. Hence it is easy to imagine what a multitude of people can be reformed if an opportunity for repentance is afforded.

Trajan's response to Pliny is brief but enlightening:

> You observed proper procedure, my dear Pliny, in sifting the cases of those who had been denounced to you as Christians. For it is not possible to lay down any general rule to serve as a kind of fixed standard. They are not to be sought out; if they are denounced and proved guilty, they are to be punished, with this reservation, that whoever denies that he is a Christian and really proves it—that is, by worshipping our gods—even though he was under suspicion in the past, shall obtain pardon through repentance. But anonymously posted accusations ought to have no place in any prosecution. For this is both a dangerous kind of precedent and out of keeping with [the spirit of] our age.[10]

The letters reveal that Trajan as Emperor had no legal precedent to appeal to with regard to Pliny's questions concerning the treatment of Christians.[11] Christians aroused suspicions for two reasons. First, they were viewed as members of an antisocial cult or, in the words of the governor, a "superstition" or "disease." Second, Christ's disciples were suspect because they refused to participate in the worship of the Emperor as a god. For a Christian, only Christ could be addressed as "Master and God."[12]

A note of caution is in order. It may surprise you, but there is no clear support for the view that Christians in the first century were being persecuted in a systematic way. However, there had been outbursts of persecution. For example, Nero's persecution of the Christians living in Rome in the mid 60s is well known. It seems reasonable to assume that Christians living outside of Rome would have grown anxious, wondering if they too would soon be attacked.

When we read through Revelation, sometimes the antagonism seems to refer to events in the recent past (2:13; 6:9-11), sometimes ongoing (1:9), and at other times there are hints of persecution to come (20:7-10). Sometimes there is lack of clarity (13:1ff.). The past and present acts of hostility hint at more difficult days ahead (13:1ff.; 14:9-13; 15:7; 17:4; 19:20). Revelation teaches that resistance will become more organized and widespread; times will become tougher for Jesus' disciples.

Cultural Seduction

We now turn to what I believe was the greatest menace facing the Christians in John's day. It was not from direct persecution, but from temptation to compromise with their culture. The threat of cultural seduction lies behind many of the passages of the book.

The specter of compromise has followed God's people throughout the centuries. For example, as the Jews in Daniel's day faced the threat of "Babylonization," so the Christians in John's day faced the threat of "Romanization." John saw Roman culture, like Babylon of old, as seductress, using all of its moral, social, economic, religious, political, and military might to lure Christians into complacency in serving God and loving one another (Rev. 14:8; 17–18). Resisting the power of cultural seduction is sounded again and again in the book.[13]

It is especially in the messages to the seven churches, though not limited to them (14:4-5; 16:15; 18:4; 21:8; 22:11, 14-15), that the reader can see the temptations facing Christians to go along with Roman culture in order to get along with their neighbors.[14] Church members in Sardis (save a minority) and Laodicea had grown complacent, having abandoned their earlier faith and zeal (3:1-4, 15-19). Their complacency had provoked little, if any, response from the communities in which they lived.

Ephesian Christians had displayed doctrinal and moral purity (2:2-3, 6), but their zeal for truth caused them to forsake the love they had for God and other disciples at the beginning of their pilgrimage (2:4-5). Perhaps they had forgotten to heed Paul's earlier counsel to speak and live the truth in love (Eph. 4:15).

Acceptance of false teachers and their teachings had resulted in Christians at Thyatira and Pergamum practicing immorality and idolatry (2:14-15, 18-23; see also 2:6). These two churches probably provide evidence of the power of trade guilds in the ancient world. It was expected that workers associated with certain occupations would worship the gods and goddesses who blessed their labors, and that worship often resulted in committing acts of immorality with the temple priests and priestesses.[15]

Only disciples in Smyrna and Philadelphia escaped censure. Ironically, their refusal to compromise had led, or was going to lead, to attempts to destroy them (2:10; 3:10).

Revelation divulges that some Christians had clearly capitulated to culture, while others had conspicuously remained ardent in their loyalty to Christ. In between these two extremes were followers who needed to be shaken from their spiritual lethargy and challenged to accept the cost of discipleship. All the churches in Asia Minor were admonished not to reflect the character of the cities in which they lived. Why? These cities were fashioned in the image of Rome, the capital of the Empire, a city noted for its depravity and violence. On the contrary, the Christians were called upon to repent and remain uncontaminated by the sins of a culture opposed to God (2:5, 16, 21-22; 3:3, 19; see also 9:20-21; 18:4).

By rejecting these lifestyles Christians highlighted the distinctiveness of their way of life: Idolatrous and licentious living were not tolerated. Their separatism combined with their customs led to misunderstandings in which Christians were accused of numerous offenses, ranging from immorality to atheism to cannibalism to anarchy.[16]

Thus Revelation presents a picture of the Roman way of life versus the Christian way of life (2–3; 9:20-21; 13:1ff.;

18:1ff.; 21:8; 22:11, 14-15). The former involved recognition and acceptance of other religions and behaviors opposed to the Christian view while at the same time supporting the right of the Empire and Emperor to command supreme allegiance through the Roman state religion (9:20-21; 13:1ff.).

The Christian faith stood in direct opposition to idolatrous claims of the state and the idolatrous and libertine living it sanctioned. To become and to remain a Christian demanded absolute faithfulness to God and the way of life ordained by him. Hence John's readers were exhorted to turn their backs on idolatry, immorality, and other practices so readily accepted by the Roman people. Moreover, Christians were admonished to spurn the state religion since they acknowledged an authority greater than the Emperor, in whom the authority of the state was incarnate.

Through many dangers,
toils and snares
I have already come
'Tis grace that brought me safe
thus far
And grace will lead me home

Yes, when this heart and flesh
shall fail
And mortal life shall cease
I shall possess within the veil
A life of joy and peace

Amazing Grace
John Newton
1779

Accordingly Christians were not acceptable to the Roman government and its people politically, religiously, and socially. Politically, Christians were viewed as a danger to the unity of the Empire by their refusal to worship the Emperor as a god. Religiously, Christians repudiated the legitimacy of other religions. Socially, Christians rejected the pagan way of life. By their very lifestyles Christians opened themselves to attack. Rejection and oppression were unavoidable. Revelation called upon believers to demonstrate the separateness of the Christian life, a life that demanded absolute devotion and obedience to God. Ironically Christians were viewed as aggressors. They sought to win converts, and, in turn, those converts were to become witnesses to the lordship of Christ.[17]

Today in Light of Yesterday

Once we have reconstructed the first-century culture in general, it is appropriate to cross the bridge to our own century. Indeed, a reading of church history reveals that the twin threats of government persecution and cultural seduction have been present throughout the centuries. Whenever we as Christians seek to be countercultural, we will be perceived to be enemies of the status quo. As a result, we should not be surprised to experience the world's enmity.

As I have stressed, the starting point for interpreting Revelation correctly and applying it meaningfully rests in understanding how it spoke to disciples in the first century. It does not take much effort to realize that the book still speaks to Christians. Rather than reading with today's newspaper in one hand and Revelation in the other and seeing contemporary events predicted in a first-century document, we should understand the "newspaper headlines" in John's day first and foremost. Our common ground for understanding the book is not current events but the interpretation of the Bible in light of ancient events, specifically the events in John's day and in the decades immediately following the writing of Revelation.

This point was driven home to me when I was in Warsaw, Poland, teaching a group of preachers how to preach the book of Revelation. It dawned on me that a Polish preacher would not necessarily preach what an American would preach, especially if the latter were using an American newspaper to interpret the scenes in Revelation. If the Polish preacher were to use a native newspaper, the conclusions could very well be different because the headlines may not be the same as those found in the American paper. For example, the week that I wrote the first draft of this book, one of the worst hurricanes in history struck southern portions of the United States. The damage from Hurricane Katrina was incalculable.[18] Many American preachers used its occurrence as a springboard to deliver dire predictions that the end of the world was near. I learned from my Polish students' e-mails that the hurricane never made it to the front pages of their newspapers. Preachers living thousands of miles away in Poland would not have been able to use a catastrophic storm that had hit the United States to indicate where history was on the prophetic timetable!

When we understand the setting of Revelation, we see that John's work emphasizes a message found throughout Scripture. The God we worship is the God of "the underdog." This theme is found in the Old Testament: Moses confronting Pharaoh; Joshua and his ragtag army fighting the forces of the Canaanites; David challenging Goliath; Elijah rebuking the prophets of Baal; Isaiah and Hezekiah rejecting the claims of Sennacherib and the mighty Assyrian army; and Daniel not bowing before the might of Babylon. The story continues in the New Testament: John and his band of Jesus-disciples refusing to compromise with Rome; Peter and John ignoring the threats of the Jewish leaders; Paul confronting the Athenians; and, supremely, Jesus himself reigning in victory in spite of all the forces of evil allied against him.

In the opening scene from Gerd Theissen's novel, *The Shadow of the Galilean*,[19] its fictional character, Andreas the Jew, has been arrested by the Romans. At his interrogation, the Roman officer in charge makes an offer: Follow the Galilean named Jesus and spy on him and report on his teachings and actions so that a case can be made against Jesus and his small band of followers. The Roman politicians were growing anxious. Is this Jesus going to mean trouble for Israel and for Rome? That is the question the officer wants answered. The Roman has made it clear to Andreas that he must accept the offer to spy on Jesus, for neither Andreas nor Jesus were any match for Roman might. Andreas challenges the Roman in the following exchange:

> "God is not like the gods of the nations. The invisible God does not deal with the powerful but with the outcasts who are driven into the desert."
>
> I saw how the officer winced.
>
> "Do you doubt that the gods are on the side of the Roman Empire? How could it have spread so far? How could a small city become a world empire?"

> "All the nations think that the gods are on the side of the victors. But we know that the invisible God can be on the side of the losers."

Nearly a century ago, the British scholar H.B. Swete wrote the following about the meaning of Revelation 12:6 where the people of God flee to escape the destructive power of the Dragon, Satan himself: "To some extent the solitary life is a necessity imposed upon Christians by their religion: to the end of the present order the Church dwells in the wilderness and is a voice crying in the wilderness."[20] Is God on the side of the underdogs, those who are driven into the desert? A decisive "Yes" is Revelation's confident retort.

The book of Revelation opens against the backdrop of Patmos where an aged apostle has been banished, all alone, where there is no city (1:9). In the succeeding chapters we read of Christians dwelling in cities, cities that lived in the shadow of the greatest city of the ancient world, Rome. And we see the forces of the imperial city, Rome itself, and the seven cities of Asia Minor aligned against the small congregations, either persecuting them or threatening to do so while always attempting to seduce them to worship false gods and what the world offered. Is it not paradoxical that John's final vision is that of the holy city, the New Jerusalem, a symbol for the people of God?

But until we dwell perfectly with God, we continue to live in cities alienated from God due to ungodly living of their citizens. We must heed the voice from heaven that warned Christians about the perils of living in Babylon: "Come out of her, my people, so that you will not share in her sins, so that you will not receive any of her plagues; for her sins are piled up to heaven and God has remembered her crimes" (Rev. 18:4-5). These verses serve as a reminder through the centuries that the people of God must never compromise their identity. Jesus' followers know that the delights found in Babylon are doomed; someday its music will cease (18:22). They also know that someday there will only be songs offered in praise to God when evil is abolished and goodness reigns (19:1ff.). Disciples of Jesus know that we must be present *in* the city, *with* and *for* the city. Why should we not be *of* the city? Because it's an earthly city, and we are a heavenly city.

I have used designations like "Babylonization" and "Romanization" to describe ancient situations facing God's people. As a Christian who is an American citizen two questions haunt me: Is one of the greatest threats to the integrity and witness of the church the "Americanization" of disciples of Jesus? Do Christ's enemies find the American church enough of a threat to bother opposing?

CHAPTER 4

LISTENING TO THE LYRICS: THE STYLE

As my collection of compact disks has grown over the years, I have chosen to arrange them according to the types of music represented. Of the approximately seventy-five types sold in music stores in the United States, I have representatives of the following: a cappella, alternative, barbershop, bluegrass, blues, boogie-woogie, calypso, chant, choral, classical, country, country-western, Dixieland, easy listening, folk, gospel, hard rock, jazz, Latin, mariachi, Motown, New Age, new country, new wave, opera, pop, progressive rock, rap, reggae, rhythm and blues, rock, rockabilly, rock and roll, swing, world music, and zydeco. At times, cataloging can be quite complex since some disks are hybrids, combining two or more styles.

My reading habits reflect a hybrid approach as well. In addition to reading works associated with Scripture (e.g., commentaries, books on theology, and so forth), I also read biographies, historical novels, thrillers, westerns, science fiction, poetry, and books dealing with politics, travel, art, and photography, to name a few.

Just as a knowledge of music and literature styles helps me better understand what I am listening to or reading, so also an understanding of Revelation's style or genre will help you appreciate that style and see how it positively impacts our reading and interpreting the book. The term "genre" refers to a group of works that bears one or more common traits.

As a child, I learned to memorize the books of the Bible in their canonical order. But I also became aware that "the Bible library" was arranged in a scheme similar to the way one would arrange a private library of books or music. I remember a multicolored library chart that hung on a wall in my third grade Sunday school classroom. All of the books of Scripture were arranged neatly on the shelves and grouped according to genre.[1] I learned that some books were labeled as law, others poetry, still others as history, and many were identified as prophecies. On the New Testament shelf, I saw that the Gospels were classified as biography, Acts was history, and that there were twenty-one letters (or epistles). Standing all by itself at the end of the shelf was the book of Revelation, and it was labeled "Prophecy." Years later, I learned that such an identification did not go far enough in identifying the last book of the New Testament. As we will see, Revelation is prophecy and more.

With regard to the importance of understanding the genre of a book, Sidney Greidanus remarks:

> Our perception of form sets our expectations and guides the questions we ask. . . . A genre mistake takes place when the genre of prophecy or apocalypse is understood as historical narrative. . . . A genre mistake leads to faulty interpretation because the interpreter will ask the wrong questions. . . . Genre mistake alerts us to the fact that one's perception of the literary form of the text determines the questions one asks."[2]

Genre matters. If we do not keep it constantly in mind as we are interpreting a book or a passage, we will likely misinterpret Scripture. For that matter, this is true for anything that we read. For example, if I showed you a week's worth of mail that I receive, you could automatically arrange the various pieces in light of the genres. In those stacks you would likely find bills, advertisements, magazines, personal letters, church newsletters, invitations to weddings, and so forth. You would be able to interpret them correctly because you know that a personal letter has a certain style and is read differently than an advertisement addressed to "Occupant." All of us do genre analysis daily, whether we recognize it or not, when we read something, listen to the radio, or watch television or a movie.

Lift up the trumpet
and loud let it ring:
Jesus is coming again!
Take heart, ye pilgrims,
rejoice now and sing:
Jesus is coming again!

Shout from the hilltops
the joyful refrain:
Jesus is coming again!
Coming in glory
the Lamb that was slain:
Jesus is coming again!

"Lift Up the Trumpet"
Jessie E. Strout
19th century

Revelation is unique; there is no other book like it in the Bible. In terms of the music metaphor we have been using, John has created a new kind of music to sing his song. It is distinctive because we see that John combines three kinds of literature that were popular in his day to communicate what he saw and heard. Separately, the three were well known. Putting them together, however, John created a new kind of book. I believe that the people who received the book would have recognized what John was doing. Furthermore, not only was such a combination appropriate from a literary perspective, but we will also see that the strategy was especially fitting for the pastoral purpose of the book.

In recent decades, numerous scholars have suggested that a comparison between Revelation 1:1ff. and 22:6ff. supports the view that the book is a hybrid work. Specifically, it contains prophetic, apocalyptic, and letterlike (or epistolary) features. That Revelation is part-apocalypse is supported by Revelation 1:1, which opens the book with the declaration "the revelation [or apocalypse] of Jesus Christ" (see also 22:6, 8). The book's prophetic nature is emphasized in 1:3 where John refers to the one who reads and those who hear "the words of this prophecy" (see also 22:6, 7b, 9, 10, 18-19). Finally, the book begins (1:4-6) like a letter: "John, To the seven churches in the province of Asia: Grace and peace to you" and ends (22:21) in a way similar to other New Testament letters: "The grace of the Lord Jesus be with God's people. Amen" (see also 1 Cor. 16:23; Gal. 6:18; Phil. 4:23). In addition, chapters 2 and 3 are written expressly to the seven churches.

More precisely, I believe that John's writing should be viewed as a Christian prophetic-apocalyptic-circular letter.[3] Such a description needs to be evaluated and its importance for interpretation highlighted. Revelation is, above all, a Christian work. It was written by a follower of Jesus, the apostle John, to followers of Jesus living in Asia Minor. Virtually every major section says something about Jesus and his church.

A Christian Prophecy

John clearly identifies his work as a prophecy (1:3; see also 22:7b, 10, 18-19; 19:10), and he is viewed as a prophet (22:9; see also 10:7, 11; 22:6). But in what sense is Revelation prophetic? Unfortunately, it is far too common for Christians to focus almost exclusively on the predictive nature of prophecy. They assert that prophets predict the future and that their predictions are found in their sermons and writings.

However, countless scholars have demonstrated that the dominant emphasis in the prophetic writings is not on predicting the future but on proclaiming God's will.[4] A simple way of putting it is that in prophetic writings there is both foretelling and forth-telling. "Foretelling" emphasizes the predictive nature of prophecy, and "forth-telling" stresses the prophet's goal to set forth the Word and will of God. Contrary to popular opinion, the emphasis is on the latter in which prophets set forth God's desires. A prophet proclaims both what God intends to do and what God intends for his people to do in light of the future.[5]

Indeed, this forth-telling emphasis with its call to obedience is the note that John sounds in the very first place where he identifies his work as a prophetic one: "Blessed is the one who reads the words of this prophecy, and blessed are those who hear it and take to heart what is written in it, because the time is near" (1:3). Unfortunately, The New International Version's rendering obscures this emphasis. The phrase "take to heart" should be translated "obeys" or "heeds." In every other place where the Greek term appears focusing on a person's duty, the NIV translators emphasize the call to obedience (2:26; 3:3, 8, 10; 12:17; 14:12; 22:7, 9; see also 16:15 which implies obedience). Why they did not do so in 1:3 is a mystery. Prophecy is to be obeyed. It is true that John provides scenes of the future (e.g., the destruction of evil kingdoms, the Final Judgment of the righteous and the unbelievers, the establishment of the new heaven and new earth, and so forth), but the future-oriented passages are meant to challenge the people of God to be an obedient people until he comes or until they die.[6]

Symbolic language is used to address the deeper spiritual realities in the battle between good and evil.

Revelation is prophetic in both character and intention. John the prophet viewed his task as involving the presentation of the Word and will of God to the people of God in a particular place at a particular time. The inspired prophetic perspective that he was given resulted in a book that helped its recipients penetrate the eternal issues behind the crisis of his day (1:9; 2:7, 11, 17, 29; 3:6, 13, 22; 17:3; 21:10). Like his Old Testament predecessors (e.g., Isaiah, Jeremiah, Daniel, Ezekiel, and others), John revealed to God's people their duties to be carried out in tough times, and he assured them that God's purposes would be fulfilled.

A Christian Apocalypse

The first word in the Greek text of John's work is translated "revelation" or "apocalypse" (1:1) and hints at a second genre.[7] The term describes the contents of the work; it is filled with visions and auditions (see also 22:8 where John testifies that he is "the one who heard and saw these things"). There is no proof that the word was used in ancient times to describe a particular type of literature. In recent decades, however, scholars have suggested that there is a body of literature that can be classified as apocalyptic. These apocalypses have similar characteristics, including other-

'Mid toil and tribulation,
and tumult of her war,
She waits the consummation
of peace forevermore;
Till with the vision glorious
Her longing eyes are blest,
And the great Church victorious
Shall be the Church at rest.

Yet she on earth hath union,
With God, the Three in One,
And mystic sweet communion
With those whose rest is won:
O happy ones and holy!
Lord, give us grace that we,
Like them, the meek and lowly,
On high may dwell with Thee.

"The Church's One Foundation"
Samuel J. Stone
1868

worldly beings communicating a revelation to humans (Rev. 1:1; 5:5; 7:13; 10:1ff.; 17:1ff.; 19:9ff.; 21:9–22:5; 22:6, 8-11, 16); an awareness of the supernatural world, as well as the natural world (4:1ff.; 9:1ff.; 12:7; 14:18; 16:15; 20:1ff.); and a view of the end when the universe (21:1ff.) and God's people (6:ff.; 7:13ff.; 21:2ff.; 22:3ff.) are completely delivered from evil.[8]

Moreover, these apocalyptic works spoke words of comfort and challenge as God's people faced suffering and defeat. Their authors wrestled with such profound questions as: Why do God's people suffer at the hands of wicked people? Does God really care? Will the faithful ever be vindicated? How should God's people behave until judgment comes?

To guide Christian readers attempting to live out their faithfulness in a hostile world, apocalyptic authors present answers to such questions in symbolic language. In order to speak about the deeper spiritual realities in the battle between good and evil, they communicated through these symbols[9] that literally permeate the apocalypses.[10] It was a language that would have been understood by the faithful. We are not certain, however, whether unbelievers would have been able to understand the works.[11] Through the use of symbolic language, authors like John proclaimed that God would have the final word: The faithful will be rescued and rewarded and judgment will be carried out against all evil powers and those who have been their allies, people included.

It appears that, primarily through the use of metaphors and symbols, the authors of apocalypses addressed the realities of the struggle of God's people. Due to the major role symbolism plays in Revelation, a separate chapter will be devoted to the language.

I remember a youth conference that I spoke for many years ago. At the end of my sermon, the sponsors showed a recently released cartoon presentation of C.S. Lewis's famous *Narnia Chronicles*, specifically *The Lion, the Witch and the Wardrobe*. During its showing, I was seated behind a dozen or more teenagers, some of whom were Christians, but most of whom were not. I recall that at the end of the movie one of the non-Christians turned to her friend and said: "So that is what the story is about! It is about Jesus and his death and resurrection."

Why had she been able to make the connection? When she first saw the movie, she told me, she had viewed it on television by herself. This time the setting was different. She was in a church building, and I had just finished preaching on Jesus as Lamb and Lion. The sermon had provided her a context in which she could understand the story's message. She had come to realize that it was not merely a story about good versus evil, but ultimately a story about Jesus. Aslan the Lion of the *Narnia Chronicles* was Jesus, and the witch was Satan. The stories of Jesus as told by both John and Lewis are a testimony to the captivating power of symbolic language.

The hyphen in the description presented above—Revelation is a prophetic-apocalyptic work—indicates a close connection between the two genres. One scholar went so far as to call apocalyptic a child of prophecy.[12] While both genres emphasized moral and spiritual truths and assured people that God was still in control, apocalypses made more extensive use of symbolism than did prophecy.

A Christian Circular Letter

Finally, Revelation should be viewed as a "circular letter." The letters found in the New Testament were written messages sent to people because the author could not deliver the message in person. In fact, the seven churches form a large circular pattern, like a delivery circuit, when viewed on a map in the order presented in Revelation 2 and 3, starting from and returning to Ephesus.[13]

John begins and ends Revelation like other letters (1:4ff.; 22:21). The body of the document would include the prophetic-apocalyptic sections (1:9–22:7).[14] It was a letter to be read during an assembly of believers (1:3; see also Acts 15:30-31; 1 Thess. 5:27; Col. 4:16). In addition, it was a letter meant to circulate among several congregations (1:4, 11; see also 2:1–3:21; see also Col. 4:16; James 1:1; 1 Pet. 1:1).[15]

If Revelation is a circular letter, then John's role as a type of pastor to the seven churches is especially highlighted. He was aware of their circumstances, and he desired to provide the watchful and responsible care they needed if they were to remain loyal to Christ. His pastorate, so to speak, ultimately included all the churches throughout the world, not just the seven mentioned in the opening chapters. And just like the other New Testament epistles, John has continued to speak to Christians throughout the ages.

Keeping in mind that Revelation is also a letter helps us appreciate the role that the doxology of 1:4-8 plays. It is generally agreed that the thanksgiving sections (Phil. 1:3-11, for example) and doxology sections (Gal. 1:1-5, especially v. 5) found at the beginning of letters give a hint of the major themes to be developed throughout the book.[16] This seems to be the case with the doxology in Revelation. The work of God, Christ, and the Holy Spirit pervades the book. Similarly the conflict between the priests of the Kingdom of God and those who reject Christ is also a major theme. Of course, the references to Christ's first coming (1:5) and the final coming (1:7) provide the context for the conflict.

Strategies Rooted in the Style

Not only did John use literary genres familiar to his readers, his unique combination of the three was especially suitable for the pastoral purpose of the book. All three genres had been used before the writing of Revelation to communicate messages to God's people who were facing various types of conflict and in need of comfort and challenge. For example,

Israel's internal and external problems are addressed in the writings of the Old Testament prophets. Books like Daniel or Ezekiel with their apocalyptic features are responses to various crises. The New Testament provides ample testimony to the use of the letter in responding to internal difficulties (e.g., 1 Corinthians) or external threats (e.g., 1 Peter).

The wedding of prophecy, apocalypse, and letter by John was an effective way of presenting the Word and will of God to Christians in Asia Minor.[17] All three contributed to making the book personal rather than detached, pastoral rather than theoretical, direct rather than roundabout, and intelligible rather than obscure. In using the three styles, John challenged the disciples to perceive the true nature of their struggle: It was a conflict involving God and his followers and Satan and his allies. God's people were exhorted to perform their responsibilities faithfully, resisting the temptation to compromise their witness to the lordship of Christ.

Awareness of the genres John used certainly challenges the way many Christians approach Revelation today. For example, the foretelling note is often emphasized to the neglect of the forth-telling emphasis. When this is done, a genre mistake is made. People misread Revelation and, therefore, misapply it. Rather than using the book to predict the future in great detail, the book should be used to guide Christians in proper living between Christ's first and final comings. Christian character, conduct, and call to witness are highlighted again and again. As I noted earlier, this emphasis is often overlooked due to an obsession for using the book to interpret current world events. To counter this, there is value in fleshing out in a general survey John's methods for comforting and challenging Christians.

It is important, then, to show how John used the three genres to influence his audience. What strategies did he adopt?[18] How was the book relevant for the first-century believers, and how does it apply to us today? If we take time to read the book carefully, asking the right questions, it becomes apparent that there is a marbling effect. John has layers of visions mingled with layers of exhortations and words of encouragement. Such artistry addresses a key concern proposed in the chapter on Revelation's storied setting, namely, how disciples of Jesus should demonstrate their commitment to God and Christ in the midst of opposition and cultural seduction. If we analyze John's techniques for interlacing visions with words of comfort and challenge, we discover that he uses at least seven strategies.[19]

First, John's designations for Christians are ultimately a reminder of who they are and what they should be doing. His most frequent name used for the disciples is saints [5:8; 8:3-4; 11:18; 13:7, 10; 14:12; 16:6; 17:6; 18:20, 24; 19:8; 20:9 (in 20:9 the NIV translates "saints" as "God's people"); see also 22:11].[20] They are to live holy lives in an unholy world. Disciples are also called priests who serve God (1:6; 5:10; see also 20:6; 22:3), God's people (18:4; 21:3; see also 5:9; 7:9), the church (1:4, 11, 20; 2:1, 7, 8, 11, 12, 17, 18, 23, 29; 3:1, 6, 7, 13, 14, 22; 22:16), servants (1:1; 2:20; 7:3; 10:7; 11:18; 15:3; 19:2, 5; 22:3, 6), fellow-servants (6:11; 19:10; 22:9), brothers (1:9; 6:11; 12:10; 19:10; 22:9), witnesses (11:3), a bride (19:7; 21:2, 9; 22:17), a city (3:12; 21:2, 10ff.). They are the called, the chosen, the faithful (17:14) as well as the righteous (22:11).

Second, there are a number of phrases used to describe Jesus' followers. They are those who are keepers of the testimony of Jesus (14:12; 22:7, 9), obeyers (12:17), and hearers (2:7, 11, 17, 29; 3:6, 13, 22; 22:17, 18; see also 1:3). They are also watchers (16:15) and keepers (16:15), fearers (11:18; 19:5) and followers (14:4). Moreover, disciples are those whose names have been written in the book of life (21:27), those who have been purchased (14:3), those who have maintained their purity (22:14), and those invited to the wedding supper of the Lamb (19:9). One phrase needs to be highlighted. "To the one who overcomes" is used more than any of the above and is a call to overcome any number of evils (2:7, 11, 17, 26; 3:5, 12, 21; 15:2; 21:7).[21]

Third, John encourages and exhorts God's people through the use of direct commands. In particular, disciples are commanded to repent (2:5, 16; 3:3, 19), to remember (2:5; 3:3), to do deeds (2:5), not to fear (2:10), to be faithful (2:10), to be watchful (3:2), to strengthen (3:2), to obey (3:13), to hold fast (2:25; 3:11), to be zealous (3:19), to leave evil behind (18:4), to rejoice (12:12; 18:20), and to praise God (19:5). In addition to these specific exhortations, Christians are challenged to hear (that is, to obey) what the Spirit says to the churches (2:7, 11, 17, 29; 3:6, 13, 22). A similar phrase is found in 13:9, 18. Four commands are found in 22:11 and two in 22:17.

All glory and praise
to the Lamb that was slain,
Who has borne all our sins,
and has cleansed every stain.

Hallelujah!
Thine the glory,
Hallelujah!
Amen!
Hallelujah!
Thine the glory;
Revive us again.

"We Praise Thee, O God"
William P. Mackay
1863

Fourth, four times we find the phrase, "This calls for . . ." In 13:18 and 17:9, Christians are called to demonstrate proper behavior in responding to evil powers. Christians need wisdom and knowledge in order to recognize the tactics of the forces of evil. Only then can they know how to conduct themselves as servants of God. The phrase is also used in 13:10 and 14:12 to summon the readers to perseverance, faith, and acceptance of God's will. As wisdom is needed to understand the nature of evil, so perseverance and faith are needed to withstand the same evil forces, namely anti-Christian government and anti-Christian religions. As we observed in the second chapter, John is speaking about the Roman Empire and the imperial cult of his day. He calls upon his brothers and sisters to demonstrate both wisdom and courage while facing the evil forces of their day. The power of evil is great; perseverance and faith are needed if the Christians are to be victorious. The strategies of the beast are both deceptive and coercive (13:1ff.). A knowledge that leads to insight is needed if the disciples are not to be deceived and are to remain faithful.

Fifth, privilege and responsibility are brought together in the so-called seven beatitudes (1:3; 14:13; 16:15; 19:9; 20:6; 22:7, 14).[22] The first and sixth beatitudes in 1:3 and 22:7 are

Rather than using Revelation to predict the future, it should be used to guide us in proper living.

virtually identical: God's servants are blessed (i.e., an approval by God that results in joyful confidence) because they have heard God's Word and obeyed. Similarly, in 16:15 the Christian must always be on guard. Christ will come unexpectedly so the Christian's character and conduct must be a life seeking to be obedient to God's will. At the final coming the righteous are blessed because they are invited to share in intimate fellowship with Christ because of their faithfulness (19:8). Finally, Jesus pronounces as blessed those who have remained pure and faithful, in contrast with those who are "the dogs, those who practice magic arts, the sexually immoral, the murderers, the idolaters and everyone who loves and practices falsehood" (22:15).

Two of the beatitudes are linked with Christians who have been faithful unto death. First, in 14:13 those who remain faithful to the Lord unto death and do not worship evil will be blessed. Because they have persevered and refused to worship false gods, their fate will not be like the death of those who worship the beast (14:11). Second, those who remained faithful unto death will be blessed because they share in the first resurrection (20:4-6). Whether one believes this passage speaks about those who will reign with Christ on earth for one thousand years, or reign with Christ upon their death, is beside the point. Those who participate in this resurrection are those who have remained faithful to Jesus. These participants include both those who were executed because they did not give in to evil forces, and those who died natural deaths and were faithful until the end.[23]

Sixth, even the formula, "if anyone," tells us something about the disciple's life. In 13:10 we read:

> If anyone is to go into captivity,
> into captivity he will go.

If anyone is to be killed with the sword,
with the sword he will be killed.
This calls for patient endurance and faithfulness on the part of the saints.

Even though there are questions concerning the precise meaning of this verse, what must be stressed is that John is informing readers how they should (or perhaps should not) respond to the beast who makes war against the saints (12:17). I take the verse to mean the disciple accepts imprisonment and even death for the cause of Christ.

The fate of those who do not remain faithful is recorded in 14:9b-10 where an angel declares: "If anyone worships the beast and his image and receives his mark on the forehead or on the hand, he, too, will drink of the wine of God's fury, which has been poured full strength into the cup of his wrath. He will be tormented with burning sulfur in the presence of the holy angels and of the Lamb." In verse 11 we read a brief description of the eternal punishment of the ones who succumb, and in verse 12 John calls upon Christians to endure, obey, and remain faithful to Jesus. Again, the conflict involves the beast (a symbol for the oppressive Roman government in John's day and perhaps any oppressive governments over the centuries) and the Christian. In 13:9-10 there is guidance concerning the proper nonviolent response to hostile government activities. The believer in 13:9-10 may experience earthly torture and even death, but the faithless one will experience everlasting separation from God if there is compromise with the beast (14:9ff.).

The formula "if anyone" appears one last time in connection with Christians in 20:15 where we read: "If anyone's name was not found written in the book of life, he was thrown into the lake of fire." The context is the Final Judgment in which both Christians and non-Christians stand before the throne of God. It serves not only as a word of comfort to the believers (their enemies will be judged), but also as a warning (Christians must not compromise). They are to remain faithful so that their names shall be found in the book of life (3:5; 13:8; 17:8).

The Bride eyes not her garment,
But her dear Bridegroom's face;
I will not gaze at glory
But on my King of grace.
Not at the crown He giveth
But on His pierced hand,
The Lamb is all the glory
Of Immanuel's land.

"The Sands of Time Are Sinking"
Anne R. Cousin
1857

Seventh, there are five lists of virtues and vices where John speaks about people's conduct. Revelation 9:20-21 focuses exclusively on the characteristics of those who refuse to repent and worship God. There are four that warn or encourage Christians. In 14:4-5 Christians are "those who have not defiled themselves with women." This clause may be referring to those who kept themselves sexually pure or to those who did not commit spiritual immorality by worshiping other gods. Regardless, they are disciples of the Lamb; they belong to God and to the Lamb; they possess integrity in their speech; and they are blameless. They shall dwell with God (14:1ff.). The three remaining lists are found in 21:8, 27 and 22:15 where John contrasts those who will dwell forever with God and those who will be forever apart from God.

The above is a sampling of the places where John speaks to Christians, reminding them who they are and what they should be doing.[24] Time and again John builds on the emphasis first introduced in 1:3. He is calling upon the disciples to be obedient to God. It would be instructive to read through the entire document and find other places and strategies where John exhorts and encourages. For example, chapters 2 and 3 could be evaluated in detail where Jesus both commends (e.g., 2:2-3, 6, 8-11, 12-13, 19; 3:4, 7) and rebukes (2:4, 5, 15, 20-24; 3:1-2, 15-17). There are threats of judgment, sometimes focusing on those who are not servants of God and the world in which they live (6:1–8:5; 8:6–11:19; 15:1–16:21). Often Jesus threatens Christians with judgment (2:16, 21-23; 3:3, 16; 14:9-13; 16:15; 18:4; 20:11-15; see also 21:8, 27; 22:15). There are promises of reward scattered throughout the book (2:7, 10b-11, 17a, 26-28; 3:4-5, 11-12, 21; 7:13-14; 11:18; 14:1ff.17:14; 19:1-10), climaxing in 21:1ff.

Using the three genres (prophecy, apocalypse, and letter), John consistently weds privileges and responsibilities as he describes rewards for those who serve God. He also writes about the punishment that awaits those who renounce Jesus. At no point are the two separated. The character and conduct of the Christian life on earth anticipates or reflects the nature of life with God in the new heaven and new earth.

When reading Revelation the question we should not ask is: How does Revelation help us plot where we are on a prophetic time line so we may know when the Lord is coming? I believe that usually such an inquiry is raised because there has been a failure to identify and interpret the book's genre. The proper question that will prove more productive and more pressing is this: In light of the future God has promised, what would he have us to do now in order to be faithful to the Lamb? Such an inquiry is natural when we recall that this perspective is at the heart of the letters, prophecies, and other apocalyptic literature found in Scripture. Indeed, such a question honors the style of the book.

If we desire to sing the lyrics before the Lamb in the new heaven and new earth, we need to begin singing them now.

CHAPTER

5

LISTENING TO THE LYRICS: THE SOURCES

In Greek mythology, Muse was "any of the nine sister goddesses presiding over song and poetry and the arts and sciences."[1] The noun has come to mean "a source of inspiration . . . a guiding genius."[2] The verb means "to become absorbed in thought . . . to turn something over in the mind meditatively."[3]

Some who write music frequently speak of their muse. Their guiding light for composing a new piece of music may be some great work of art, a special friendship, or an experience that transformed a life, for good or bad. John's ultimate source of inspiration was God (Rev. 1:1; 22:6). But no doubt John became so absorbed in what he saw and heard that he turned the images and words over and over again as he meditated on them. Like the other inspired works of Scripture, we have an intermingling of the divine and the human. John received the revelation from God, but he recorded what he heard and saw in his own distinctive style. In other words, he received, he reflected, and then he reported the message using language familiar to him and the other disciples. He communicated with artistry, as we saw in the last chapter, by combining three genres (prophecy, apocalypse, and circular letter) to present God's message. He also called upon special sources and made extensive use of symbolism to describe what at times was indescribable. We cover these subjects, the sources and the symbolism, in this chapter and the next.

One of the major reasons we fail to understand Revelation is that we lack an awareness and knowledge of the sources

Holy, holy, holy,
Lord God Almighty!
Early in the morning
our song shall rise to thee.
Holy, holy, holy,
merciful and mighty,
God in three persons,
blessed Trinity.

Holy, holy, holy!
All the saints adore thee,
Casting down their golden
crowns around the glassy sea.
Cherubim and seraphim
falling down before thee,
Which wert and art
and ever more shalt be.

"Holy, Holy, Holy"
Reginald Heber
1826

John used to communicate God's message to the disciples in Asia Minor. More pointedly, we lack a sufficient knowledge of the Old Testament Scriptures that permeate the book from beginning to end. Indeed, if we would realize that John was using language and imagery familiar to the original recipients, perhaps there would be less of a tendency to read current events back into a first-century text.

When we seek the sources for John's presentation, we are faced with a doubly challenging task. First, we need to reconstruct the original setting of the Old Testament passages written to people before Christ. Then we need to see if and how John modified those passages to communicate the message to God's people who followed Christ.

Before I pursue this issue of John's use of the Old Testament any further, let me share a story. While I was working on this book during the summer of 2005, I was blessed with an opportunity provided by a Christian couple to spend some time at their cabin located near Lake Michigan where I could withdraw to pray and write. On the four-hour trip from my home to the Michigan village, just over Indiana's border, I decided to listen to *Messiah* by George Frederick Handel (1685–1759). In the English-speaking world, *Messiah* is perhaps the most loved of all classical compositions. Even though I knew a little about the life of Handel, I had taken time to review it in more detail before I listened again to the work in one sitting.

From reading the compact disk's liner notes of the performance, I learned that one Charles Jennens had written to

Edward Holdsworth, on July 10, 1741, detailing a request he had made of Handel:

> Handel says he will do nothing next winter, but I hope I shall persuade him to set another Scripture collection I have made for him, and perform it for his own benefit in Passion Week. I hope he will lay out his whole Genius and Skill upon it, that the Composition may excel all his former Compositions, as the Subject excels every other Subject. The Subject is Messiah.[4]

Describing the libretto[5] as "another Scripture collection," Jennens hints at an earlier work, no doubt *Israel in Egypt*, which Handel composed in October 1738. Jennens desired that the work by Handel be presented during Holy Week. He compiled the Scriptures that were to be the foundation for the piece, using the 1611 King James Version as his prime source. His goal was to drive home a central doctrinal point—the identification of the founder of Christianity as the Messiah, the anointed king promised by the ancient Hebrew prophets. Essentially, the events of the New Testament are related and explained through the language of the Old Testament prophecies, something the early Christians would have done as they used those Scriptures to present Jesus as the Messiah.

Handel agreed to Jennens's request, and the first performance of *Messiah* was given on April 13, 1742, in Dublin, Ireland. There are three parts. Part I has references to Christ's entry into Jerusalem and the blessedness of his followers. Part II offers a reflection on Christ's suffering and death and proclaims that Christ died to atone for the sins of mankind. The dominant theme is the personal agony of the rejected and despised Christ. It tells of his ascension, his reception in heaven, the spread of the gospel, the resistance to the gospel, and the vision of its ultimate triumph. Part III teaches the promise of resurrection and eternal life, a life opened to all people by Christ's conquest of death.

Before I began listening to the music, I reviewed the contents of the three sections and noticed that each piece of music contained one or more verses from either the Old or

New Testaments. In Handel's day, Scripture was more a part of daily life than it is today. I began to wonder if Christians today, myself included, would miss much of the beauty of the composition because of our biblical illiteracy. Accordingly, I decided to give myself a test. I was anticipating writing this chapter on John's sources and emphasizing the fact that many of us simply do not know the Scriptures well enough to realize when John is alluding to an Old Testament passage. I observed that there were fifty-three recitatives,[6] or, when subtracting the overture, fifty-two solos and chorus presentations. I wanted to know in how many of the fifty-two I could detect the Scripture being sung. At the end, I scored around seventy percent. I was able to identify every one of the New Testament passages and even some of the Old Testament ones:

17[7] Glory to God in the highest, and peace on earth, good will toward men.	Luke 2:14
46 Since by man came death, by man came also the resurrection of the dead. For as in Adam all die, even so in Christ shall all be made alive.	1 Cor. 15:21, 22

2 Comfort ye, comfort ye my people, saith your God; speak ye comfortably to Jerusalem; and cry unto her, that her warfare is accomplished, that her iniquity is pardoned. The voice of him that crieth in the wilderness: Prepare ye the way of the Lord, make straight in the desert a highway for our God.	Isa. 40:1-3
28 He trusted in God that He would deliver Him; let Him deliver Him, if He delight in Him.	Ps. 22:8

But I failed to recognize where the following Scriptures are found:

7 And He shall purify the sons of Levi, that they may offer unto the Lord an offering in righteousness.	
29 Thy rebuke hath broken His heart; He is full of heaviness. He looked for some to have pity on Him, but there was no man, neither found He any to comfort Him.	
29 Behold, and see if there be any sorrow like unto His sorrow.	

I knew the above were from the Old Testament, but I did not know they were from Mal. 3:3, Ps. 69:20, and Lam.1:12, respectively. It was embarrassing. I have been a student of Scripture for years, and I was only average on this particular test!

Unfortunately, until several years ago, I would have felt the same embarrassment if asked to identify the scores of allusions to the Old Testament John makes in Revelation. Why? I was raised in a heritage that stressed that Christians are a New Testament people, and the Old Testament was supplemental at best. What I have been reminded of over the years is that we truly need to be a Bible people if we are to understand any passage, New or Old. Far too often the cleanest pages in our Bible are those found in the Old Testament.

Let me give you a test. Would you be able to identify the Old Testament allusions in the following passages from Revelation?

To him who loves us and has freed us from our sins by his blood, and has made us to be a kingdom and priests to serve his God and Father . . .	Rev. 1:5b-6a
And you will suffer persecution for ten days. . .	Rev. 2:10
They . . . sang the song of Moses the servant of God and the song of the Lamb: "Great and marvelous are your deeds, Lord God Almighty. Just and true are your ways, King of the ages, Who will not fear you, O Lord, and bring glory to your name? For you alone are holy. All nations will come and worship before you, for your righteous acts have been revealed."	Rev. 15:2-4

A conservative estimate is that there are more than five hundred allusions to the Old Testament writings in John's work. One scholar proposes that of the 404 verses in Revelation, only 126 contain no allusions to the Old Testament.[8] Unlike passages such as Matthew 2:6, Luke 4:18-19, and Acts 2:17ff., John never formally quotes the Old Testament. He only alludes to a clause or a phrase. He assumes that the recipients will know the passages he is alluding to, as well as the layers of context and the story or stories behind those passages.

Old Testament Allusions[9]

In general, John employs Old Testament allusions in a variety of ways. He uses them to describe who Christ is, including what he has done in the past, what he does even now, and what he will do in the future. Allusions from the Old Testament describe God's majesty, power, and so forth. He uses Old Testament language to describe and address the church, including the designations, commands, commendations, threats, and promises. Powerful Old Testament images are used to portray the forces of evil and those who are aligned with those forces.

Space does not permit an extensive presentation of the references to the Old Testament, but we may start with the three examples given above. Following a brief discussion of them, I will cite some specific resources that will aid in locating them.

John employs Old Testament allusions to describe who Christ is – past, present, and future.

The first allusion is found in 1:6a where John writes that Christ "has made us to be a kingdom and priests to serve his God and Father." Undoubtedly, this is an allusion to Exodus 19:6 where God addresses the people under the old covenant in the Desert of Sinai with the words "you will be for me a kingdom of priests and a holy nation."[10]

This allusion to a declaration of blessing fits in perfectly with the situation John and his brothers and sisters were facing. Just as God called his people out of Egypt to serve him, John sees God calling his people out again. This time, it is not out of Egypt, but out of Rome (see Rev. 18:4, where Babylon is a symbol for Rome and the Empire).[11] The world does not belong to Rome but to God, and his servants must be faithful to him and not to the idolatrous claims of Rome. The Kingdom of God is greater than the kingdom of Rome, and the priests of God are to represent him in a hostile and seductive world.

The second allusion is found in a message to one of the seven churches. What Old Testament passage provides the background for the declaration by Jesus that his followers in Smyrna "will suffer persecution for ten days" (2:10)? Using a concordance and tracing the use of "ten days," we discover that there are just a handful of references. Even though such passages as Num. 11:19, 2 Chr. 36:9, and Jer. 42:7 refer to ten days, their relevance for understanding Revelation 2:10 is not apparent.[12] It is only when we turn to Daniel 1:12ff. that

The Son of God goes forth to war,
A kingly crown to gain;
His blood red banner
streams afar;
Who follows in His train?
Who best can drink
His cup of woe,
Triumphant over pain,
Who patient bears
His cross below,
He follows in His train.

A noble army, men and boys,
The matron and the maid,
Around the Savior's
throne rejoice,
In robes of light arrayed.
They climbed the steep
ascent of heav'n
Through peril, toil, and pain;
O God, to us may grace be given
To follow in their train.

"The Son of God Goes Forth to War"
Reginald Heber
1827

we find a likely link. You may recall that Daniel and his three friends were being tempted to compromise with pagan religion by eating food from the king's table. They refused to do so because such behavior would have indicated that they had pledged their allegiance to a pagan king, something unthinkable for a faithful Jew. They asked to be tested for ten days, confident that God would bless their faithfulness. And God did.

Once again, we can see why John would use such an allusion to the first chapter of Daniel. It speaks powerfully to the people of God who lived in a reborn "Babylon," as they were attempting to be faithful to Jesus, the Messiah. Just as the Babylonian gods were not to be worshiped, for John's recipients Caesar was not Lord, only Jesus.

The third Old Testament allusion is the song of Moses that John highlights in 15:3-4. It is likely that John is echoing, in part, one sung in Exodus 15:1-18. As Israel under the old covenant praised God because he delivered them from Pharaoh's army, so God will be praised when he defeats the beast that threatens the followers of Jesus. By referring to the song that is also the Lamb's song, John is emphasizing a much greater deliverance (Rev. 1:5ff.; 7:14; 12:10ff.). Particularly, the earlier victory at the Red Sea as recorded in Exodus anticipated an even greater victory achieved by the death and resurrection of the Lamb (1:5b-6).

The song of Moses is a song about judgment and may also be tied to Deuteronomy 32 (Deut. 31:19, 22, 30; 32:44). Both

Exodus 15 and Deuteronomy 32 refer to judgment. Interestingly, in Deuteronomy 32, God promises to punish idolatrous Israel along with the pagan nations that have oppressed Israel.

The song in Revelation 15 is a bit more complex than the previous examples. The actual contents of the song do not come from one primary source, either Exodus 15 or Deuteronomy 32. For example, we can compare 15:3b-4a with Jeremiah 10:7, 15:4 with Psalm 86:9-10, and 15:4c with Psalm 98:2. Over and over John creates visual and auditory collages by drawing together a variety of Old Testament passages to describe what he had seen and heard.

We need to make one final observation about the three examples, an observation that will guide us whenever we find an allusion to the Old Testament. In all three passages, God's people who follow Jesus are connected with God's people of old. Just as God expected the people under the Old Covenant to serve him as priests because he was king, likewise he expected the same of the people of the New Covenant. Revelation teaches that God has established a new Kingdom with priests who serve him (1:5b-6; 5:9-10). Just as God delivered people like Daniel and the three young men (Dan. 1:3ff.), so God will deliver the people of the New Covenant. According to Revelation, God will protect his people when they choose to be faithful to him in the face of persecution. Just as God delivered old Israel from Pharaoh, so God will deliver the followers of Jesus from any enemy, including Satan himself. According to Revelation, God is to be praised because of his righteous acts of judgment against the wicked. We need to recognize and explore such continuity wherever John makes a connection between an Old Testament passage or story and the story he is telling in Revelation.

It cannot be emphasized enough that it is not sufficient to simply find a parallel to a Revelation phrase or statement in some Old Testament book. The contexts of both books need to be examined. Also the stories behind the passages need to be kept in the forefront. We saw this when we considered both the story of Daniel and the events associated with the

Exodus. Furthermore, John may modify or adapt a passage or story to suit his inspired purposes, much the way he does with many symbols, so we must be keenly aware of the original text.

In pursuing John's use of the Old Testament, you will discover that he uses familiar Old Testament themes, stories, patterns, persons, places, and events to express distinct ideas. At times he uses the texts informally to show their fulfillment in the New Testament. As we saw above, he constantly incorporates core Old Testament meanings to teach New Testament truths.

Typology

We need to examine a special use of the Old Testament found in the New Testament. Even though "typology" may be a term that many may not be familiar with, it is, nevertheless, an important method of interpretation found in the New Testament. The word refers to an approach that links Old Testament events, persons, or things to similar events, persons or things in the New Testament. When this technique is used in the New Testament, the term "type" describes an event, person, or thing that is the past reality. The "antitype" is the new reality that corresponds to that past reality. Furthermore, typology shows that God works in similar ways throughout history to bring redemption or judgment. We could say that typology is basically a more specialized form of analogy. Some examples will make the above clearer.[13]

Jesus himself uses typology. In John 3:14, the lifting up of the image of the snake in the desert is the type (Num. 21:8-9); the antitype is the lifting up of the Son of Man on the cross. Or in Matthew 12:39-41, the deliverance of Jonah from the belly of the huge fish is the type and the resurrection of Christ is the antitype (Jonah 1:17; Matt. 16:4).

In 1 Peter 3:20-21, Peter writes that Noah's family was saved in the ark and that the ark was borne up by water. He suggests that the water is the type and baptism the antitype. The deliverance by water of Noah and his family in the ark anticipated the higher reality of salvation associated with baptism by water (Gen. 7:13ff.).

> *Revelation is ageless because it speaks to Christians of all centuries who live in cultures that seduce and oppose God's people.*

Typology is found in the examples from Revelation explored above. The ten days of testing experienced by Daniel and his colleagues are the type (Dan. 1:12ff.); the testing of the Christians in Smyrna is the antitype (Rev. 2:9ff.). Other examples may be cited. The unfaithful in Pergamum are the antitype (Rev. 2:14ff.) to those Old Testament people who followed the teaching of Balaam and Balak who enticed the Israelites to worship false gods and practice immorality (Numbers 22–24). The story of Jezebel in 1–2 Kings is the type; the so-called prophetess "Jezebel" who is misleading Christians of Thyatira is the antitype. In the writings of Jeremiah and Daniel, Babylon is powerful in seduction and opposition and is the type. For John and his audience, Rome is the antitype, a Babylon reborn (Rev. 14:8; 17:1–18:24; see also 1 Pet. 5:13).

It is helpful for us to highlight a major Old Testament event that is developed in the book of Revelation as we consider type and antitype. The book of Exodus contains the story of God's liberation of the people of Israel from slavery in Egypt. Few events of the Old Testament are as important historically and theologically as those described in Exodus. Historically, the exodus event was the birth of Israel as a nation. Theologically, the deliverance of the Jewish people from Egypt was interpreted as a prototype for God's freeing all his people.

This story of the Exodus is a fascinating theme to trace in Revelation. The type-antitype approach is developed in a significant way. The Exodus is a prominent motif elsewhere in the New Testament (Matt. 2:13-15; 1 Cor. 5:7ff.; 1 Pet. 1:19ff.), but in no other New Testament writing is this great event from Israel's past developed more fully than in

Revelation. If we are not aware of the narrative, we will miss the creative ways in which John weaves his story. It concerns the "exodus" of God's people to a better world as well as the "exodus" of evil.

A few examples will show the significance of the event. As we have seen above, there are clear allusions to the Exodus in 1:5b-6—becoming a kingdom and priests (Exod. 19:6; see also Rev. 5:9-10; 20:4-6; 22:3-5), 12:13ff.—carried out on eagle's wings (Exod. 19:3ff.), and 15:1f—singing Moses' song stressing God's reign (Exod. 15:1ff.; see also Deut. 31:19ff.). Other references include:

- The mention of "hidden manna" in 2:17 is to be linked to Exodus 16:31ff.
- The washing of the robes in 7:14 is likely an allusion to Exodus 19:10, 14.
- There is a reference to the oppressive power of Egypt in 11:8 (Joel 3:19; Ezek. 20:4ff.), a passage that describes the world's opposition to the church (under the symbol of the two witnesses, one of those witnesses is portrayed in terms associated with Moses and the power displayed in the ten plagues; see Exod. 7–11).
- The language used to describe the seven bowls in 16:1ff. is drawn from the events associated with the Exodus (Rev. 16:1-2 with Exod. 9:9-11; 16:3-4 with Exod. 7:17-21; 16:8-9 with Exod. 9:23 and Deut. 32:24; 16:10-11 with Exod. 10:22; 16:12-16 with Exod. 14:21-22; and 16:17-21 with Exod. 9:22-34).

Truly, the Exodus anticipated by John is far greater than the one experienced by the Old Testament people of God.[14] This analogy between God's Final Judgment on human history and the deliverance of Israel from Egypt shows that through all of the blood and thunder the purpose of God continues always to be a saving purpose. As in the Exodus, the plagues come as God's reply to the prayers of his suffering people crying out for vindication against their persecutors (Exod. 2:24ff.; see also Rev. 6:9ff.; and 8:1ff.). The final Exodus will not be one that merely liberates God's people from earthly powers but from all of Satan's powers, and the freedom to come is not just for Jews but those "from every nation, tribe, people, and language" (Rev. 7:9).

We also see the connection between Revelation and the events of the Exodus when we consider the battleground. Rome was forcing Christians to worship the Roman Emperor as a god. At the heart of the battle between Moses and Pharaoh was this same issue of worship. Moses stated that the people of God needed to be liberated from Egypt in order to worship God: "Afterward Moses and Aaron went to Pharaoh and said, 'This is what the LORD, the God of Israel, says: "Let my people go, so that they may hold a festival to me in the desert"'" (Exod. 5:1). As we know, Pharaoh refuses (15:2). Peterson's insight is helpful:

> Moses' task was to lead his people in worship. Pharaoh's sin was that he prevented them. The judgment plagues are visited over this issue, and this issue alone. The greatest evil that people of faith face from outside is the obstruction of worship. The greatest evil that they face from inside is the subversion of worship.[15]

It is no wonder that the theme of worship is emphasized in Revelation. The book of Revelation promises that God will judge Rome if the Empire stands in the way of people worshiping God, just as he did in Egypt (Revelation 17–18).

John is convinced that what people do in their worship lies behind what they do in the world. Worship is not to be limited to a gathering of believers on a certain day of the week; the worship or service to God is to be offered continually. Indeed, John agrees with Paul's notion that Christians are to present their lives daily to God in complete submission to his will (Rom. 12:1). It's a complete heart-surrender. If God is truly acknowledged in all that Christians say and do, the *war at the heart of things is won because the war of the heart is won.*

I believe John's typological use of the Old Testament is a key to helping us see Revelation's timelessness. In using typology, John demonstrates the enduring value of the Old Testament Scriptures. Similarly, Revelation is ageless because it speaks to Christians of all centuries who live in cultures that seduce and oppose God's people. Babylon of old is a type; Rome becomes the antitype. In turn, ancient Rome becomes a type for any godless culture that still today persecutes God's servants or attempts to lead them into compromising relationships. Because of this, Revelation is more flexible and timeless in its application. In describing the downfall of Rome for his readers, John sets it up as a type for the destruction of all godless cultures leading up even to the destruction of the world when Christ comes in glory.

Resources for Studying John's Sources

As you make this pilgrimage in studying Old Testament allusions, you may want to make your own separate concordance for the way a book like Daniel is used in Revelation, noting the specific passages in Daniel that are alluded to in Revelation. You will want to place the allusions within the contexts of both Daniel and John in order to determine the meaning.

With regard to resources that will help you find allusions, the starting point is one's own personal knowledge of Scripture. Martin Luther challenged his students to read and study the Bible so that they became fit concordances, able to locate passages readily. Christians need to study the content and context of the entire Bible as well as individual books. Of course, this is a pilgrimage that never ends.

A second study aid is a good concordance.[16] For those with knowledge of the original languages, Hebrew and Greek concordances are needed. For all students, exhaustive concordances on one or more English translations will prove invaluable.

Another resource is a Bible with an extensive cross-referencing system. It would be helpful for those who can use Greek to consult the best Greek texts and make a list of all of the allusions listed in the margins. Good study Bibles in English will be of help as well. Knowledge of the Old Testament allusions is so crucial, in fact, that I have included at the back of this book a detailed list of them.[17]

Bible software can greatly facilitate the study task, due to comprehensive search capabilities along with specialized reports. More and more resources are becoming available in electronic form, including Bible versions, Bible dictionaries, and commentaries.[18]

Finally, the best commentaries available on Revelation are those that discuss the allusions. For those who know Greek and Hebrew, I believe the finest commentary that assesses the use of Old Testament allusions in Revelation is *The Book of Revelation* by G.K. Beale.[19] Even those who do not know the biblical languages will be able to use Beale's work to a limited degree.

In closing, that John alludes to the Old Testament so extensively should not surprise us. After all, as we saw in the previous chapter, he uses three genres, two of which are found in the Old Testament, the prophetic and apocalyptic. It was quite natural to use the language employed by the authors of these genres (for example, Isaiah, Daniel, and Ezekiel) to communicate what he saw and heard. John communicated marvelous truths revealed to him by God through word pictures that were familiar to the original recipients. At times, the images are modified, at other times, they are not.[20] He used them to show that what was going on in their world and in their lives was not unusual. It involved the perpetual struggle between God and his followers and Satan and his allies.

Crown Him with many crowns,
The Lamb upon His throne;
Hark! How the heav'nly
anthem drowns
All music but its own!
Awake, my soul, and sing
Of Him who died for thee,
And hail Him as thy
matchless King
Through all eternity.

Crown Him the Lord of love!
Behold His hands and side,
Those wounds, yet visible above,
In beauty glorified:
All hail Redeemer, hail!
For Thou hast died for me:
Thy praise and glory
shall not fail
Throughout eternity.

"Crown Him with Man Crowns"
Matthew Bridges
1851

In Revelation, God gave to John on numerous occasions a timeless point of view that sees all history in a flash, from the first coming of Christ to the final coming. It is in those flashes of revelation that we receive comfort and challenge. God has always had the final word in dealing with the cultures of this world, and he always will. And such a record ought to stir our hearts and minds to be faithful until he speaks, "The End." What a rich heritage we participate in when we appreciate and understand the way John uses the Old Testament in Revelation and when we become more knowledgeable of that portion of God's Word!

Perhaps we should spend more time saturating our minds with Old Testament Scriptures rather than with contemporary events. What we need to do is renew our commitment to being a people of the book, a book that embraces both the Old and the New Testaments. We need to study the whole Bible so that we become like that fit concordance, knowing where verses, phrases, clauses, and even words are found.

The lyrics that we sing now reflect the rich heritage of songs that have been sung down through the centuries and anticipate the lyrics that will be sung before the Lamb forever and ever.

CHAPTER 6

LISTENING TO THE LYRICS: THE SYMBOLISM

As the previous chapter on sources flows naturally from the conclusions on genre, this chapter on symbolism builds on the previous two. We have seen that symbolism especially abounds in apocalyptic works. Furthermore, we have been reminded that much of that symbolism finds its roots in the Old Testament Scriptures. This chapter addresses the fundamental divide in centuries-long debates among Bible students: Should Revelation be read "literally" or "symbolically?"

As I have written earlier, I love to listen to all types of music. In recent years, I have become interested in a particular genre of music, the so-called spirituals sung by slaves in nineteenth-century America. Over the years, as I have listened again and again to these songs, their symbolism has moved me deeply. Why? Because I understood the historical setting in which they were composed and performed. For example, I remember listening to a soloist who was halfway through "Wade in the Water" when I recalled a comment I heard a preacher make. This call-and-response chant sung by Southern slaves was telling them how to escape: "Wade in the water, children," so that Master's bloodhounds can't pick up your scent. "Wear black," said another verse, to escape detection at night.

I began to wonder what other secret-meaning songs were sung in the fields while clueless overseers kept watch. "Follow the Drinking Gourd" told fugitive slaves how to follow the Big Dipper north to freedom. "The Gospel Train"

Well, who's that a-writing?
John the Revelator
Who's that a-writing?
John the Revelator
Who's that a-writing?
John the Revelator
A book of the seven seals.

Tell me what's John a-writing?
Ask the Revelator
What's John a-writing?
Ask the Revelator
What's John a-writing?
Ask the Revelator
A book of the seven seals.

19th century Spiritual

told about the Underground Railroad. "Swing Low, Sweet Chariot" told slaves to find Ripley, Ohio, where a "band of angels" would bring a "sweet chariot" to carry them across the dangerous Ohio River. "Balm in Gilead" pointed to the prophet Jeremiah, who said: "Woe to him who builds his palace by unrighteousness, his upper rooms by injustice, making his countrymen work for nothing, not paying them for their labor" (Jer. 22:13; see also 8:22; 22:6; 46:11).[1]

The masters thought Christian songs would pacify their slaves and train them to suffer quietly. Instead, the spirituals became their "liberation theology," training captives for freedom, with escape instructions and with a promise that the liberating God of Exodus was coming for them.

Just as the nineteenth-century slave masters thought the slaves were disruptive, John knew, and the Romans were beginning to learn, that the Christian faith was disruptive, even subversive. Our faith is about transformation. It speaks about a new creation, a new Kingdom, new names, new identities, new homes, and a new way of life—blessings the slaves yearned for. The Christian faith is about movement, not standing still. The faith points forward, not backward. It is about following the Messiah-Lamb (14:4ff.) and not the Dragon or his allies. Such a faith is a threat to any earthly kingdom that casts its lot with the forces of Satan, whether first century, nineteenth century, or today.

Not only is symbolism found in spirituals, we observe it in many of the church's great hymns that were not written as a response to slavery. Often these hymns allude to Scripture without directly quoting it. Moreover, many of their symbols need interpreting. Unless we are familiar with Scripture, we may well miss the biblical allusions in many of those songs. And if we do not understand what the symbols represented, meaning will escape us.[2]

To appreciate fully the music we hear, we must first hear each of the notes. Each individual note represents a distinct sound that, when strung together with other notes, creates a melody or a song. The many symbols of Revelation are the many notes that create its overall song. The symbols that make up the lyrics must be properly understood within their context, just as notes are properly understood within the rules of music.

Even though I love music, if I were shown a sheet of music with lyrics and notes, I might well be able to understand the lyrics, but the musical notes would be incomprehensible to me. Why? I don't read music. And because I do not, I certainly should not assign tones or sounds to the notes in an arbitrary way. To do so would be nonsense. Neither should we do so when determining the meaning of a word. I can even misinterpret the lyrics if I ignore the symbolism a writer may have used. The same is true with Revelation.

Literal or Figurative?[3]

Do I interpret Revelation literally? I am asked this frequently. Such a question is really not a good one. The word "literal" comes from the Latin word *littera* that means "letter." When we interpret something literally, it means we pay attention to the *littera,* that is, the letters and words that are being used by an author or speaker. What does this mean? It means that the natural meaning of a passage is to be interpreted according to the rules of grammar, speech, context, and the genre of the writing.

It is often assumed, however, that passages describing Christ's final coming and events associated with it must be interpreted literally. With such a claim, the term "literal" takes on the meaning that words are used in a straightforward way. After all, some declare, weren't the passages associated with Christ's first coming fulfilled literally? But were they? Surely, no interpreter believes that John the Baptist was a reincarnation of Elijah (Mal. 3:1-4; 4:5; Matt. 11:7-15; 14:5; Mark 11:32; John 1:20-24)! In reading the Gospels, one gets the impression that neither the religious teachers of the day nor the twelve disciples were able to interpret the Messianic prophecies properly.

If an Israelite living a generation or two before Christ's first coming had written a commentary on the prophecies he thought portrayed the coming of the Messiah, would Jesus' coming have proved him correct? Or what if that Israelite had used the Old Testament prophecies to write a novel on the coming of Christ? Do you think the novelist would have used the prophecies to write about the virgin conception, the nature of the Kingdom, and the Messiah coming as a servant? For that matter, would the central character, the Messiah, have been portrayed as a suffering servant? Would the novel have included the story of the death, burial, and resurrection of the Messiah? Hardly!

I believe the Messianic prophecies as they were fulfilled in Jesus would have been unimaginable to such a commentator or author. Indeed, the Gospels reveal the ignorance of those who lived when Jesus came. Both his opponents, such as the religious teachers, and his own twelve disciples were shocked at the way his first coming fulfilled Scripture. John reminds us on the occasion of the triumphal entry that "At first his disciples did not understand all this. Only after Jesus was glorified did they realize that these things had been written about him and that they had done these things to him" (John 12:16; see also Luke 18:34; 24:13-35, especially vv. 25ff.). The shock effect continues even into the book of Acts with the gift of the Holy Spirit, when the universal nature of the Kingdom (not for Jews only) was made clearer (Acts 1:6ff.; 8:25; 10:34ff).

Surely, such surprises should make us pause. Jesus brought salvation in a way that shocked everyone. So, I believe, will his final coming be full of surprises. No doubt the Scriptures associated with that coming will become clearer after the event.

Until then, we must be humble as we approach a book like Revelation. We are reminded that no interpreter ultimately knows the unsearchable mind of God when dealing with either the first or the final comings of Christ.

No serious student of the Bible would deny that its authors used symbols and metaphors. From beginning to end, Scripture is filled with them. It is not a matter of interpreting Revelation literally or figuratively. Instead it is a matter of interpreting Revelation, or any book of Scripture for that matter, *naturally* in light of the genre or genres of a book. Plus, we must remember that a particular genre may express truth in either literal (if by literal we mean a word's normal meaning) or nonliteral (that is, symbolic or figurative) ways. A true literal method of interpreting Scripture acknowledges that a word can take on a straightforward meaning, or it may be used as a symbol or metaphor. Bruce Metzger's insight is extremely helpful: "John does not mean what he writes, he means what he means."[4]

As Revelation 1:3 ties the prophetic genre to the call to obedience,[5] likewise 1:1 links another genre, apocalypse, with the use of symbolism. The New International Version obscures this connection when it proposes the translation: "The revelation of Jesus Christ, which God gave him to show his servants what must soon take place. *He made it known by sending his angel to his servant John*" (italics mine). Contrast the italicized words with the italicized portion in The King James Version: "The Revelation of Jesus Christ, which God gave unto him, to shew unto his servants things which must shortly come to pass; *and he sent and signified it by his angel unto his servant John*" (italics mine). The rendering "made it known" is not as clear as "he . . . signified it." The Greek verb translated "signified" means "to make known in symbols."

The same verb ("to signify") is used in John 12:33 in the same sense as Revelation 1:1. Jesus states that he will be "lifted up." John explains that this is a symbol for Jesus' being lifted up on a cross. Once again, The King James Version conveys this sense in its translation of 12:33: "This he said, signifying what death he should die."[6]

It is paradoxical, yet true, to state that the revelation (remember, the Greek term in Rev. 1:1, "apocalypse," means an unveiling, a disclosure) given to John was communicated in symbols. After all, apocalyptic works imparted their message not in plain language but in symbols. When we realize this, we will be better prepared to interpret the book properly. As a result we will realize that Revelation is a revelation, after all. In truth, there is not a chapter in the book that does not contain words that are meant to be interpreted as symbols. John writes in symbols not to conceal but to reveal the deeper spiritual realities at work.[7] John's symbols are not meant to obfuscate but to elucidate God's message. One scholar's assessment is right on target when he observes that Revelation "is a word of a different sort: an acted word, a word dramatized, painted, set to music—a word you can see and feel and taste,"[8] and, I will add, hear.

To say that a work uses symbolism does not diminish the work in the least. It does not imply that the events are any less real or historical than when a writer communicates in a nonsymbolic way. John is describing real people, events, circumstances, and so forth, but he describes most matters in symbolic (or metaphorical) terms. By using symbolic language, John is attempting to describe how historical events have happened, are happening (in his day) and will happen. For example, the symbols used to describe the forces of evil do not literally describe evil, but they create in our mind the awfulness of evil. The symbols are not the message, but rather they are the powerful vehicles in which God's message is the truth or reality to which the symbols refer. Yet it remains true that the reality symbolized is beyond present human understanding or experience.

The same is true with symbols used to describe God, Christ, the church, heaven, Satan, and hell. Generally speaking, symbolism challenges us to determine what theological truths or event in the history of God's redemptive acts are being portrayed in the symbols. For example, at the first coming, Christ came as a male-child (Rev. 12:1ff.); at his final coming he will come as a warrior on a white horse

(19:11ff.). What matters is that he came, and he is coming again. The Christmas story is filled with symbols stressing humility (Bethlehem, a manger, shepherds, and poor Mary and Joseph). The Second Advent is filled with symbols emphasizing power and majesty (a warrior lamb, a sword, a white horse, and many diadems).

The Christian faith is about movement, not standing still.

Moreover, Revelation was God's response to the profound questions John and other followers of Jesus were asking, especially the question: Where is God in an age of evil and suffering? By using symbols John was able to address in a powerful way the deeper realities of the cosmic struggle in which the people of God found themselves as they lived in a hostile and seductive world.

Even though John communicates God's message in words of a different sort, it needs to be underscored that John's message does not contradict the other New Testament writings. Often what John does is offer a fuller picture than other biblical authors. For example, whereas Paul speaks about principalities and powers in Ephesians 6:10ff., John has a more developed and thorough presentation of the nature and work of those forces of evil.[9]

Paul also writes about Satan masquerading as an angel of light (2 Cor. 11:14), while we read in Revelation a more detailed discussion of the deceitful ways of Satan who manifests himself in attractive ways. Even though Paul spoke a message of wisdom, as far as we know even he did not see or hear what John heard and saw (1 Cor. 2:9).[10]

Some Examples of Interpreting the Figurative

How, then, do we interpret the symbols found in Revelation? First, we must be reminded that symbols represent reality. It is generally recognized that a symbol both points beyond itself and participates in what it symbolizes. In Revelation, symbols are used to represent God, Christ, the Holy Spirit, the church, Satan, Christians, those who are not Christians, heaven, hell, and so forth. Concrete images like colors, animals, and numbers, as well as events, persons, and places are used by John to represent something else. In essence, a symbol is a code word, and it is not meant to paint a literal picture. For example, is Christ going to return with a sword sticking out of his mouth, or does the symbol stress the power of Christ's pronouncements (1:16)?

Another way of expressing this concept is that symbols point to spiritual realities. When reading Revelation, we need to use our ability to think by means of images and intuition coupled with our knowledge of John's world and the literary world of the Old Testament. A mind saturated with Scripture as well as a knowledge of ancient history will serve as a control for our imagination and intuition.[11] Only then can Revelation's message be understood and applied.

Obviously, John had a Scripture-soaked mind. It is also apparent that he knew the world in which he lived and the conditions of the Christians living in the shadow of the Roman Empire. I believe that John heard messages and saw visions.[12] Perhaps we could suggest that what he heard he wrote down verbatim. But what he saw he had to describe by drawing on his knowledge of Scripture and his own creative skills. He saw images and symbols in known and, at times, strange or different combinations. Hence, he used analogies to describe the experience. It is no wonder that the word "like" (a term that is not synonymous with "is") permeates the book (72 times).[13]

Three examples will illustrate what I have been saying about symbolism. One focuses on the meaning of a single word. The second addresses one of Scripture's favorite numbers. The final example reveals how John sheds light on a familiar story by retelling it in an unfamiliar way.

Example 1. Consider the use of the term "door" in Revelation. According to the dictionary a door is usually a "swinging or sliding barrier by which an entry is closed and opened."[14] Does John adapt this meaning to communicate another reality? It will be helpful to list all of the places where the word is used (italics mine):

3:8 I know your deeds. See, I have placed before you *an open door* that no one can shut. I know that you have kept my word and have not denied my name.

3:20 Here I am! I stand *at the door* and knock. If anyone hears my voice and opens the door, I will come in and eat with him, and he with me.

4:1 After this I looked, and there before me was *a door standing* open in heaven, and the voice I had first heard speaking to me like a trumpet said, "Come up here, and I will show you what must take place after this."

The use of "door" in these three passages illustrates that a symbol may have more than one meaning. A key idea associated with a door, that it is an entrance to something or someone, is preserved in all of the verses. But there are some more precise meanings pointing to deeper spiritual realities. In fact, when we consider the context (John's and often the Old Testament's), it appears as if the expression has three different meanings.

Consider the word's use in 3:8. The context (3:7-13) suggests that the small number of Christians in Philadelphia were experiencing opposition from the Jews who stressed that they (the Jews) were the true synagogue of God (3:9), not the Christians. Specifically, the Jews had access to God, not the followers of Jesus.

John appears to be alluding to the door in Isa. 22:22. The king, Eliakim, has absolute political power over the Davidic throne, and God says: "I will place on his shoulder the key to the house of David; what he opens no one can shut, and what he shuts no one can open." Whereas Eliakim was appointed to his royal office by God, Christ has been appointed to a higher royal office: He is King of kings (3:7; see also 1:5; 17:14).

Evidently, the Jews in Philadelphia were still claiming to be the people of the covenant; only they could have access to God. Consequently, only they were truly God's synagogue.

Symbols point to spiritual realities.

Jesus reminds the Philadelphian Christians that only *he*, with his absolute spiritual power, holds the power over salvation and judgment. *He* has the keys to let people enter into a life with God, and those keys[15] will be used to usher them into the house of David (3:7) and make them a pillar in the temple (3:12), symbols for the presence of God. The door is open and *no one* can shut it.

There is an intriguing possibility that John's imagery of door in Revelation 3:8 is paralleled in a story told in John 9–10, the only other place where "door" appears in the Johannine writings as a symbol (see 10:1, 2, 7, 9; cf. 18:16; 20:19, 26 where a literal door is in view). The story begins in John 9 where Jesus heals the man who has been blind since birth. After investigating the healing, the Pharisees become irate over the man's refusal to side with them by calling Jesus a sinner. In John 9:34 the man is excommunicated from the synagogue because of his defense of Jesus (9:30-33). Then Jesus speaks about spiritual blindness, with the teaching continuing into John 10 where Jesus links the image of the door with that of the good shepherd and identifies himself as being both. This is a challenge directed to the Pharisees who viewed themselves as shepherds and gatekeepers for those who wished to be in a right relationship with God. Both the blind man and the believers in Philadelphia were considered insignificant and rejected by the Jews. To both Jesus says he is the way to God. If the connection between John 9–10 and Revelation 3:7ff. is not deliberate, it is at least remarkable.[16]

On the other hand, the twice-mentioned door in Revelation 3:20 is not the door that admits one into a new relationship with God (as in new disciple or convert). To the contrary, it is a symbol used to describe the believer who repents and desires to renew a relationship with Christ and is willing to submit to him.[17]

Finally, the door in Revelation 4:1 is a door that grants

John the entrance into the heavenly throne room so that he may view the affairs of the world from a different perspective. Entering through the door leads to even more visions that John must communicate to the people of God.

***Example* 2.** This example focuses on an important number. Most Christians know that Revelation is a book filled with numbers (for example, the adjectives "first" and "third" or "a third"; and the numbers "four," "a fourth," "seven," "ten" [and its multiples], and "twelve" [and its multiples]). In Scripture as a whole, only the book of Numbers surpasses Revelation in the use of numbers! But just like colors, animals, jewels, pieces of furniture, clothing, and even weather conditions, we must determine the meaning of the symbolism of the numbers, and we must not think of Revelation as being a mathematically precise book.

If we seek such precision with numbers, we shall end up with nonsense. For example, in Matthew 18:22 Jesus teaches that we are to forgive seventy times seven. He does not mean that we have to forgive exactly four hundred and ninety times, and if a person sins one time beyond that number, forgiveness is not granted. His point is that we must always forgive.

Even in our own culture, we see the significance of numbers. We hear people speak about 24/7/365. What is meant? The combining of the numbers emphasizes totality, completeness.

So it is with the use of "seven" in Revelation. Nearly two-thirds of the occurrences of "seven" in the New Testament appear in Revelation. We read of seven churches, seven spirits, seven angels, seven seals, seven trumpets, seven thunders, seven bowls, seven plagues, seven lampstands, seven stars, seven lamps, seven heads, seven crowns, seven horns, seven eyes, seven mountains, seven kings, and even the slaying of seven thousand.[18] What does the number symbolize? Consensus among scholars is that we should think in terms of "completeness" or "totality," perhaps finding its origin in the seven days associated with creation.[19]

***Example* 3.** For a final example, consider the story found in Revelation 12:1-6.[20] A while back, I published an article on this passage entitled "Christmas on Patmos."[21] In the piece, I suggested that Matthew and Luke present their renditions of the Christmas story, but an overlooked one is the story told by John in these few verses. The big picture is that in six verses John tells the entire earthly story of Jesus, beginning with his birth and ending with his ascension. John begins telling the story by stating that he saw a sign (the noun is related to the verb translated "to signify" in Rev. 1:1).

On the basis of Old Testament symbols for the tribes of Israel, we can identify the woman of 12:1-3 as a symbol for Israel, God's people.[22] Out of Israel shall come the Messiah (Rev. 5:5).

The dragon as a symbol (the noun "sign" is found in 12:3 as well) is easy to identify, not only because John does so for us (12:9) but also because of rich allusions to the Old Testament's depiction of God's and his people's nemesis.[23] The Devil, as a representative head of all evil powers, tries to destroy the child. Ultimately, Herod was the dragon's henchman (Matt. 2:16ff.).

There is no debate about the identity of the child in 12:5; he is Christ (see also Ps. 2:7-9; Isa. 66:7). Satan is not successful in destroying the child at his birth and even on the cross. In 12:5 John summarizes the death, burial, resurrection, and ascension of Christ. Jesus, the male-child, is victorious over the dragon.

Some Guidelines[24]

Committing ourselves to studying all of the symbols in Revelation can appear to be an overwhelming task. But if we follow some guidelines, it is not impossible. To be sure, our study of Scripture over the years only enriches our understanding of the various symbols, even after we have completed an initial study like the ones given above. I offer seven guidelines to help you in your study of symbols:[25]

First, a symbol must be interpreted in light of the immediate context in which it appears. Make every effort to understand the author's intention by noting the symbol in its rich

Finish then Thy new creation,
Pure and spotless let us be;
Let us see Thy great salvation
Perfectly restored in Thee:
Changed from glory into glory,
Till in heaven we take our place,
Till we cast our crown before Thee,
Lost in wonder, love, and praise.

"Love Divine, All Loves Excelling"
Charles Wesley
1747

layers of context.[26] Care must be taken to see the core idea behind the symbol. This is only accomplished when we look at a word's straightforward meaning and see how biblical authors used it in one or more symbolic ways. Attention must focus first on how the symbol is used in Revelation and then proceed to study its use in other biblical writings (starting with the Old Testament and other writings by John and moving to other biblical and nonbiblical writings).[27]

Paying close attention to how a symbol is used within Revelation alone pays abundant dividends. For example, Revelation appears to use parody to highlight the difference between good and evil. A parody is a feeble or ridiculous imitation. The beast out of the sea is a parody of the Lamb (13:1ff.). The beast has horns, heads, crowns, and a fatal wound that had been healed. The power of its feet and mouth are stressed, and it has universal authority and is worshiped. This is evil's attempt to mimic similar attributes associated with Christ (1:14ff.; 5:5ff.; 19:11ff.). Another example of parody is detected when we compare the descriptions of the Whore and Babylon in Revelation 17:1ff. with the attributes of the Bride and the New Jerusalem in Revelation 21:1:ff.[28]

Second, seek to discover whether the symbol has a traditional meaning. For example, in the ancient world, dragons were not viewed as friendly creatures but rather were consistently associated with evil.[29] Even in examining the use of the symbol in other biblical writings, the student must be sensitive to the possibility that John may have modified the meaning and thus transformed it into a new image with a new meaning. That does not appear to be the case with dragons, however.

Third, look for those places where John himself explicitly explains the meaning of a symbol. He does so numerous times (e.g., 1:20; 4:3; 5:8; 7:13-14; 12:9; 13:18; 17:9, 12, 15, 18; 19:8; 20:4-6, 14). But for many Bible students, John does not do it enough, especially with those passages we perceive to be the more difficult ones to decipher (e.g., 666 in 13:18 or Armageddon in 16:16). And yet, can you imagine him explaining every symbol? The book's beauty would be diminished. Something happens when you turn all symbols into prose. Can you imagine doing this with poetry? The power of the words, namely their ability to capture the imagination, would be weakened.

Fourth, we need to realize that John also uses other devices to explain the visions. For example, worship is the dominant theme in Revelation 4–5. Yet the motif could possibly be overlooked if we attempted to determine the symbolism behind each jewel or weather condition. The songs sung by the various members of the heavenly court focus on God's power and majesty as holy creator (4:8, 11). Christ, on the other hand, is worshiped because he has redeemed people (5:9-10, 12, 13).

Sometimes summary statements either at the beginning or the end of a vision provide a clue to the big picture. For example, Rev. 21:1ff. promises that God will dwell among the redeemed in the new heaven and new earth. Rather than focusing on such details as the measurements of the city and the jewels, the opening verses stress the key idea, namely intimacy with God and absolute security.[30] The garden imagery of 22:1ff. takes us back to the beginning of the story, where God and Adam and Eve dwelled in perfect unity.

Fifth, we should beware of stressing the details. Indeed, the particulars may belong to the overall picture or be used for dramatic effect. On the one hand, it is possible that the twenty-four elders introduced in Revelation 4:4 may be angels who are identified with the twelve tribes and twelve apostles. They represent the redeemed of the old and new covenants. On the other hand, the precise meaning of describing God who sits on the throne in terms of jasper, carnelian, and a rainbow may elude us. The throne imagery, however, surely stresses power and might.

Perhaps a nonbiblical illustration will clarify what I am proposing. In the Fall of 1982, my family and I were living in Aberdeen, Scotland. One Saturday we decided to visit the small village of Balmoral since the Queen of England and members of the royal family were scheduled to make an appearance at the Balmoral Highland Games where athletes competed for prizes. Early that morning, the trumpets sounded. As we stood on the outside of a racetrack, on the opposite side from where we were, the gates swung open, and the royal entourage came out in horse-drawn carriages. The crowds cheered. My four-year-old son watched in wonderment as the parade passed by us within a few feet. When I asked him what he had observed, he simply replied he had seen wheels, horses, and soldiers atop the carriages. We had taken him to see the Queen and her family, and my son failed to do so. I think this is what we do with many scenes in Revelation. We cannot see the forest for the trees. We miss the big picture and do not see what God would have us see.

Accordingly, in Revelation some details may be added for dramatic effect or to clarify the picture as a whole. It is critical to focus on the essence (i.e., the foundational nature or quality of what John is revealing) of the vision if the exactness cannot be determined. In other words, look for one central meaning of the picture. You cannot know if the details are important until you have studied them as thoroughly as possible. Is John describing exactness or essence? This question must be repeatedly asked as you study the symbols of Revelation.

Also you should attempt to discover the relationship of the symbol to the main theme being treated. It is obvious in Revelation 4:1ff. that worship is the key theme; God is to be worshiped because of his beauty, power, majesty, and, above all, because he is creator. In Revelation 5:1ff., Christ is worshiped because of the redemption he brings to people. We know that the essence of the dragon (Rev. 12:1ff.) and the two beasts (e.g., Rev. 13:1ff.) is evil: They coerce; they deceive; and they seduce. Ultimately, they are opposed to God and his servants.

We must be constantly asking: What did the author intend by the symbol he used?

Sixth, we should interpret the obscure by the clear. This sounds logical, but it is remarkable how many people often interpret relatively clear passages by more difficult ones. For example, some suggest that the angel associated with each church in chapters 2 and 3 is the pastor who leads the church. Yet every other time where the term appears in Revelation, it is referring to those heavenly beings who serve God.[31] Why would the meaning change in the messages to the seven churches? I believe this is an instance of reading our present understanding of church leadership back into a first-century document.

Or consider another example. Who are the "seven spirits before the throne" in 1:4? Note that the seven spirits are associated with God and Christ in 4:5 and 5:6 and that seven times the Spirit speaks to the seven churches. Because seven often denotes completeness or totality, perhaps John is reminding his recipients of the complete power of God's Spirit. The Old Testament allusions support the view that the Holy Spirit is portrayed in this symbol (Zech. 4:2ff.; Isa. 11:2ff.).

Seventh, simplicity should be the norm and the principle of humility employed. There are limits to what God has revealed (e.g., Rev. 10:4), as well as limits to what we can understand due to our ignorance of John's day or our prejudices. The precise interpretation of some of the symbols still eludes us (e.g., 13:18). We should study the Bible in the context of the Christian community, and this means that we should consult the contributions other Christians have made to our understanding of the book.[32]

As I come to the end of this section, a word of caution is called for. We do not understand the symbols by merely following specific steps or principles. Comprehending the

Bible is not only a matter of developing a fine studious mind; it is also a matter of the heart. We must desire to have seeing eyes and listening ears, coming to Scripture with a desire to hear what God wants to say. We must beware of imposing our agendas and conclusions, even finding answers to our questions that God never intended to answer. Revelation reveals its message to those who do their best in study and have an open heart and mind; it continues to conceal its meaning when we approach the text with poor principles and a closed heart and mind, or when we seek to reveal what God still conceals.

The Timelessness of the Symbols

A question remains. If these symbols meant something to John and his audience, do they continue to speak to disciples of Jesus long after Rome has fallen? More pointedly, do they still speak to us or is much of the book irrelevant for us today? How can we apply all of Revelation responsibly? We must not forget that this issue of application to today is pertinent to studying any book in the Bible. The Psalms, Isaiah, and Hosea still speak to us today, centuries after they were composed. How do they continue to speak? Not many of us encounter Judaizers today, so how do we apply Galatians where they are referenced? Not many of us are members of a congregation where there is tension between Jewish followers of Jesus and Gentile followers of Jesus. So how do we apply Romans?

With Revelation, some would believe that the problem of application is compounded because of the symbolism. To the contrary, I believe appreciating the richness of the symbols makes application easier. The above guidelines stress that Revelation can be properly understood only in light of the meaning given by the author himself. Accordingly, one should remain with the context of Revelation as well as with the situation of the first-century church. We should not impose a meaning from outside (either from our twenty-first century or even Old Testament times). Essentially, we must be constantly asking: What did the author intend by the symbol he used? What clues does he provide, either directly or indirectly, either within the immediate context or the larger scriptural context?

To illustrate, the two beasts of Revelation 13 meant something to John's people. Most scholars agree that the beasts refer to the Roman government and the cult that worshiped the Emperor as a god. Together, anti-Christian government and anti-Christian religion harassed and persecuted the people of God at the end of the first century. Such opposition has continued throughout subsequent eras.

This reminds us that there is a fluidity to the symbols. John actually saw scorpions, beasts, and other evil forces along with the forces of good; but the emphasis is on the reality they symbolized. John is speaking of realities beyond human descriptive experience. He points to something real, but the images are not reality itself. This underscores the reason it is crucial to determine what the symbols represent.

Therefore, I believe that we can maintain that the symbols are flexible and pliable. There can be other Jezebels, whores, and beasts throughout history just as there are others like Antipas and the faithful living in Smyrna and Philadelphia or those struggling in Ephesus, Pergamum, Thyatira, Sardis, and Laodicea. As symbolic of spiritual realities, these realities can be reborn over and over through the centuries. To be sure, they spoke to John's readers, but they are not limited only to John's day and the decades thereafter. Babylon, for example, meant the Roman Empire for John's audience. The Babylon of the first century reflected ancient Babylon of Daniel's day. And perhaps we can go a step farther and say that Babylon has taken many forms throughout history. Thus, the events depicted in Revelation are perpetually relevant, from John's day to the end of history. They are greater than their historical context.[33]

I have emphasized that we must never read Revelation in one hand and the newspaper in the other. We must not think that John saw visions of helicopters, communism, nuclear weapons, and the most recent military conflict in the Middle

East. It needs to be repeated: The visions must have had meaning for John and the other followers of Jesus. Therefore, we must seek to know first and foremost what the meaning would have been for John and his recipients before we seek to know what the meaning is for us.

The quest to determine how the symbols spoke to John's audience does not mean we should not seek to discern how evil is at work today and how those symbols help us identify similar forces at work in our day. Yet we must be cautious. It is easier for us to see Babylon-like cultures in countries where totalitarian governments rule, but it is not so easy to see it close to home. To be sure, it is more comforting to see other evil cultures seducing God's people, attempting to bring them to a lower level of living without realizing how toxic our own culture is. But as I write these words, it appears to me that my own country is betraying similar characteristics, and I am not confident that a major change for the good in my culture is on the horizon. We must exercise caution when applying the book, but when we follow proper principles and when we study in Christian community, we stand a better chance of discerning what the book meant to the original recipients and what it means to disciples today.

Why Symbolism?

Several times in this chapter I have emphasized that symbols represent spiritual realities. John uses symbols to describe as best he could the indescribable, to provoke, to enrich, to stimulate, to motivate, to irritate. Symbols appear to the eye, ear, heart, and mind. Symbols can leave imprints on our minds in a vivid way. They conjure up in our imagination pictures of things real and unreal, helping us grasp more clearly the thoughts being conveyed. Modern communication theory holds that we understand and retain far more of what we see than what we only hear or read. Symbols helped John express realities when his language was reaching the breaking point and straightforward words simply could not express what he had seen and heard. But I repeat:

The symbols are not the reality; they point to a deeper reality. Let me illustrate.

Let's say that a ten-year-old boy in 1985 discovers his father's electric typewriter in the attic and is fascinated by it. The child is told how the father used the machine to write all of his papers when he attended college. The father then puts in a piece of paper, and the boy is delighted to type away. When he is finished, the son asks the father if he could have a typewriter when he goes to college, and the father agrees to get him one. The years pass, and it is graduation day, 1993. On that day the father gives the boy a laptop computer with printer. The typewriter has long since been forgotten. Did the father keep his promise? If we insist on a strict "literal" understanding, then the answer is no. But did he really keep the promise? Yes, but in a much richer and fuller way.

Likewise, God describes goodness and evil, righteousness and unrighteousness, and holiness and unholiness in symbols. God is actually even more majestic and powerful than the picture that is presented to us. Jesus is more powerful and majestic than the depiction of him as a resurrected Lamb. The Devil is far more terrifying than a red dragon. Hell is much worse than a lake of burning fire. And heaven will be much better than walking on streets of gold.

Phillips reminds us that when we try to interpret and translate the symbols, we have "but the slightest foothold in the time-and-space world with which he [John] is familiar. He is carried not into some never-never land of fancy, but into the ever-ever land of God's eternal Values and Judgments."[34] Through the use of symbolism John hoped to provide comfort and challenge to his fellow disciples. They were in poor shape and needed that reassurance. What better way to stir the hearts and the minds than by using symbolism!

Reconnecting with our metaphor involving music, we are reminded that music is emotive; it has the power to move people, making them stop and reflect. When we pay close attention to the power of Revelation's symbols, we are touched.

We experience a rhapsody not unlike that of a stirring piece of music. We bow in wonder before God Almighty who sits on the throne. We are moved by the sacrificial Lamb who stands. We may be tempted to tremble before the power of the dragon and the two beasts, but we know that victory belongs to the Lamb and his followers. We rejoice when we are given a glimpse of the wedding of the bride and the Bridegroom. We marvel when we see the crystal clear water of the river of life. And we celebrate that the God who has come among us invites us to listen to the lyrics of the Lamb.

The symbols are not the reality: they point to a deeper reality.

CHAPTER 7

LISTENING TO THE LYRICS: THE STRUCTURE

More than thirty years ago, I evaluated two commentaries on Revelation that have profoundly influenced my understanding of the book's organization. In 1974, when I read William Hendriksen's *More Than Conquerors,* a work written in 1939 and still in print,[1] I felt liberated. Revelation no longer frightened me. The overall approach taken by Hendriksen was that Revelation is divided into parallel sections. The sections span from the first coming to the final coming of Christ, repeating the same material in an ever intensifying way. Bible scholars use the word "recapitulation" in a specialized manner to describe Hendrickson's approach. I will be using this same term "recapitulation" and will explain it more fully in this chapter.

The other work was a commentary by G.B. Caird, *The Revelation of St. John the Divine.*[2] I recently reread Caird, and I noticed that I had double-underlined an insight on structure that I had forgotten had profoundly influenced my thinking: "The unity of John's book . . . is neither chronological nor arithmetical, but artistic, like that of a musical theme with variations, each variation adding something new to the significance of the whole composition."[3]

Nearly twenty years after reading Caird's insight, I was asked to address the issue of the book's organization for a study Bible. His influence is seen in an observation I made:

> Each of the sevenfold series seems to lead us to the end of the world. How do they fit together? John is not a chronologist so, for example, the trumpets do not necessarily follow the

> seals in strict chronological order. It may help to see John as an artist or musician. If his "musical theme" is the end of the world, then each series . . . is a "variation" that adds to the composition. Each one heightens and intensifies the final, climactic confrontation between God and the forces of evil. It is the theological message not a strict chronology that really counts. The seals remind us that evil exists only by permission from God. The trumpets call people to repentance. The peals of thunder emphasize God's judgments (8:5).[4]

If I could rewrite my explanation of these events in Revelation 5 and the following chapters, I would elaborate, emphasizing that the various sections of Revelation are not successive chronologically, but instead each one includes the one preceding it and goes beyond it in detail.

The basic approach that I present in this chapter is not new but goes back to the third century A.D. An early opponent of reading Revelation chronologically was Victorinus of Pettau, a bishop who was martyred about A.D. 304. Victorinus concluded that ultimately "order is not to be looked for in the Apocalypse, understanding is to be looked for."[5] Even though the approach that argues for repetition and recapitulation in Revelation is not a new one, to date it has not received the attention it deserves.

A Book's Structure and Its Message

We need to be reminded that Revelation is not different from any other biblical book with respect to structure. All of the books of the Bible have a design. A book's message is enhanced by its organization. Indeed, we can understand the message better if we understand the structure.[6] Clearly, we can see the organization of some books easier than others. And yet, even in those books that appear fairly simple to outline, when we probe more deeply, we see complex arrangements often overlooked. Nevertheless, most scholars would agree that John's composition is much more complex than the other books of the Bible.[7]

Many Christians mistakenly believe that Revelation should be read as if the events happen in chronological order.[8] They prefer to think that John sings a simple, singable tune. They do not want any surprises or fancy arrangements, thank you. Sing your message, John, with a straightforward melody, they say. They see his composition as starting in the first century and moving through the centuries until it reaches the generation right before Christ returns. First, one event happens, then the next, still another, leading us up to the end. Some even go so far as to suggest that chapters 2 and 3 in Revelation break history into seven periods, one for each of the churches, and that the generation right before Christ comes to establish an earthly kingdom is the age of Laodicea. Not surprisingly, proponents of this position frequently think they are living in that age of lukewarmness. Advocates of this sequential approach confidently say that most of the book is meant only for Christians living in the days immediately before Christ returns.

The King shall come
when morning dawns
And light triumphant breaks,
When beauty gilds
the eastern hills
And life to joy awakes.

The King shall come
when morning dawns
And light and beauty brings.
Hail, Christ the Lord!
Thy people pray;
Come quickly, King of kings!

"The King Shall Come"
Early Greek hymn

Even though many attempt to structure Revelation as if it were history-written-in-advance, such efforts, I believe, are doomed to failure. You could check out of a library any number of commentaries that have taken a chronological approach to the book. Or visit a bookstore and you will find on the clearance table books on Revelation that used current events to incorrectly explain John's visions. The authors of those works do not even agree among themselves as to what events John was predicting. Such authors are part of a long heritage going back to the earliest centuries, a heritage that is riddled with failure. Any reader could cite some well-known

> *Many Christians mistakenly believe that Revelation should be read as if the events happen in chronological order.*

preacher or author who has attempted to predict when Christ was going to come. Such predictors have one thing in common: They have all been wrong. Surely, this should make us pause and question such an approach.

I believe it is possible to understand the overall strategy of John: It is one that combines repetition and recapitulation. Repetition is what it sounds like, namely, the repeating of a word, a phrase, a main clause, a sentence, or even an entire section. Poets use it when they repeat a line of poetry. Authors may repeat a portion of text. Musicians often repeat lyrics or a melody line. John also repeats.

On the other hand, recapitulation is repetition and more, repetition ratcheted up, on steroids so to speak. It is found in both musical and written compositions. The composer or author repeats or restates themes or ideas introduced earlier, but with progression in some way. The strategy is to describe the same events in different ways and with ever-increasing intensity.

Specifically, I am proposing that Revelation does not move forward in a strictly chronological way. The various sections of Revelation are concurrent rather than successive.[9] The book appears to move back and forth; moving forward, pausing, moving forward again, and then circling back to the original point. It "sounds" like a piece of jazz. Jazz goes round and round and round. The book of Revelation has that kind of momentum. It circles and builds, circles and builds, while being both simple and complex at the same time.

The implications of this approach are as obvious as they are profound. Recognizing such a scheme means we must not read Revelation in a sequential way. John is not laying out in great detail a blueprint for events that are to happen before Christ returns a final time. The various sections (e.g., the seven seals in 6:1ff.; the seven trumpets in 8:6ff.; and the seven bowls in 15:1ff.) are not successive, but they overlap—

while intensifying at the same time—always bringing us to the end of the world.

Artistic Arrangements: Repetition in Scripture

Repetition and, to a lesser degree, recapitulation are found throughout the Bible on both macro and micro levels. We may find it when comparing two or more books as well as sections within a book. Let's consider the following examples, covering first the Old, and then the New Testament.

We find repetition involving entire books in the Old Testament. 1–2 Chronicles repeat material from 2 Samuel and 1 and 2 Kings. Why? The latter books were written to a people in exile. The people were wondering how and why they got there. First and Second Chronicles were written to a people returned from exile. They wrestled with the issue of whether or not they still fit into God's plan.

Within individual Old Testament writings we see repetition. We can cite several examples that represent the major genres. In the Pentateuch we see repetition in the two accounts of creation in Genesis 1–3. Genesis also refers several times to the covenant God established with Abraham (Gen. 12:1ff.; 15:1ff.; 17:1ff.). There are two accounts of the giving of the Ten Commandments (Exod. 20 and Deut. 5).

Scholars have long acknowledged that repetition abounds in the Psalms, especially in the form of parallelism. This "is a construction in which the content of one line is repeated, contrasted, or advanced by the content of the next [line]."[10] Some representative examples are found in Pss. 8:1-9; 19:1-14; 118:1-4 and 136:1-26.

We find repetition in the historical and prophetic writings. Several times in Judges we are told that Israel did what was evil in the sight of the Lord (2:11; 3:7, 12; 4:1; 6:1; 10:6; 13:1). Three times we find the story of Sennacherib's siege of Jerusalem and the roles that Hezekiah and Isaiah played (2 Kgs. 18–19; 2 Chr. 32; Isa. 36–37). In addition, ponder the repetition of the formula in Amos: "For three sins of . . . even for four" (1:3, 6, 9, 11, 13; 2:1, 4, 6).

Daniel and Ezekiel come to mind as specific examples of recapitulation. It is commonly accepted that John alludes to Daniel and Ezekiel at numerous points. I believe it is significant to note that these three books share similarities in organization as well. Daniel's visions and dreams in chapter 2 have basically the same content as those in chapter 7.[11] Similarly, Ezekiel 16 and 23 cover the same subject matter, the history of Israel's apostasy.[12] Chapter 23 is much more graphic than 16.

We also see repetition in the New Testament. Three synoptic Gospels (Matthew, Mark, and Luke) give a common view of Jesus. Mark's arrangement of the life of Jesus and most of Mark's content are found in Matthew and Luke, with the latter two adding material that fits their inspired purposes.

On a micro level, in Matthew we see repetition of the formula "When Jesus had finished saying these things" (7:28; 11:1; 13:53; 19:1; 26:1). It highlights five major teaching blocks that weave in and out between narrative and teaching. We also have repetition of the phrase "From that time on . . ." in Matt. 4:17 and 16:21 to show another way of dividing Matthew. The first time this phrase appears, the theme of the Kingdom is introduced. The second occurrence emphasizes the suffering Jesus must undergo since he has proclaimed God's vision of the Kingdom.

In Acts we find Peter and Paul both healing a lame man (3:1ff. and 14:8ff.), both being thrown into prison and being miraculously released (12:1ff. and 16:16ff.), and both raising individuals from the dead (9:36ff. and 20:7ff.), perhaps emphasizing the legitimacy of both apostles' ministries. This would be especially important for Paul since he was called to minister specifically to the Gentiles. He and Peter were both empowered by God to carry out their respective ministries.

We also discover repetition in the letters. In one of Paul's earliest letters, references to the final coming of Christ and its desired effect on Christian living abound (1 Thess. 1:10; 2:19; 3:13; 4:13-18; 5:1-11, 23). Repetition of the phrase "Now concerning . . ." in 1 Corinthians highlights some of the issues where the Corinthians had requested guidance from Paul (7:1, 25; 8:1; 12:1; 16:1, 12).

From this brief survey we see that repetition is pervasive throughout the Bible. Its use in Revelation, then, is not to be unexpected.

Artistic Arrangements: Repetition in Revelation—Micro Level

Revelation has repetition in every major section. We are going to see it on the micro level in this section. Several examples follow:[13]

1. The descriptions of Christ in 1:12ff. are repeated in the messages given to the seven churches in chapters 2 and 3.
2. There is repetition of a threefold formula in 1:4 ("from him who is, and who was, and who is to come;" see also v. 8); 4:8 ("who was, and is, and is to come"); and 17:8 ("The beast . . . once was, now is not, and will come up").
3. Seven times Jesus announces: "I am coming" (2:5, 16; 3:11; 16:15; 22:7, 12, 20).
4. There are seven blessings in the form of beatitudes (1:3; 14:13; 16:15; 19:9; 20:6; 22:7, 14).
5. The phrase "the testimony of Jesus" is repeated in 1:2, 9; 12:17; 19:10(2×); 20:4; see also 6:9; 11:7; 12:11.
6. Many of the numbers are repeated (4, 7, 10 and its multiples, and 12 and its multiples).
7. Even the word "Behold!" is repeated and plays a significant role by calling upon the recipients to lift their eyes to consider what God is doing or is going to do (1:7, 18; 2:10, 22; 3:8, 9(2×), 20; 4:1, 2; 5:5; 6:2, 5, 8; 7:9; 9:12; 11:14; 12:3; 14:1, 14; 16:15; 19:11; 21:3, 5; 22:7, 12).
8. John begins and ends the book with "Amen!" (1:6, 7; 22:20-21), and the word is found at key points in between as well (3:14; 5:14; 7:12(2×); 19:4).

9. Chapters 2 and 3 reflect a structure that is built around repetition. The historical context is underscored with the same formula, "To the angel of the church in . . ." (2:1, 8, and so forth). Something about the character and/or conduct of Christ is found (2:1b, 8b, and so forth), with each description looking back to the previous description in 1:12ff. Christ then offers either a positive or negative (usually both!) assessment of the church, usually praising and censuring, sometimes only praising, and at least once only rebuking, but always challenging disciples to a deeper commitment (2:2-6, 9-10, and so forth). There is the sevenfold repetition of the phrase "To the one who overcomes" as well as the call "He who has an ear, let him hear . . ." (2:7, 11, and so forth). Each message ends with a promise to the faithful (2:7, 11, and so forth).

10. In addition to the above analysis of chapters 2 and 3, John appears to use a technique called "chiasm" in presenting the messages to the seven churches. A chiasm is "a literary device in which words, clauses, or themes are laid out and then repeated, but in inverted order."[14] The focal point of the chiasm is at the point of the arrowhead, in this case "C." The material associated with the focal point is often the crux or theme that the author is highlighting or emphasizing. This pattern is called "chiasm" because it is patterned like the Greek letter "Chi" (pronounced "key"), which looks like our letter "X." To see this, envision the letter "X" with its right side lopped off. Then you have something that looks like an arrowhead pointing to the right. We can take lines of text and arrange them next to this arrowhead pattern, so that successive lines are indented first to the right, and then to the left, as below:

A—Ephesus
    B—Smyrna
        C—Pergamum, Thyatira, Sardis
    B´—Philadelphia
A´—Laodicea

When applied to Revelation 2–3, the chiastic structure that surfaces is as follows:

LISTENING TO THE LYRICS: THE STRUCTURE

A—Ephesus—Christians receive some commendation but they had lost their first love and were heading toward decline like Laodicea.

B—Smyrna—Christians receive no harsh criticism from Jesus, but he encourages them to remain faithful in facing persecution from the Jews.

C—Pergamum, Thyatira, and Sardis—*Even though some praise is given, Christians in these cities were guilty of either compromising with their culture through idol worship and immorality (Pergamum and Thyatira) or becoming complacent in living out their faith (Sardis).*

B´—Philadelphia—Christians receive no harsh criticism from Jesus, but he encourages them to remain faithful despite their perceived powerlessness and the opposition they are facing from the Jews.

A´—Laodicea — Christians receive no commendation from Jesus but are rebuked for their lukewarmness.

Here, the focal point of the chiasm is "C," showing that John's primary concern is that Christians are being seduced by culture. As pointed out in chapter 2, there is a lack of references to persecution on a widespread scale at this time. In John's day, the real pressure Rome exerted on the churches was a subtle seduction that targeted the exclusiveness of Christians, tempting them to adapt their moral and religious principles to the society at large.

This analysis does not minimize the problems faced by the other churches. On the one hand, the Ephesian and Laodicean churches are paired in the chiasm because they share a diminishing commitment to Christ. On the other hand, while the congregations in Smyrna and Philadelphia remain true to Christ, they are paired because they face present or impending opposition from the Jews.

Artistic Arrangements: Repetition in Revelation – Macro Level

In analyzing John's artistic arrangements, we will focus on five macro-level organizational features he uses. The first supports the unity of the work. The second is a key for unlocking the book's design. The last three focus on repetition, in major sections as well as the entire book. Finally, we will look at the relationship between repetition and typology.

1. *"Inclusio" or Bracketing*

Certain New Testament documents begin and end in similar ways, thereby reinforcing major themes. The technical name given to this literary device is "*inclusio*" (Latin for "inclusion") and refers to a bracketing or framing where some key concepts are found at the beginning of a unit of Scripture (or an entire book) and repeated at the end. The device reinforces the importance of what is repeated.

For example, Matthew 1–3 begins the story of Jesus by introducing the reader to certain themes like king and Kingdom (1:6; 2:1-2, 6), opposition and worship (2:7, 11, 16-18), baptism (3:6, 11), and discipleship (4:18-22). In the final chapters, Matthew comes full circle in telling the story of the death, burial, and resurrection. Here, he refers to themes of the king and Kingdom (27:11, 37), opposition and worship (26:47ff.; 28:17), baptism (28:19), and discipleship (28:19).

Scholars have noted that John's Gospel adopts a bracketing strategy.[15] For example, one of my colleagues convincingly argues for the use of *inclusio* in John 1 and 21.[16] He points out that both Peter (1:40, 44 and 21:2, 3, 7, 11, 15, 17, 20, 21) and Nathaniel (1:44-51 and 21:2) are mentioned in each passage, along with two unknown disciples (1:37 and 21:2). Johnson suggests that this device supports the view that John 21 is not a mere appendix to John's Gospel as is argued by some scholars. The bracketing shows that John considered chapter 21 an integral part of the Gospel, emphasizing the important theme of discipleship with which he had begun his Gospel.

The opening and closing verses of Revelation function like

bookends. John introduces and concludes the book, as he does his Gospel, with a call to obedience and faithfulness as disciples (1:1ff. and 22:6, 8; 1:3 as well as 1:4-6 and 22:21). There are even hints identifying the genres John has used: 22:7 emphasizes the prophetic nature of the book; 22:8 stresses that, like other apocalypses, John saw and heard things; and 22:21 ends, like many of Paul's letters, with a reminder about God's grace.

When you are aware of the inclusio, you are aware of the unity of the book. The inclusio introduces the major themes of the book and restates them at the end. Because a careful study reveals the continual resurfacing of those very themes, the unity of the work is confirmed.

A final word is in order. Jesus' identification of himself as "the Alpha and the Omega" at the beginning and the conclusion of the book (1:8 and 22:13) is a key part of the inclusio. Why? Because it emphasizes that the unity of the book is ultimately found in Jesus, who is the First and the Last.

2. *The Role of Revelation 1:19*

The second organizational feature is found in 1:19. John is commanded: "Write, therefore, what you have seen, what is now, and what will take place later." Does the verse provide a key to understanding the structure of the entire book? The majority of scholars I have examined would answer yes, but its meaning is debated. Many proposals have been made, but two have surfaced as the major options.[17]

Some suggest that this verse divides the contents of the entire book into three parts. For example, 1:19a ("Write, therefore, what you have seen") refers to the entire vision, 1:19b ("what is now") refers to the description of the churches in chapters 1–3, and 1:19c ("what will take place later") refers to the rest of the book, chapters 4–22. In other words, chapters 4–22 follow historically after the description of the churches in John's day.

Such an understanding assumes that the book is to be read chronologically. But we have already suggested that John describes the same events several times, repeating with

The various sections of Revelation are concurrent rather than successive; it "sounds" like a piece of jazz.

intensification (recapitulation). If John uses repetition and recapitulation, it does not appear that a chronological outline of the entire book is feasible. Furthermore, there are exceptions to a chronological sequence in chapters 4–22. Past events are referred to in places like 5:5ff. and 12:1ff., the latter including a description of Christ's birth. This passage is a special problem for those who read the book chronologically. The story of Jesus' first coming is certainly not a future event and is out of place if a strict chronological reading is held.[18]

The second option is to see 1:19 referring equally to the entire book, the option I favor. This view suggests that there is an intermingling of past, present, and future events, especially focusing on the present and future. The last two clauses ("what is now" and "what will take place later") describe the overall nature of the contents of Revelation. John is writing what is already and what is not yet. The phrase "Write . . . what you have seen" in 1:19 repeats the commission "Write . . . what you see and send it to the seven churches" found in 1:11. What John sees concerns what is already present and what is not yet present. The present and the future, in other words, are intermingled throughout the book.

There is no nice, neat movement from past to present to future in the book. Perhaps one commentator's translation clarifies the meaning: "Write, therefore, the things you are about to see, that is, both what now is and what lies yet in the future."[19] The weaving of the past, present and future is found throughout the book. James Moffatt summarizes the matter well when he obsèrves that "the contents of the vision . . . consist of what is and what is to be."[20]

3. *Comparing the Trumpets and the Bowls*

The third organizational feature focuses on repetition in the accounts of the trumpets and the bowls. Here, we find additional support for the theory of recapitulation, namely, that the events in Revelation do not all form a continuous series, but rather some scenes recapitulate the events of other scenes. Similar vocabulary between each of the trumpets and bowls suggests recapitulation.[21] The chart below confirms this:

THE SEVEN TRUMPETS	THE SEVEN BOWLS
1. Hail and fire, with blood, cast to the earth a third of the *earth* is burned (8:7)	1. Poured out upon the *earth*—evil boils appeared on men who had the beast's mark (16:2).
2. A mountain of fire is cast into the *sea*. A third of the sea is turned to *blood* (8:8-9).	2. Poured out upon the *sea*—it became *blood*, and all life died (16:3).
3. A burning star called Wormwood falls on a third of the *rivers and wells of water* (8:10-11).	3. Poured out upon *rivers and wells of water*—they became blood because the blood of saints and prophets was shed (16:4-7).
4. A third of the *sun, moon, and stars* are darkened (8:12).	4. Poured out upon the *sun*—it burned people, but they did not repent or give glory to God (16:8-9).
5. A demonic locust plague. The sun was *darkened*. Locusts were given authority to injure people as from the sting of scorpions (9:1-12).	5. The kingdom of the beast was *darkened*—although in great pain, people blasphemed the God of heaven and did not repent of their works (16:10-11).
6. Loosing of angels at the *great river Euphrates*. An army of two hundred million horses with tails like serpents with power to kill people. People did not repent (9:13-21).	6. The *great river Euphrates* was made bitter. A way was opened for the kings of the east. Froglike spirits gathered all kings to the great war of Armageddon (16:12-16).
7. "The kingdom of the world has become the kingdom of our Lord and of his Christ" (11:14-19).	7. "It is done." The Final Judgment upon Babylon, with giant hailstones. Yet people still blasphemed God (16:17-21).

An intensification or progression in the judgments occurs. The first four of each group of catastrophes show God's sovereignty over all the realms of his creation (compare with the first four seals in 6:1-8). The last three are heightened so as to strike directly at people. With the breaking of seals five and six (6:9–7:17), those who do not worship God experience his wrath (6:12ff.) while those who do worship God experience security and salvation (7:1ff).[22] The silence of 8:1 is to be viewed as a continuation of the Final Judgment described in 6:12ff. The imagery of silence is frequently linked with God's judgment (Hab. 2:20; Zech. 2:13; see also Isa. 23:2; 41:1-5; 47:5; Ezek. 27:32; Amos 8:2-3; Lam. 2:10-11).[23] Like the seventh seal (8:1ff.), the seventh trumpet and the seventh bowl bring us to the ultimate completion of God's purposes in history. The end results in positive triumph, not merely in judgment (11:15; 16:17).

Additional support for this notion of progression occurs in the expansions of the series. Specifically, with each series of seven there is an intensification of the judgment imagery (e.g., moving from one fourth [the seals] to one third [the trumpets] to totality [the bowls]). As mentioned before, it is possible that highlighting one-fourth and one-third is a literary device showing that John is not yet ready to bring the book to an end because the vision had not ceased.

4. The Relationship between Revelation 12–14, Revelation 15–16, and Revelation 17–20

The fourth organizational feature, which we will highlight in our analysis of Revelation 12–20, also supports recapitulation. Consider this brief outline:

CHAPTER	CONTENTS
6–8	7 SEALS
8–11	7 TRUMPETS
12–14	*Dragon – 2 Beasts Babylon*
15–16	7 BOWLS
17–20	*The 4 Evil Forces Destroyed*

Notice there are two large units where we do not find a series of seven, namely chapters 12–14 and 17–20. The seven seals in chapters 6–8 flow into the seven trumpets in 8–11, but the seven trumpets do not flow into the seven bowls recorded in 15–16. Chapters 12–14 interrupt the series. Just as the seals, trumpets, and bowls brought us to the end of the world, if we review the content of chapters 12–14 and 17–20, we find that they also take us to the end. Instead of presenting the end-time scenario only once, as you would expect in a chronological work, John brings us to the end of the world four times.

The interlude separating the seven trumpets and the seven bowls begins in 12:1 and ends at 14:20. One of the purposes of this interlude appears to be to introduce the main antagonists to God and his servants: We read about the dragon (12:1ff.); the two beasts in 13:1ff., and Babylon the Great (14:8). Beginning with 15:1ff., we have the pouring out of the seven bowls that emphasizes totality of judgment. John then becomes more specific as to who or what is judged totally: He zeroes in on the antagonists, who are judged and dispensed with in the reverse order they were introduced. Babylon is judged in 17:1–19:10, next the two beasts in 19:11-21, and then finally Satan and his followers are the focal point in 20:1-15, a passage that ends with the Final Judgment.

This sequence has a chiastic structure, evident in the outline below:

- **A**—The Dragon (12:1ff.)
  - **B**—The Two Beasts (13:1ff.)
    - **C**—Babylon the Great (14:8)
      - **D**—The Seven Bowls (15:1–16:21)

        The pouring out of the seven bowls emphasizes total judgment of creation, including those who do not serve God. It also anticipates the total judgment of the antagonists who are dismissed in reverse order: Babylon, the two beasts, and the dragon.
    - **C´**—Babylon's Destruction(17:1–19:10)
  - **B´**—The Two Beasts' Destruction (19:11-21)
- **A´**—The Dragon's Destruction (20:7-10)

When Christ shall come
with shout of acclamation
And take me home,
what joy shall fill my heart!
Then I shall bow
in humble adoration,
And there proclaim,
my God, how great Thou art.

"How Great Thou Art"
Stuart K. Hine
1949

The focus of a chiasm is found at the crossing point of the "X," the point on the arrowhead, in this case at "D—The Seven Bowls." Here the emphasis is on total judgment. Presumably Babylon, the beasts, and the dragon were tolerated until the sins of the people reached a level God judged as enough. With total judgment on the earth and mankind, then, Babylon, the two beasts, and the dragon have become actors with no stage. Their doom is already spelled.

John speaks of destruction coming upon a fourth and a third of certain parts of creation. By using the formulas one-fourth (6:8) and one-third (8:7, 9, 10, 12), as I indicated earlier, fractions are used to encourage the recipients to keep on reading or listening; the vision continues. Even 6:9ff. shows this, since more saints will die. Beginning in chapter 15, John is wrapping things up, so to speak, because the vision is coming to an end. No fractions are used in association with the bowls in 16:1ff.; all creation and all humanity are affected. Ironically, more attention is devoted to the judgment of Babylon than to the two beasts. The dragon is simply dismissed in a handful of verses. Because of such brevity, perhaps we could argue that John is showing contempt for the nemesis of God and his servants. Or in the words of Luther, "One little word shall fell him."

5. A Synthesis

We need to keep in mind the first four features as we turn our attention to the final one. In light of the details presented above, I want to expand on the comments I made in the study notes on Revelation as published in *The Quest Study Bible.* John is not a chronologist in the sense that he is setting forth in great detail the events that are to take place before Christ's final coming. Countless times efforts have been made to read Revelation this way, and as we have observed, they have all failed.

I believe it helps us to see John as a composer. His *Theme* is stated—a message of warning for those who do not worship God and a message of hope for those who do—and then it is restated in different ways. In composing a musical piece based on the form of *Theme and Variations*, elements of the *Theme*—its melody, rhythm, and instrumentation—will be varied while retaining the theme. Accordingly, if John's *Theme* is the end of the world (an end which brings either salvation or punishment), then each series of seven (seals, trumpets, and bowls), and even the interlude found in chapters 12–14,[24] is a *Variation* that adds to the composition. Each series of seven, as well as the interlude, moves the reader closer to the end. This is not because each follows the preceding series in a purely chronological sense, but because each heightens and intensifies the final and climactic confrontation between God and his people and Satan and his allies. The fate of Satan and his allies is eternal punishment. But God and his people will dwell together forever.[25]

The following outline illustrates this:

Verse	Comment
1:1–3:22	The Messages to the Seven Churches, each ending with a promise to the overcomer, a promise that will be completely realized when the new heaven and new earth are established (2:7, 11, 17, 26-28; 3:5, 11b-12, 21).
4:1–8:5[27]	The Seven Seals lead up to the end, with 6:12-17 depicting the fate of those who are not followers of Christ. They (along with the rest of creation) will experience the wrath of God.[28] With regard to the fate of the redeemed, they are sealed and will be able to stand before God (7:1-17). Note also that there is an interlude in 7:1-17 that stresses the security of God's people on the Day of Judgment. In the midst of the chaos, God's people are secure.

Verse	Comment
8:6—11:19	The Seven Trumpets lead up to the end of the world, with the end depicted in 11:17ff. in which God is praised: "We give thanks to you, Lord God Almighty, the One who is and who was, because you have taken your great power and have begun to reign." It is significant that unlike 1:4, 8, and 4:8, the clause "who is to come" is omitted.[29] Why? Because God has come and his perfect reign has begun. Note again that there is an interlude between the sixth and seventh trumpets from 10:1–11:14, with an emphasis on the responsibility of John and the church (symbolized by the two witnesses) to witness to God's power despite the hostile world's response. In the midst of evil forces that attempt to destroy the church, God's people must be faithful in their witnessing.
12:1–14:20	This is an interlude introducing the main antagonists of God and his people. It is found between the seals and trumpets (which have taken the reader up to the end, but in showing that only one-fourth or one-third have been affected by the judgment, John has indicated that he is not ready to bring the revelation to a close just yet.) The purpose of this interlude is to take the readers deeper and introduce them to the true nature of the conflict they are involved in. It is not merely Rome who is opposing them but the Dragon (12) and its two allies (anti-Christian government and anti-Christian religion—the imperial cult) along with Babylon the Great (14, the whore, i.e., Roman culture in all its manifestations). Thus, John introduces us to the key antagonists. Their fate will be explored more fully with the pouring of the seven bowls (15:1–16:21) that in turn leads to an even more detailed description of the complete defeat of the above evil powers. But in the meantime, those who worship the beasts will be punished (14:9-20), still another reference to the end.

15:1–16:21	The Seven Bowls lead up to the end of the world, depicted in 16:17-21. There is a final interlude, albeit brief, in 16:15 in which there is an exhortation to be vigilant and faithful. As the forces of evil gather to make one last effort to destroy the church (20:7-10), God's people must be watchful and loyal.[30]
17:1–20:15	The seven bowls and their emphasis on total judgment are a transition to the total judgment on Babylon, the two beasts, and the Dragon (in the reverse order in which they were introduced).
21:1–22:5	John is given a description of the new heaven and new earth and the people of God symbolized by the bride and the New Jerusalem.
22:6-21	The epilogue brings the revelation full circle, emphasizing the book's genres and a final call to obedience.

THE STRUCTURE OF REVELATION REFLECTING ITS EMPHASIS ON THE END OF THE WORLD[26]

The chart provides a summary of the whole book, supporting the theory of recapitulation. This view suggests that the events in Revelation do not all form a continuous series but the series of sevens (seven seals in 6:1–8:5, seven trumpets in 8:6–11:19, and seven bowls in 15:1–16:21) repeatedly bring us to the end of the world, when Christ comes in judgment to either reward or punish. As noted earlier, even the interlude of Revelation 12–14 begins with the first coming of Christ (12:1ff.) and ends with the Final Judgment (14:14-20).[31] There is "chronology" in the sense that *within* each series of seven (the seals, the trumpets, and the bowls), and also *within* the interlude of Revelation 12–14, the reader is brought to "the end."[32] Thus, once again we see that a chronological reading of Revelation is not possible.

Imagine the following scenario. After John received the revelation, no doubt copies of it were made by hand. Let's say that over the decades, for whatever reasons, chapters 8–22 had been omitted by those responsible for copying the document. If Revelation had ended at 7:17, readers would have been satisfied. The big picture is found in the first seven chapters: God judged the wicked and rewarded his faithful followers. Indeed, the book could have ended at numerous points, namely, 11:15-17; 14:14-20; 16:17-21; and 17:1–20:15. Therefore, if the book could have ended at 7:17, we have another indication that the book is not to be read in a purely chronological way.

Another way of viewing Revelation is to say that there is a spiraling effect in Revelation in the sense that each section returns to the point from which it began, but higher up, so to speak. Each series of seven moves the reader closer to the end, not because each follows the preceding series in a chronological sense but because each heightens and intensifies the final and climactic confrontation between God and the forces of evil.[33]

Moreover, even though the visions are parallel in many respects, they are also cumulative visions of history. Evil will grow worse and worse along with increasingly severe judgments on the world until there is a point of no return. But the point of no return is not the point when evil has the final victory, but when God has the last word. All of God's judgments on evil cultures through the centuries are leading up to the Final Judgment.[34]

Repetition, Recapitulation, and Typology

The previous analysis of recapitulation fits in with the earlier discussion on typology.[35] I suggest that with each series of seven, as far as the judgment aspect is concerned, John is describing the end of the world in terms of the end of the Roman Empire. By bringing the reader to the end of the Empire, the end of the world is being foreshadowed. Indeed, we could argue that the destruction of Rome is a model for the destruction of any godless culture, leading up to the destruction of the whole universe and the judgment of all humankind.[36] John is describing the end of the world not only in symbols the people were familiar with, but he is using the Roman culture as a type for any and all godless cultures leading up to the final godless culture in which God will bring history as we know it to a halt.[37]

Why Repetition and Recapitulation?

Why so much repetition? Why use recapitulation as a literary device to communicate the book's theme? Perhaps there are two reasons.

First, God has a history of using repetition in communicating his Word. It is his style. Let me illustrate with two examples from the Old Testament. The first is in the story of Joseph and his brothers in Genesis 37. Joseph had two dreams. In the first dream, Joseph saw his brothers' grain bowing down to his grain (v. 7). When he told his jealous brothers, they were furious, and asked, "Do you intend to reign over us?" (v. 8). They had clearly seen the symbolic implications of the dream.

Later Joseph has a second dream with the sun, moon, and eleven stars bowing down to him. This time his father Jacob rebuked him, asking him if he thought his mother, father, and eleven brothers would bow down to him. Once again the dream was interpreted properly.

When we look at the two dreams, we can make some observations. There were two dreams, and they used different imagery, sometimes to represent the same thing (e.g., both the grain and the stars represented the brothers). They spoke of the same eventuality, but in a progressive way. The first dream showed only the brothers bowing down and this happened (42:6). The second dream showed the full family bowing down. Although Genesis does not record Joseph's father and mother bowing to him, perhaps this is fulfilled when the entire family moves to Egypt and comes under Joseph's leadership (Gen 46:1ff.).

The second example is recorded in Genesis 41 and is more

difficult to interpret. Pharaoh had two dreams. In the first dream, seven fat cows were grazing and then seven gaunt cows came and ate the fat cows. In the second dream, seven healthy heads of grain were growing and then seven scorched heads of grain swallowed up the healthy heads. Joseph interpreted Pharaoh's dreams as meaning there would be seven years of abundance and then seven years of famine. Joseph provides us valuable information when he goes on to say, "The dreams of Pharaoh are one and the same. God has revealed to Pharaoh what he is about to do" (Gen. 41:25). Joseph further says, "The reason the dream was given to Pharaoh in two forms is that the matter has been firmly decided by God, and God will do it soon" (Gen. 41:32).

Why are these examples relevant for our study of Revelation? First of all, they show that God uses repetition as a style. Furthermore, God discloses one of his purposes for repetition: that the events depicted are firmly set and will take place. This shows God's ultimate sovereignty.

Applying this to Revelation, John's readers needed to hear the message that God is in control, despite what they saw. Two issues are addressed: 1) God's persecuted people may have felt abandoned, and God reassures them that he still reigns, and 2) God's people may have been tempted to compromise with the world, and God reminds them that there is a better world coming, one inhabited only by his holy servants.

The second reason for repetition and recapitulation is to reinforce the message and make it clearer. This is especially helpful in a culture where people would be *listening to,* rather than *reading,* a message. The tradition in New Testament times was for a literate person to read to those who did not know how to read. Many feel this is the background for Revelation 1:3: "Blessed is he who reads and those who hear the words of the prophecy, and heed the things which are written in it; for the time is near" (NASB).

Why does God repeat or recapitulate? Perhaps for reasons other than literary ones. Years ago, a student of mine from the Czech Republic shared with me a saying in his country: "Repetition is the mother of wisdom." To say a thing twice or more is to intensify it. To repeat something means to underline it. In other words, repetition emphasizes the attitude or action the author most wants to implant in the hearts and minds of the recipients. The purpose of hitting the same nail several times is to drive it home.

God knows how we have to be challenged to focus, lest we forget. God knows that we have short attention spans. John wants to drive home the point: The Romelike cultures of this world come and go, and God will always judge. And all of his judgments throughout history are foreshadowing the Final Judgment. For our own sakes as disciples of Jesus and for the sake of a hostile and seductive world, we cannot hear such warnings too often. Neither can we preach the warnings too much.

I'm just a poor,
wayfaring stranger,
A-traveling through
this world of woe;
But there's no sickness,
toil nor danger,
In that bright world
to which I go.
I'm going there
to see my Savior,
I'm going there,
no more to roam,
I'm just a-going over Jordan,
I'm just a-going over home.

"I'm Just a Poor,
Wayfaring Stranger"
American folk hymn

But as we preach the warnings to ourselves and others, we remind ourselves that the challenges of Revelation are balanced with the comfort in Revelation. The judgment scenario sounds like a funeral dirge following horrendous scenes of destruction and death. But the other side to judgment is God's promise to make things right. For those of us who are tempted and oppressed while living in idolatrous and immoral cultures, we still hear the cry of Revelation 6:10, "How long, Sovereign Lord, holy and true, until you judge the inhabitants of the earth and avenge our blood." Revelation's call to faithful obedience and perseverance finds comfort in the promise that one day through God's righteous judgment all evil will be banished, and finally, finally God's people will abandon their laments, claim a new set of heavenly lyrics, and sing a song of victory with the Lamb.

EPILOGUE

AN INVITATION TO LISTEN TO THE LYRICS OF THE LAMB—FOR ETERNITY

When we learn to listen to John's music, we learn to live with the end in view. This notion is true with all we do in life. The end! We hear the ring of finality, of closure. The end of the day . . . the end of a season . . . the end of another year . . . the end of a meal . . . the end of a song . . . the end of a book. . . .

The constancy of living with the end in view is often summed up in a variety of emotional statements: When will this end? I wish this would end! I wish this would never end! Why does this have to end?

If our ears are properly tuned and if we listen closely enough to Revelation, we will see that it is a book that guides us in living with the end in view: the end of history as we know it . . . the end of the world, indeed the universe . . . the end of our earthly lives . . . the end of evil and suffering.

We have seen that John is constantly reminding us of the end. He is intent on getting us caught up in the end. Why? Because he knows that the end is really the beginning, a beginning that knows no end. For the followers of the Lamb, it is a beginning that leads to life everlasting, perfectly. It is a beginning of a deeper and richer life with God and with one another in the most marvelous of settings, a new heaven and a new earth.

If we listen to John, we learn that in the end you, I, indeed, everyone, will have a new beginning, either the most wonderful or the most awful beginning of all. It is an ending that leads to rhapsody because we stand before the reigning

Lamb of God, who takes away
the sins of the world,
Have mercy on us.
Lamb of God, who takes away
the sins of the world,
Grant us peace.

Agnus Dei (Lamb of God)
Seventh century

Lord and the redeeming Lamb or to woe because we are banished forever from their presence.

In the end, what makes the difference is the song we sing. The song that makes all the difference is one found in Revelation that we have either chosen to sing or refused to sing. On the Sunday afternoon in 2005 that I listened to Handel's Messiah, I was startled as the choir finished singing the famous "Hallelujah Chorus" (based on Rev. 11:15; 19:6, 16). The composition did not come to a finish; other songs followed. I was stunned. I had completely forgotten that the work concluded with other words from John's last writing:

> Worthy is the Lamb that was slain, and hath redeemed us to God by His blood, to receive power, and riches, and wisdom, and strength, and honor and glory, and blessing. Blessing and honor, glory and power, be unto Him that sitteth upon the throne, and unto the Lamb, for ever and ever. (Rev. 5:12, 13, KJV)

Even with the words "for ever and ever," Handel's piece does not come to a close. Nor does Revelation close with a "for ever and ever." It has no thunder, no lightning, no hailstones, and there are no heavenly choirs praising God, only a hush. Rhapsody and hush are brought together. Handel's last word is John's last word: "The grace of the Lord Jesus be with God's people." Near the end, we are reminded of God's grace in Jesus, John with the simple word and Handel with the song about the Lamb. Grace, both authors tell us, takes us home. Grace takes us to the end. Grace enables us to listen to the song about the Lamb and the lyrics given by the Lamb. It is God's saving and sustaining grace that allows us not only to listen to, but to live out the lyrics of the Lamb.

Over the years I have been to countless concerts. Before a performance begins, the lights dim, the people stop talking, and silence invades the auditorium. Once the concert starts, the instruments ring out: The trumpets sound, the cymbals clang, the harps reverberate, the bells ring, and the audience is caught up in the moment. Our hearts soar, and sometimes I feel as if the oxygen has been removed from the room. I am spellbound. At the end of the performance, when the applause has died down, a kind of silence once again invades the concert hall. There is a hush.

Both Handel and John use a single word to end their works. Even though it is a little word, it is a powerful word, a word of confidence, comfort, and challenge based on grace. It is an expression that weds rhapsody and hush. It is a word that can only be joyfully spoken by those who know and heed the lyrics of the Lamb. It is, Amen!

NOTES

Prologue

1. See *Jesus Means Freedom*, trans. by F. Clarke (Philadelphia: Fortress Press, 1970) 139.
2. When I use a technical term that I think needs defining, I will do so either in the text or in an endnote. At the end of the book there is a glossary that defines several technical terms.
3. In contrast with J.S. Bell and S. Campbell, *The Complete Idiot's Guide to the Book of Revelation* (New York: Alpha, 2001).

Chapter One

1. G.K. Chesterton, *Orthodoxy* (New York: Lane, 1908) 17.
2. M. Strom, *The Symphony of Scripture* (Downers Grove, IL: InterVarsity, 2001).
3. Tools such as Bible dictionaries and encyclopedias, commentaries, and other special studies enrich our understanding of God's Word. Specific resources that will aid you in your study will be mentioned throughout the book.
4. I am well aware that some teach that Jesus will come twice, but this is a scenario unknown to the New Testament. Simply put, Jesus will return once (Heb. 9:27-28).
5. *Merriam-Webster's Collegiate Dictionary*, 11th ed., s.v. "lyric."
6. The use of "lamb" is John's favorite way to symbolize Christ. It is a powerful image in Revelation (5:6, 8, 12, 13; 6:1, 16; 7:9, 10, 14, 17; 12:11; 13:8, 11; 14:1, 4(2×), 10; 15:3; 17:14(2×); 19:7, 9(2×); 21:14, 22, 23, 27; 22:1, 3, all referring to Christ, with 13:11 being the exception, a reference to the beast being a parody of Christ the Lamb). Furthermore, the form of the word for "lamb" possibly stresses that John is writing about a "little lamb." Consider the paradoxes: A "little lamb" defeats a monstrous Dragon (12:7ff and 20:7-10), and people follow a "little lamb" (14:4). Other paradoxes include the wrath of the Lamb (6:16),

the Lamb as shepherd (7:17), and people as an offering to the Lamb (14:4). The Old Testament background for using the "lamb" to refer to Jesus is both the Passover lamb and the Messianic prophecy concerning the sacrificial lamb described Isaiah 53:7ff. In a book about the conflict disciples of the Lamb find themselves in as they face the Dragon (Satan) and his allies, surely it is paradoxical that Jesus is presented primarily as a Lamb who has conquered evil because of self-sacrifice.

7. J. B. Phillips, *The Book of Revelation: A new translation of the Apocalypse* (London: Geoffrey Bles, 1957) xiv.

8. Ibid., xiv-xv.

9. Especially helpful is the article on "Music" in L. Ryken, ed., *Dictionary of Biblical Imagery* (Downers Grove, IL: InterVarsity, 1998) 576-578.

10. John sometimes uses the word "say" (4:8) instead of "sing," (5:9). The places cited above suggest that the two verbs are used interchangeably. Hence, the word for speaking is consistent with singing. At points there is no introductory verb (7:15-17). The editors of The New International Version arrange the above passages with indented lines and with separate stanzas, underscoring their hymnic nature. Some scholars believe that these hymns (or portions of them) were actually sung by the early Christians and became a part of their service of worship. See R.P. Martin, *Worship in the Early Church* (Grand Rapids: Eerdmans, 1974) 42-46. See also L. Morris, *The Revelation of St. John* (Grand Rapids: Eerdmans, 1969) 100. A good devotional study that focuses on the songs in Revelation is by R. Coleman, *Singing with the Angels* (Grand Rapids: Baker, 1998).

11. Even though the word "storied" may be a new one for some readers, it is a helpful one to describe what needs to be considered in studying any work of Scripture.

12. See G.D. Fee, *Listening to the Spirit in the Text* (Grand Rapids: Eerdmans, 2000) 14.

13. G.K. Chesterton, *Varied Types* (New York: Dodd, Mead, 1908) 126.

Chapter Two

1. U. Eco, *The Name of the Rose*, trans. by W. Weaver (San Diego: Harcourt, 1994) 303.
2. For a concise discussion of the battle for Revelation's inclusion within the New Testament, see I. Boxall, *Revelation: Vision and Insight* (London: SPCK, 2002) 146-150.
3. For a good survey of the love-hate affair with Revelation, see C.R. Koester, *Revelation and the End of All Things* (Grand Rapids: Eerdmans, 2001) 10-26.
4. The writer introduces himself simply as John in Rev. 1:1, 4, 9 (see also Rev. 22:8). To discuss the complex issue of authorship and the question of the relationship between Revelation and the Johannine writings (The Gospel and Epistles of John) is not necessary in order to accomplish our purpose. Even though I believe John the apostle wrote the five documents, F.F. Bruce reminds us that "Whoever the seer of Patmos was, he was deemed to be a suitable messenger to convey the apocalyptic warnings and encouragements to the churches of Ephesus and other Asian cities." See *Peter, Stephen, James, and John* (Grand Rapids: Eerdmans, 1979) 149.
5. Some scholars date the book during the time of Nero (mid 60s), while others date it during the reign of Domitian, around A.D. 95 or 96. There is nothing in the book that demands an early date, and there is no evidence that discredits the testimony of the early church teachers who believed that the book was written at the end of the first century. If you want to pursue the issue, please examine the commentaries listed in the back of my book.
6. For numerous illustrations, see R. Kyle's *The Last Days Are Here Again: A History of the End Times* (Grand Rapids: Baker, 1998).
7. A concordance lists in alphabetical order words of a given Bible version with their location and context. There are three kinds of concordances: exhaustive, complete, and analytical. An exhaustive concordance lists all words in a given translation, giving under each word its occurrences in context, except for words like articles ("the"), conjunctions ("and"), and so forth. A complete concordance lists all words in a given translation,

giving under each word representative (and for some words, all) occurrences in context. An analytical concordance goes further by grouping word occurrences under the original language source word (Hebrew, Aramaic, and Greek), showing one or more ways the original language word is translated in that version. Lately, publishers have blurred some of these distinctions by adding original language material to exhaustive concordances, to aid the reader (e.g., *The Strongest NIV Exhaustive Concordance*, ed. by E.W. Goodrick and J.R. Kohlenberger [Grand Rapids: Zondervan, 2004]).

8. Matthew 24:6, 13, and 14 use "the end" to refer to the destruction of Jerusalem, an event that took place in A.D. 70 and was a fulfillment of a promise made in 24:34 in which Jesus said that the first-century disciples would live to see the catastrophic event ("I tell you the truth, this generation will certainly not pass away until all these things have happened."). Elsewhere in Matthew's Gospel, the phrase "this generation" always refers to the first generation of followers who lived to see Jerusalem destroyed (11:16; 12:41, 42, 45; 23:36; see also 12:39; 16:4; 17:17). It *never* refers to the generation of disciples who will be living before Christ's final coming.

9. *The Oxford English Dictionary*, Vol. III (Oxford: Clarendon Press, 1933) 284.

10. The Greek word *parousia,* meaning "coming," "arrival," or "presence," often refers to the final coming of Jesus (1 Thess. 2:19; 3:13; 4:15; 5:23; 2 Thess. 2:3; James 5:7; 2 Pet. 1:16; 3:4; and 1 John 2:28).

11. This is done apparently because the narrow definition of the term has been adopted.

12. See A. König, *The Eclipse of Christ in Eschatology: Toward a Christ-Centered Approach* (Grand Rapids: Eerdmans, 1989).

13. See *Salvation in History*, trans. by S.G. Sowers (New York: Herder & Herder, 1967) 13; and *Christ in Time,* trans. by F.V. Filson (Philadelphia: Westminster, 1950) 17-19, 72, 81-82.

14. See *Christ in Time*, 84.

15. Cullmann, *Salvation in History*, 172. For a thorough treatment of this concept, see A.J. Conyer's *The Eclipse of Heaven* (Downers Grove, IL: InterVarsity, 1992).

16. In *Christ in Time* (87), Cullmann asserts: "The hope of the final victory is so much the more vivid because of the unshakably firm conviction that the battle that decides the victory has already taken place." Despite such conviction or hope, the New Testament authors did not commit themselves to any time-scale. They stressed the urgency of the time in which they lived, suggesting that we must be ready for Christ's final coming at any time (1 Thess. 5:1ff.; Heb. 10:23ff.; 1 John 2:18ff.).

17. Some of the passages that I link with the final coming of Christ at this point (e.g., 11:15ff., and so forth) may appear questionable, but in the chapter on structure I will show that they do indeed refer to his *parousia*.

18. The theme of the kingdom and Christians reigning is an important one (1:9; 5:10; 11:15; 12:10; 16:10; 20:4, 6; 22:5, and so forth), as well as the imagery of Christians being priests who serve God (1:6; 5:10; 20:6; see also 3:12; 7:14; 22:3).

19. The Greek word is *nikē*, and outside the New Testament it is used to refer to the Roman goddess of military victory. *Nikē* is the winged goddess emphasizing Rome's vision of victory and imperial conquest. It is a politically loaded term. John boldly uses the verb to describe Christ (5:5) and Christians (2:7, 11, 17, and so forth). Rome conquered by war or killing; Christ conquered by faithful witnessing and dying a sacrificial death. Likewise, Christians follow in Christ's steps (12:11; 14:4ff.).

20 I believe there are hints that the conflict will intensify before Jesus' final coming (Rev. 20:7ff.), but it is difficult to speculate when it will occur (or even if it is occurring in our time).

21. Eugene Peterson, *Reversed Thunder: The Revelation of John and the Praying Imagination* (San Francisco: Harper & Row, 1988) 21.

22. From the Greek *protos*, meaning "first," and *logos*, meaning "word."

23. C.G. Rossetti, *The Face of the Deep*: A *Devotional Commentary on the Apocalypse* (New York: E. & J.B. Young, 1895) 551.

Chapter Three

1. Michael Card, *Unveiled Hope* (Franklin, TN: Word Entertainment, 1997).

2. See S. Smith and M. Card, *Unveiled Hope: Eternal Encouragement from the Book of Revelation* (Nashville: Thomas Nelson, 1997) x-xii. This book is an excellent example of application based on proper study.
3. Ibid., xii.
4. The credibility of such approaches is challenged by Kyle in *The Last Days Are Here Again: A History of the End Times*. Other helpful resources include: D.J. Lewis, 3 *Crucial Questions about the Last Days* (Grand Rapids: Baker, 1998); B.R. Rossing, *The Rapture Exposed: The Message of Hope in the Book of Revelation* (Boulder, CO: Westview Press, 2004); T.P. Weber, *On the Road to Armageddon: How Evangelicals Become Israel's Best Friend* (Grand Rapids: Baker Academic, 2004); and D. Wilson, *Armageddon Now* (Grand Rapids: Baker, 1977).
5. D.T. Niles, *As Seeing the Invisible: A Study of the Book of Revelation* (New York: Harper and Brothers, 1961) 19.
6. The conflict between Jews and Christians is possibly reflected in the presentation of Christians as the true Jews in such passages as Revelation 1:6; 7:4ff.; 14:1ff.; and 21:12. Indeed, there is not a designation associated with Christians in Revelation that is not also linked with the descriptions of God's people in the Old Testament. See D.E. Aune, "St. John's Portrait of the Church in the Apocalypse," *The Evangelical Quarterly* 38 (1966) 131-149.
7. Evidence that Jewish persecution continued on into the second century is provided in the account of the martyrdom of Polycarp (between A.D. 155–160), bishop of Smyrna. The Jews living in Smyrna joined forces with the Romans in opposing Christians. For fascinating reading, see "The Martyrdom of Polycarp" in *The Apostolic Writings. A New Translation and Commentary*, 6 vols., ed. by R.M. Grant (Camden, NJ: Thomas Nelson, 1967). In the story about Polycarp's death, we see the Jews approving of his punishment because he refused to worship the Emperor as a god.
8. We will consider the response of the Roman people in general when we discuss the temptation Christians faced to compromise with their culture.

9. B. Witherington III, *Revelation*, The New Cambridge Bible Commentary (Cambridge: Cambridge University Press, 2003) 23ff., represents the consensus of scholars. See also S.J. Friesen, *Imperial Cults and the Apocalypse of John* (Oxford: Oxford University Press, 2001) 122ff.

10. See *Roman Civilization Sourcebook II: The Empire*, ed. by N. Lewis and M. Reinhold (New York: Harper & Row, 1955) 582-585.

11. The persecution of Christians by Nero around A.D. 64 was limited to those who lived in Rome. The Roman historian Suetonius provides information about Domitian's demand to be addressed as "Our Master and God," but there is no proof that Christians were persecuted extensively during his reign because of their refusal to participate in the cult. See J.B. Lightfoot, *The Apostolic Fathers* (London: Macmillan, 1890), part one, 74ff. The persecution of the church reached its climax under Diocletian (A.D. 284–305) and did not come to an end until the time of Constantine (A.D. 306–337). Therefore, it is best to conclude that persecution had been or was in John's day, at most, occasional and selective. Nowhere does Revelation clearly reveal the actuality of rampant and systematic persecutions at the time of writing. John does, however, foresee an era in which the refusal of Christians to participate in the imperial cult would result in Rome functioning as jailer (13:10a), boycotter (13:16-17), and executioner of Christians (13:10b; see also 20:4). The local trouble experienced in Pergamum (2:13) foreshadowed the universal storm to come. Persecution was inevitable, and it would be sustained, systematic, and widespread. Of course, even beyond Roman times, this has often been the case throughout history up to our own century.

12. This is in contrast with the claims of Domitian, the emperor who reigned when John wrote Revelation (A.D. 81–96). In *Domitian*, XIII, the ancient Roman historian Suetonius (ca. A.D. 69–122) wrote about Domitian: "With no less arrogance he began as follows in issuing a circular letter in the name of his procurators, 'Our Master and our God bids that this be done.' And so the custom arose of henceforth addressing him in no other way even in writing or in conversation." *Suetonius*, vol. 2, Loeb Classical Library, ed. by T.E. Page, et al. and trans. by J.C. Rolfe.

13. The situations faced by the early Christians were not unlike those faced by ancient Israel in both the Old Testament (the influence of the Canaanites, Assyrians, Babylonians, and so forth) and intertestamental times (the period between the last of the Old Testament writings and the coming of Christ where Greek influence especially was a threat). Fidelity to God when confronting adversaries and alluring cultures was a note sounded time and again in the Scriptures. Hence, it is not surprising that John uses the language and images from Old Testament writings like Ezekiel, Isaiah, Jeremiah, and Daniel to portray the nature of the conflict and the demands made of God's people. This topic will be explored more fully in the chapter dealing with John's sources.
14. For a detailed analysis of the historical setting of each of the churches the work by Colin Hemer is indispensable. See *The Letters to the Seven Churches of Asia in Their Local Setting* (Grand Rapids: Eerdmans, 2001).
15. Ibid., 107-109, 120-121, 127-128.
16. For a discussion of these charges, see F.F. Bruce, *New Testament History* (Grand Rapids: Eerdmans, 1969) 378ff.
17. Writing about Roman aggression, W.C. Frend observes that "Persecution . . . is the other side of aggression, the inevitable outcome of a truly missionary spirit; the two are linked together as action and reaction." See *Martyrdom and Persecution in the Early Church: A Study of a Conflict from the Maccabees to Donatus* (New York: Anchor Books, 1967) 20.
18. August 29, 2005.
19. G. Theissen, T*he Shadow of the Galilean: The Quest of the Historical Jesus in Narrative Form*, trans. by J. Bowden (Philadelphia: Fortress Press, 1987) 8.
20. H.B. Swete, *The Apocalypse of St. John* (Grand Rapids: Eerdmans, 1908) 158.

Chapter Four

1. We must beware of a danger when we speak about "the Bible." To do so does not mean that the sixty-six books found in the

single volume are all alike. As noted above, we find a host of genres. It is like buying a collection of the best short stories written in any given year. When we open the volume, we may well find a variety of genres ranging from science fiction to western to mystery to romance.

2. See *The Modern Preacher and the Ancient Text: Interpreting and Preaching Biblical Literature* (Grand Rapids: Eerdmans, 1988) 17. Two other helpful books that discuss principles for interpreting different genres are G.D. Fee and D. Stuart, *How to Read the Bible for All Its Worth*, 3rd ed. (Grand Rapids: Zondervan, 2003); and D.B. Sandy and R.L. Giese, Jr., *Cracking Old Testament Codes: A Guide to Interpreting the Literary Genres of the Old Testament* (Nashville: Broadman & Holman, 1995).

3. I discuss the genre of prophecy first because the book is more clearly identified with that genre than with writings viewed as apocalypses or letters. As noted above, John identifies himself as a prophet and his work as a prophecy. Yet as I show in this chapter, prophecy and apocalypse are related. That the book is to be viewed as a letter is made clear in 1:4, and yet the characteristics of a letter do not reappear until 22:21. It is a letter, but a different kind of letter, when compared to the letters by Paul and others.

4. In *Plowshares and Pruning Hooks: Rethinking the Language of Biblical Prophecy and Apocalyptic* (Downers Grove, IL: InterVarsity, 2002) 130ff., D.B. Sandy argues that prediction is the least prominent characteristic of the prophetic literature and that the emphasis is on prosecution and persuasion. As to persuading, the prophets realized that a key function was to enforce the historic covenant between God and the Israelites. The prophets' other key role was to awaken the people of God from their self-sufficiency, and to reorient their worldview in line with God's. Concerning prediction, he notes that its "function was to make the prosecution and persuasion more convincing" (see p. 131). For a study of the exhortation character of the promises and assurances found in the prophetic writings, see C. Westermann, *Basic Forms of Prophetic Speech*, trans. by H. White (Louisville, KY: John Knox/Westminster, 1991).

5. See also G.V. Smith, *The Prophets as Preachers: An Introduction to the Hebrew Prophets* (Nashville: Broadman and Holman, 1994) 14, who observes: "Before a prophet can communicate God's way to live, God must reveal knowledge about His plans for a group of people and send a prophet to deliver that message."

6. J.P.M. Sweet expresses the matter well: "A prophet in the biblical sense is not simply one who predicts the future, but one who sees into the realities that lie behind the appearances of this world and sets them out, with the consequences he sees, so that people may act accordingly. . . . Revelation uncovered the missing dimension, so that Christians should act according to the will of God they could not see, rather than of the Caesar they could—so that at whatever cost, they should put eternal destiny before apparent security and prosperity in the present." See his *Revelation*, rev. ed., TPI New Testament Commentaries (Philadelphia: Trinity Press International, 1990) 2.

7. The word means "an unveiling" or "a disclosure."

8. There are portions of Daniel and Ezekiel that are considered apocalyptic. Apocalypses not found in our Bible, but written by Jews who wrestled with explaining the hard times that had come upon God's people, include 2 Baruch, the Apocalypse of Abraham, 1 Enoch, and Fourth Ezra (which is actually chapters 3–14 within 2 Esdras in the Old Testament Apocrypha). The nonbiblical books were written anywhere from second century B.C. to second century A.D.

9. John is fond of metaphors (Rev. 1:17-18; 5:5; and so forth), "a figure of speech in which an aspect of one thing is pointed out by implicitly comparing it with something else or by simply identifying it as the thing to which it is being compared." M.S. DeMoss, *Pocket Dictionary for the Study of New Testament Greek* (Downers Grove, IL: InterVarsity, 2001) 84. Similes are found throughout the book as well (Rev. 1:15; 21:18; and so forth). A simile is "a comparison of two basically unlike things, frequently using the word *like* or *as*." Ibid., 113.

10. G.R. Beasley-Murray offers us an analogy concerning the use of symbolism in apocalyptic works: "The closest modern parallel to this mode of communication is the political cartoon, which

has gained an established place in the popular press all over the world. The purpose of a cartoon is to embody a message relating to a contemporary situation, whether it be of local, national, or international import. Many of the symbols employed by cartoonists are stereotyped (like John Bull and Uncle Sam). Frequently the situations depicted are deliberately exaggerated, and even made grotesque in order that the message may be made plain. But no one complains—except perhaps the people represented." *The Book of Revelation,* rev. ed., The New Century Bible (Greenwood, S.C.: The Attic Press, 1978) 16-17.

11. It is inconceivable to me that a Roman citizen who was not a Christian would have failed to see Rome being described in such passages as Revelation 17–18.

12. H.H. Rowley, *The Relevance of Apocalyptic* (Greenwood, SC: Attic Press, 1980) 15-43.

13. See Hemer, *The Letters to the Seven Churches of Asia in Their Local Setting,* 14-15; and W. Ramsay, *The Letters to the Seven Churches of Asia* (London: Hodder and Stoughton, 1904) 171-196.

14. Similar to some of Paul's letters (e.g., 1 Thess. 5:12ff. and 2 Tim. 4:9ff.), John has an extended conclusion (22:8ff.). Properly speaking, it is obvious that chapters 2 and 3 are not seven letters since they do not contain the epistolary features we see elsewhere in the New Testament. They are Christ's messages to the seven congregations.

15. Even though a church is singled out at the beginning of each message, we find a common exhortation near the end of each message in Revelation 2–3 in which all the congregations are addressed: "let him hear what the Spirit says to the churches." The repeated call provides additional support for the idea that the message of the book is to have a wider audience. Many scholars have pointed out that the number seven probably denotes completeness or wholeness. Accordingly, the book is ultimately addressed to the church wherever it may be found.

16. See W.G. Doty, *Letters in Primitive Christianity,* Guides to Biblical Scholarship (Philadelphia: Fortress Press, 1973) 31-33, 45.

17. Nearly a century ago, Swete observed: "The Apocalypse of John

is the letter of an exiled prophet to the Christian congregations to which he ministered. He writes under the conviction that he has a message for them from the Supreme Prophet and Pastor of the Church and his primary purpose is to deliver this message. It has come to him in a way of revelation and under the form of a succession of visions, and he delivers it as it was given; his letter consists solely of visions and revelations of the Lord, which he has been not only permitted but commanded to transport. . . . It is a genuine outcome of the time, written with a view to the special needs of a particular group of Christian societies; it portrays the life of those societies, and ministers to their spiritual necessities. In form it is an epistle, containing an apocalyptic prophecy; in spirit and inner purpose, it is a pastoral." See *The Apocalypse of St. John*, xciv.

18. For an assessment of John's methods, see P.S. Minear's *I Saw a New Earth: An Introduction to the Visions of the Apocalypse* (Washington, D.C.: Corpus Books, 1968) 213-227.

19. I have found it helpful to read through the entire book and underline in color the passages that reveal strategies John adopted to emphasize comfort or challenge. Perhaps one color could be used to underline commands, another for names, and so forth. When this is done, John's concern to guide becomes even more apparent.

20. This term stresses the holiness of God's people and their special relationship to him. On the other hand, it is significant that John's favorite designation for those who are not saints is found in the phrase often translated "those who dwell upon the earth" (3:10; 6:10; 8:13; 11:10(2×); 13:8, 12, 14(2×); 17:2, 8). These individuals are loyal to the forces of evil because their focus is living on earth, getting as much as possible out of life. Christians, on the other hand, are those concerned with holiness and faithfulness to God.

21. See note 36.

22. The term "beatitude" is derived from Latin and means "blessedness," referring to those who are right with God and experience such blessings as forgiveness and the love and favor of God.

23. In contrast with The New International Version, The New American Standard Bible's translation suggests that two groups are in view rather than martyrs only: "And I saw the souls of those who had been beheaded because of the testimony of Jesus and because of the word of God, and those who had not worshiped the beast or his image, and had not received the mark upon their foreheads and upon their hand."

24. Minear observes: "The prophet did in fact seek to produce certain changes in the attitudes and actions of his audience, and one of these changes was the replacement of terror by courage in the face of persecution. But when one isolates the hortatory sections of his book, and analyzes the thrust of these sections, he is impressed with the diversity of external conditions, the variety of Christian response, and the manifold shape of the author's purpose. It is clear that the document would never have been written apart from John's desire to produce changes in thought and behavior. It is true that no vision is intelligible apart from this desire, and that the recapture of purpose is essential to every student's work." *I Saw a New Earth,* 213-214. The word "hortatory" refers to those passages that exhort or urge.

Chapter Five

1. *Merriam-Webster's Collegiate Dictionary,* 11th ed., s.v. "muse."
2. Ibid.
3. Ibid.
4. See M. Steinberg's notes on *Handel's Messiah* performed by The Robert Shaw Chorale & Orchestra (Broadway, New York: BMG Music, 2004) 7ff of the liner notes.
5. The text of the work (as an opera) for the musical theater. *Merriam-Webster's Collegiate Dictionary* 11th ed., s.v. "libretto."
6. A recitative is a narrative song that describes some action, thought, or emotion.
7. The number before each quotation represents what recitative is being cited.
8. D. Guthrie, *New Testament Introduction,* 4th ed. (Downers Grove, IL: InterVarsity, 1990) 966.

9. DeMoss offers the following definition of allusion: "An indirect, imprecise or passing reference in which verbal correspondence to the source text is relatively remote. A citation or quotation, on the other hand, contains a portion of the source text that is obvious and normally relatively longer. Also called an echo." *See Pocket Dictionary for the Study of New Testament Greek*, 17. In contrast with the way many of the direct quotations are introduced in other New Testament writings, an allusion is not introduced by a formula clearly stating that a particular portion of Scripture is being cited. For example, in his Gospel, John uses a formula like the one in 2:17, "His disciples remembered that it is written . . ." and it is followed by a quotation from Ps. 69:9, "Zeal for your house will consume me." See also John 6:31, 45; 10:34; 12:14-15; 15:25; 19:36-37. This formula and similar ones are never found in Revelation.

10. It is interesting to note that in this same passage there is the following statement: "You yourselves have seen what I did to Egypt, and how I carried you on eagle's wings and brought you to myself." Recall the scene in Rev. 12:13ff. where the woman (i.e., a symbol for the people of God who follow Jesus; see Rev. 12:17) is pursued by the dragon (i.e., Satan; see 12:9), and God delivers the followers of Jesus just like he delivered old Israel: "The woman was given the two wings of a great eagle, so that she might fly to the place prepared for her in the desert, where she would be taken care of for a time, times, and half a time, out of the serpent's reach" (Rev. 12:14a). Note that the phrase "for a time, times and half a time" is an allusion to the Old Testament as well (see also Dan. 9:26; Rev. 11:2, 6; 12:14). The result is that John combines allusions to Exodus and Daniel in the same verse, and in both situations the common denominator is that the people of God were being oppressed not by Egypt, Babylon, or some other earthly power but ultimately by Satan.

11. First Peter 5:13 uses the image of "Babylon" to describe Rome. There are several points of contact between 1 Peter and Revelation. First, both documents are addressed to Christians living in Asia Minor (1 Pet. 1:1; Rev. 1:4). Second, both are written

to Christians who are suffering for Christ (1 Pet. 4:13; 5:1; Rev. 1:9). Third, both authors provide guidance on how to be faithful to Jesus in tough times.

12. And yet the number ten, when linked with words other than "day," is used in the Old Testament to refer to testing (e.g., Gen. 24:55; 31:7, 41; the ten Exodus plagues; and Num. 14:22; Job 19:2-3. See also Rev. 12:3; 13:1; 17:3, 7, 12, 16 in which the number ten is based on Dan. 7:1ff.).

13. Paul uses typology as well (Rom. 5:14; 1 Cor. 10:1ff) as does the author of Hebrews on an extensive level.

14. References to the Exodus are also found in the places where John, apparently seeing the heavenly tabernacle, mentions items associated with the tabernacle (and later the Temple), namely, the golden lampstands (1:12; Exod. 25), the hidden manna (2:17; Exod. 16), the altar of incense (8:3-5; Exod. 3), the holy of holies (11:1; 15:8; Exod. 19), and the ark of the covenant (11:19; Exod. 9).

15. Peterson, *Reversed Thunder,* 144.

16. See note 7, ch. 2, for a discussion of concordances available for Bible study.

17. See "Appendix A: Old Testament Allusions in Revelation," p. 176.

18. Some of the finest electronic Bible software, tools, and resources today are produced by Logos Bible Software of Bellingham, Washington, the world's largest developer of Bible Software. Logos Bible Software may be found at **http://www.logos.com.**

19. *The Book of Revelation,* The New International Greek Testament Commentary (Grand Rapids: Eerdmans, 1999). See pp. 76ff. for an overview and virtually every page where Beale comments on individual verses. A commentary that is sensitive to John's use of the Old Testament and is not as technical as Beale's is M. Wilcock's *The Message of Revelation* (Downers Grove, IL: InterVarsity, 1975).

20. The guidelines for interpreting symbols will be presented in the next chapter, and they also will be of help in evaluating the way John uses the Old Testament.

Chapter Six

1. See J.W. Johnson's *The Books of the American Negro Spirituals* (Cambridge, MA: De Capo Press, 2002), and **www.negrospirituals.com.**
2. For a helpful summary of the way Revelation is quoted or alluded to in hymns, see Koester's *Revelation and the End of All Things*, 31-38.
3. One of the most important books I have read on this subject is Sandy's *Plowshares and Pruning Hooks.*
4. See *Breaking the Code: Understanding the Book of Revelation* (Nashville: Abingdon, 1993) 26. Earlier in the book (see p. 11) Metzger observes: "The book of Revelation is unique in appealing primarily to our imagination—not, however, a freewheeling imagination, but a disciplined imagination. This book contains a series of word pictures, as though a number of slides were being shown upon a great screen. As we watch we allow ourselves to be carried along by impressions created by these pictures. Many of the details of the pictures are intended to contribute to the total impression, and are not to be isolated and interpreted with wooden literalism."
5. We do not "obey" predictions, but we obey God's Word and will, if we desire to be faithful to God.
6. The verb is used in John 18:32 (similar to 12:33) and 21:19. In the latter passage, John refers to the kind of death Peter was to experience.
7. Symbols are found in John's use of numbers, colors, animals, furniture, musical instruments, jewels, and so forth.
8. Wilcock, *The Message of Revelation*, 24-25.
9. Whereas Peter writes about the devil prowling around like a roaring lion looking for someone to devour (1 Pet. 5:8), John writes about Satan being a dragon, roaring and roaming.
10. If Paul is describing in 2 Cor. 12:1ff. an experience he had, it is ironic that he heard things that could not be told (12:4), but John could tell what he saw and heard.

11. Of course, such knowledge is required to study any book of the Bible.

12. Many scholars argue that John did not actually see or hear what he recorded. The book, they say, is a product of his own fertile imagination. To the contrary, D.S. Russell observes: "All these experiences are so true psychologically that it is difficult to see in them nothing more than the expression of literary convention; their very nature argues strongly that they reflect the actual experiences of the apocalyptic writers themselves." *The Method and Message of Jewish Apocalyptic* (Philadelphia: Westminster, 1964) 165-166.

13. 1:10, 14(3×), 15(2×), 16, 17; 2:18, 24, 27, 28; 3:3, 21; 4:1, 6, 7; 5:6; 6:1, 6, 11, 12(2×), 13, 14; 8:1, 8, 10; 9:2, 3, 5, 7(2×), 8(2×), 9(2×), 17; 10:1(2×), 3, 7, 9, 10; 12:15; 13:2(2×), 3, 11; 14:2(3×), 3; 15:2; 16:3, 13, 15, 21; 17:12; 18:6, 21; 19:1, 6(3×), 12; 20:8; 21:2, 11, 21; 22:1, 12.

14. *Merriam-Webster's Collegiate Dictionary*, 11th ed., s.v. "door." Please remember that English dictionaries are seldom helpful in defining terms used in the Bible. I use it here because of the timeless meaning of "door."

15. "Key" is a symbol for power (Isa. 22:22; see also Rev. 1:18; 9:1; 20:1 where keys convey the same meaning).

16. A popular interpretation of this verse is that it should be linked with the way Paul uses the imagery of the "door" in Col. 4:3. In that verse it is a symbol for an opportunity to share the gospel. If this is the meaning, the Christians in Philadelphia are being challenged by Jesus to evangelize. But John's context does not support this interpretation. We must beware of imposing a meaning of a word assigned by Paul. We must let John define that word. To impose a meaning assigned by Paul comes into conflict with the way John uses the word in Revelation. See J.R.W. Stott, *What Christ Thinks of the Church* (Wheaton: Harold Shaw, 1990) 96ff., who sees the door as a symbol for evangelistic opportunity.

17. Often this verse is taken out of context, and the plea of Christ is directed toward the person who needs to become a Christian. The context clearly shows this plea is directed toward those

who already claim to be followers of Christ, in this case, the members of the Christian community in Laodicea.

18. The number "seven" does not have to be explicitly mentioned. For example, in Revelation several times we have groups of seven attributes associated with Christ ("power and wealth and wisdom and strength and honor and glory and praise" in 5:12), seven parts of creation ("a great earthquake . . . the sun . . . the whole moon . . . the stars . . . the sky . . . every mountain and island" in 6:12-14), and seven divisions of humanity ("the kings . . . the princes, the generals, the rich, the mighty, and every slave and every free man" in 6:15).

19. Contrary to popular opinion, according to Scripture seven is not "the perfect number." Nor is it always associated with good. As the above illustrates, seven is often associated with evil in the book of Revelation (see 11:13; 13:1; 17:3, 7, 9, 10, 11).

20. The commentaries and other special studies listed at the end of this book will be of help to the Bible student as symbols are studied. It is critical for a student to do a personal study and then consult those works and others to check their conclusions. On a personal note, if there is the desire to see how I have interpreted many of the symbols, the notes on Revelation in *The Quest Study Bible* reflect my study.

21. R. Lowery, "Christmas on Patmos," *The Christian Standard* (19 December 2004) 14-15.

22. See Isa. 7:14; 26:17–27:1; 60:19-20; 61:10; and 62:3, 5 for the allusions found in 12:1. See Jer. 4:3; Isa. 26:16-17; 52:2; 54:1-6; 61:10; 62:1-5; Micah 4:9-10; 5:3; and Hos. 13:13 for the allusions found in 12:2. See Isa. 7:10, 14 for both verses.

23. See Pss. 7:13-14; 89:10; Isa. 27:1; 30:7; 51:9; Ezek. 29:3; 32:2-3; Dan. 7:7, 24; 8:10 and Hab. 3:8-15.

24. In addition to the commentaries and special studies on Revelation listed in the bibliography, two indispensable tools are *Dictionary of Biblical Imagery*, ed. by L. Ryken, and Sandy's work.

25. See "Appendix B: A Key to Select Symbols in Revelation," p. 199.

26. Fee reminds us that "God's Word is very closely tied to the intentionality of the divinely inspired author. . . . [A]uthors are

intentional, and that meaning resides ultimately in that intent. . . . And since most authors also have at least normal egos, they do not take kindly to being misquoted, misinterpreted, or misconstrued—and all of that in light of what they understand to have been their own intentionality." See *Listening to the Spirit in the Text*, 9-10.

27. Numerous scholars also attempt to trace the use of a word in ancient Greek and Hebrew literature, outside of Scripture, for example in nonbiblical apocalyptic works like 2 Esdras. This can be helpful, but Scripture seems to me to be the best place to start since we can assume that is what the early believers would have used. Nevertheless, uses in extrabiblical writings can enrich our understanding of how a symbol was used in similar or different ways.

28. We should not be surprised that Satan and his allies engage in parodying (see 2 Cor. 11:14, where Paul emphasizes that Satan masquerades as an angel of light). Parody is one of the major tactics Satan and his allies use to deceive, and deception is, perhaps, at the core of evil (Rev. 12:9; 13:14; 18:23; 19:20; 20:3, 8, 10).

29. "Dragon" can refer to any one of a number of monstrous land and sea creatures. It does not refer to the huge, fire-breathing, winged reptile of Western lore. One Hebrew word is sometimes translated "sea monster" or "sea creature" (Job 7:12; Ps. 74:13; 148:7; Isa. 27:1). The same word that is translated "monster" elsewhere likely means "crocodile" (Isa. 51:9; Ezek. 29:3; 32:2). In Revelation "the Dragon" is clearly a symbol of Satan (12:3ff.; 13:2, 4, 11; 16:13; 20:2).

30. Contrary to popular views, I believe the symbols of the New Jerusalem and the bride are synonyms. Note that in 21:9 the promise is made to reveal to John the bride, a symbol for the people of God. In the following verses, rather than describing the bride, John describes the city. Both symbols express a core idea about intimacy between God and his people (21:3).

31. The conclusion by Hanns Lilje is helpful: "In the countless hosts of the heavenly multitude there is always at any particular time one angel who directly connects a particular church with the

throne of God. Each particular church on earth, in its sorrow, tribulation, struggle, and distress has its own heavenly representative. He is here addressed, and in him the whole church, as once more in the individual churches the whole church is being addressed. For it is one of the most daring ideas of the primitive church that each local church represents the whole church, as indeed the Greek word for 'church' is the same for the local body in any particular place." What a word of comfort Lilje provides! See his *The Last Book of the Bible*, 4th ed., trans. by O. Wyon (Philadelphia: Muhlenberg Press, 1957) 64-65.

32. The commentaries recommended at the end of this book are especially helpful in determining possible meanings of the symbols. See Appendix C, p. 205.

33. To illustrate the timelessness of the symbols, I often have students read through Revelation and categorize the images under such topics as clothing, wealth, sex, speech, weather, and so forth. These are issues of concern in any culture, and studying the symbols associated with them proves enlightening.

34. *The Book of Revelation: A new translation of the Apocalypse*, ix.

Chapter Seven

1. *More Than Conquerors* (Grand Rapids: Baker, 1939).

2. *The Revelation of St. John*. Black's New Testament Commentary (Peabody, MA: Hendrickson, 1966).

3. Ibid., 106.

4. See *The Quest Study Bible*, rev. ed. (Grand Rapids: Zondervan, 2004) 1779. There is no mention of the seven bowls in this comment because I was asked to comment on Rev. 5–10. Today, I would add that the seven bowls emphasize totality of God's judgment. Whereas the seals stressed one fourth and the trumpets stressed one third, there is an emphasis on "all" with the bowls in Rev. 16:1ff. In other words, the bowls emphasize the same message as the seals, trumpets and thunders: God is going to judge the world, but with the bowls we are coming not only to the end of the world but to the end of the book, and thus John emphasizes the complete judgment of evil and the wicked. Additional observations on this are found later in the chapter.

5. Victorinus is one of the first known scholars to suggest that John does not give a linear presentation with one sequence of events but rather a series of repeated presentations of the conflict (i.e., recapitulation, in which there is repetition of the conflict and resolution). To those who align themselves with the forces of evil, judgment awaits; to the good, reward. In particular, he proposed that the seven bowls of 15:1–16:21 do not sequentially follow the seven trumpets (8:2–11:18) as part of a continuous series. Instead, the trumpets and bowls are parallel accounts or recapitulations of the same event. See *Commentary on the Apocalypse* 8:1-2, as cited by W.C. Weinrich, ed., Revelation, New Testament XII, Ancient Christian Commentary on Scripture (Downers Grove, IL: InterVarsity, 2005) 121; see also p. xx. A lay theologian and student of Scripture from North Africa, Tyconius (A.D. 370–390), argued for recapitulation as well (ibid., xxiiff.). Augustine of Hippo (d. 430), who was influenced by Tyconius, took a similar approach (ibid., xxiv).
6. A work that compares various views for understanding Revelation's structure and message is S. Gregg, ed., *Revelation: Four Views, A Parallel Commentary* (Nashville: Thomas Nelson, 1997).
7. 7. E.F. Scott observed that a perfectly logical apocalypse would be nothing short of a contradiction in terms (*The Book of Revelation* [New York: Charles Scribner's Sons, 1940] 26.). For centuries, scholars have attempted to unravel the intricate structure of John's writing. Their efforts reveal that no proposal answers all the questions by tying up the book into a nice, neat package. To put it bluntly, no scheme for organizing Revelation is without difficulties. I believe there will always be loose ends in our analysis of its structure. But then, I believe this will be the case with any book of the Bible. In light of these cautions, this chapter will be especially demanding. I do not pretend to have solved all of the problems, but I believe that the proposal outlined, though not new, is one that students of the book must be aware of.
8. Two popular study Bibles take a chronological approach: C.I. Scofield, *The Scofield Reference Bible* (New York: Oxford University Press, 1945), and C.C. Ryrie, *The Ryrie Study Bible:*

The New American Standard Bible Translation (Chicago: Moody Press, 1976). See also J. Walvoord, *The Revelation of Jesus Christ* (Chicago: Moody, 1966).

9. For representatives of this approach, see Beale's *The Book of Revelation* and Wilcock's *The Message of Revelation*.
10. *Nelson's New Illustrated Bible Dictionary* (1995), s.v. "POETRY."
11. See A.A. Di Lella, *The Book of Daniel*, The Anchor Bible (Garden City, NY: Doubleday, 1978) 208ff., and J.E. Goldingay, *Daniel*, Word Biblical Commentary (Dallas: Word Books, 1989) 322ff.
12. See D.I. Block, *The Book of Ezekiel*, The New International Commentary on the Old Testament (Grand Rapids: Eerdmans, 1997) 24ff., and J.W. Wevers, *Ezekiel*, The New Century Bible Commentary (Grand Rapids: Eerdmans, 1982) 133.
13. The list is not exhaustive. You will discover additional repetitions as you go deeper into the book. Of course, either an exhaustive concordance or a computer with Bible search capability is indispensable for tracing words and phrases that are repeated.
14. DeMoss, *Pocket Dictionary for the Study of New Testament Greek*, 29.
15. See M.W.G. Stibbe, *John's Gospel* (London and New York: Routledge Press, 1994), and P.F. Ellis, "*Inclusio*, Chiasm, and the Division of the Fourth Gospel," *St. Vladimir's Theological Quarterly* 43 (1999) 269-309.
16. B.D. Johnson, "The Disciple Who Follows: An *Inclusio* of John 1 and 21," Unpublished paper delivered at the Midwest Regional Evangelical Theological Society 49th Annual Meeting, Lincoln, Illinois, March 19, 2004.
17. For an excellent summary of the issues involved, see Beale, *The Book of Revelation*, 152-170 and 215-216.
18. Beale (161) observes that the main problem with the view that 1:19 presents a straightforward chronological division of Revelation into three historical periods is "that it interprets Revelation without sufficient sensitivity to its literary form, giving a straightforward, literal reading of the book, rather than using a figurative approach, which would be more appropriate to the book's symbolic genre. Furthermore, since chs. 2–3

(which supposedly describe only the 'church' age) and chs. 4–22 (the future 'great tribulation') contain repeated references both to the past and the future, neither section can be understood as strictly chronological. Not only do chs. 4–22 describe the events of past, present, and future, but the subsections of that large section recapitulate the same events in different ways."

19. R.H. Mounce, *The Book of Revelation*, rev. ed., New International Commentary on the New Testament (Grand Rapids: Eerdmans, 1998) 62.

20. J. Moffatt, "The Revelation of St. John the Divine," in *the Expositor's Greek Testament* (Grand Rapids: Eerdmans, 1951), 5:347.

21. The seven seals are not closely matched with the trumpets and the bowls. A possible reason is that the seals represent the events that must take place before the scroll (Rev. 5:1ff.) is opened. If the content of the scroll is the consummation of the Kingdom of God (e.g., Rev. 11:15ff. and so forth), then the seals end up at the same point as the seven trumpets and seven bowls, the end of the world where evil is completely defeated and God's rule is perfectly and completely realized.

22. Scenes which are an answer to the questions raised by the saints in 6:9-11: "How long . . . until you . . . avenge our blood?"

23. Beale observes that "the main point is the horror of divine judgment, which has such an awesome effect that no human is able to verbalize a response. However brief the description, this idea of judgment composes the seventh seal." *The Book of Revelation*, 447.

24. It could even be argued that each message in Revelation 2–3 takes the reader to the end of the world, with the various promises made to the ones who overcome, promises that are developed more fully in passages like Rev. 7:9ff. and Rev. 21:1ff. where we are given a glimpse of life eternal with God in the new heaven and new earth.

25. At various points in my book I have noted the importance of the theme of worship in Revelation. It would be instructive for you to explore the significance of the way this theme weaves its way throughout the book, especially in light of the fact that

each series of seven (the seven churches, the seals, and so forth) is bracketed by images of worship (Rev. 1:9ff. and 4–5 bracket chapters 2–3; 4–5 and 8:3-5 bracket 6–8:2; 8:3-5 and 11:16ff. bracket 8:6–11:15; and 15:1-4 and 16:17ff. bracket the seven bowls described in 15:5ff.).

26. Many scholars support the repetition and recapitulation analysis when they propose a breakdown of Revelation into two halves. Revelation 1–11 presents the visible conflict between the church and the Roman Empire, with an emphasis on judgment that is both partial and final. Revelation 12–22 presents a more focused explanation of the true nature of the conflict; it is one involving the evil forces of Satan (the Dragon) and God and his followers. The emphasis shifts to totality of judgment (especially from chapter 15 to the end of the book).

27. Since it appears that we are brought to the end of the world in light of the scenes depicted in 6:12–7:17, it is possible that the seventh seal (8:1-5) is a literary device, so to speak, leading the reader into the next series, the seven trumpets.

28. As pointed out in the chapter on symbolism, with the opening of the sixth seal, we are given a glimpse of judgment day. Seven categories of creation (6:12-14) and seven categories of humanity (6:15) will come under God's judgment. As we saw earlier, the number "seven" emphasizes totality or completeness. This is strong support that we are brought to the end of the world with the opening of the sixth seal.

29. The King James Version adds the phrase, "which art to come," found in some manuscripts. The phrase, however, is not found in the earliest and best manuscripts. In this setting, the Kingdom has come completely.

30. The same verb is used in Rev. 16:17 ("It is done!") and in Rev. 21:6 ("It is done!"). The former focuses on the final judgment of the wicked, while the latter refers to the final reward for God's people.

31. John describes four sets of "seven": the seven messages to the churches (2–3), the seven seals (6–8:5), the seven trumpets (8:6–11:19) and the seven bowls (15:1–16:21). Some have

attempted to divide the book into seven sections (e.g., W. Hendricksen, *More Than Conquerors*, 28ff., and J.L. Blevins, *Revelation as Drama* [Nashville: Broadman Press, 1984]), but such proposals appear forced. We should avoid imposing a connection among all of the series that is greater than the text indicates. For example, in general, the seals, trumpets, and bowls appear to take the reader to the end of the world, but when one compares the contents of each of the series, there is closer connection between the trumpets and the bowls than there is between the seals, trumpets, and bowls. As noted in this chapter, there appear to be interludes between the sixth and seventh seal, trumpet, and bowl. Other linkages are explored in this chapter.

32. I believe that a key theological theme associated with the seven seals is God's permissive will. The use of the verb "was given" (6:2, 4(2x), 8, 11; 7:2; see also 8:2) stresses that God is in control. With regard to the seven trumpets, Rev. 9:20-21 teaches that the horrors associated with the trumpets were meant to bring people to repentance. Finally, when the seven bowls are poured out, God's retributive justice is being stressed.

33. Even though we have four sets of seven—the seven seals, seven trumpets, seven thunders, and seven bowls—we cannot say much about the seven thunders since their contents were sealed (10:1-5, specifically verses 3-4). At most, we can say the thunders are related to judgment in general, since that is the context in which thunder is found elsewhere in the book (4:5; 6:1; 8:5; 11:19; 14:2; 16:18; 19:6).

34. Perhaps another analogy sheds light on understanding the structure. Rather than viewing the scenes in Revelation like a film showing the unfolding of history in detail, the reader is to see John presenting the scenes like slides, depicting the same landscape, yet from different angles.

35. See pp. 92-96.

36. Throughout history, between Christ's first and final comings, we should expect many Babylons leading up to a final Babylon, many judgments from God leading up to the Final Judgment, and many blessings for believers leading up to perfect blessings.

37. To describe the Final Judgment, John is using the culture the recipients were most familiar with to describe a culture and a time they would never live to see. Neither John nor his immediate audience knew whether Christ would come in their lifetime, but they had been promised that there would be a day of reckoning.

APPENDIX A

OLD TESTAMENT ALLUSIONS IN REVELATION

We observed in the chapter on John's sources that he nowhere formally quotes an Old Testament passage. Instead, he uses allusions. Scholars have identified a large number of them. I have drawn upon their work to compile a list of these allusions, included here for your benefit.[1]

To help you make full use of this extensive list of allusions, I offer three suggestions. First, when you identify an Old Testament allusion, you need to look at the context surrounding that allusion. For example, Revelation 2:10 alludes to Daniel 1:12. The story that surrounds Daniel 1:12 is the testing of Daniel and his Jewish brothers. They ask to be tested for ten days. John uses the "ten days" as a symbol for the period of testing of the Christians in Smyrna.[2] Daniel and the others were tested and refused to compromise their faith. On the other hand, the Christians in Smyrna will be tested because of their refusal to compromise. The "ten days," therefore, becomes a symbol for the testing of God's people. Second, you need to study the symbols in the Old Testament allusions because they will give clues to interpreting similar symbols in Revelation. Third, you need to consult good commentaries that discuss the Old Testament allusions.

You will see at various points in the allusions listed below two standard conventions often used by scholars. First, you may see a number in parenthesis. English Bibles will sometimes have a slightly different chapter or verse division when compared to the Hebrew text. For example, Psalm 89 in the English is Psalm 88 in the Hebrew text. In the list below I show the Hebrew reference in parentheses after the English reference. For example, this is used in the Revelation 1:5 citation of Ps. 89(88). Second, "LXX" is a symbol for the Septuagint, the Greek translation of the Hebrew and Aramaic Old Testament.

Revelation	OT Allusion
1:1	Dan. 2:28-30, 45-47
1:1-2a	Isa. 48:6; Dan. 2:28-29, 45
1:2	Dan. 2
1:3	Dan. 12:4
1:4	Gen. 1; Exod. 3:14; Lev. 26:18-28; Isa. 11:2; 41:4; 43:10; 44:6; 48:12; Zech. 3:9; 4:2-7, 10
1:5	Exod. 24:8; Lev. 16:14-19; Pss. 2:7-8; 89(88):27, 37; 130 (129): 8; 2 Sam. 7:13-16; Isa. 1:16, 18; 40:2; 55:4; Jer. 42:5
1:5-6	Exod. 24:4-8; 29:10-21
1:6	Exod. 19:6; Deut. 28:9; Pss. 89(88):19-32; 89:28; Isa. 43:10-13; 51:6; 61:6; Dan. 7:22, 27; Zech. 4:11-14
1:7	Isa. 40:5; 52:10; Dan. 7:13-14; Zech. 12:10, 12
1:8	Exod. 3:14; Isa. 41–48; 41:4; 44:8; Amos 3:13 (LXX); 4:13 (LXX)
1:10	Ezek. 3:12
1:10-11	Exod. 19:16, 19-20; Ezek. 2:2; 3:12, 14, 24; 11:1; 43:5
1:11	Exod. 17:14; 34:27; Isa. 8:1; 30:8; Jer. 36:1; 37:2; Hab. 2:2
1:12	Exod. 20:18-19; 25; 37; 40:4; Num. 8; 1 Kgs. 7:48-49; Zech. 4:2, 9-10
1:13	Exod. 25:7; 28:4, 31[27], 39ff.; 29:5, 9; 35:9[8]; Lev. 8:7; Isa. 22:21-22; Ezek. 1:26; 8:2; 9:2, 11; Dan. 3:25; 7:13; 8:15; 10:5-6, 16, 18; Zech. 4:2, 11-14
1:13-15	Dan. 7; 10
1:14	Dan 7:9; 10:6
1:14-15	Dan. 10:6
1:15	Ezek. 1:7(LXX), 24, 27; 43:2; Dan. 3:24-25; 10:6
1:16	Exod. 34:29; Judg. 5:31; Isa. 11:4; 49:2; Dan. 10; 12:3, 6-7; Zech. 4
1:17	Josh. 5:14; Ps. 90:2; Isa. 41:4; 44:2 (LXX), 6; 48:12; Ezek. 1:28; 3:23; 43:3; 44:4; Dan. 8:17ff.; 10:5-12, 17-20
1:18	Deut. 32:40; Job 38:17; Isa. 22:22; Dan. 4:34; Hos. 13:14

APPENDIX A

Revelation	OT Allusion
1:19	Isa. 48:6(LXX); Dan. 2:28, 29, 45
1:20	Dan. 2:29, 45
2:4	Jer. 2:2; Ezek. 16:8; Hos. 1–3
2:5	Exod. 25:30-31; 40:4; Num. 8:1-4; 1 Kgs. 7:48-49; Zech. 4:2-8
2:6	Ps. 139:21
2:7	Gen. 2:8(LXX), 9; 3:22, 24; Prov. 11:30; Isa. 6:9-10; Ezek. 3:27; 28:13(LXX); 31:8-9 (LXX); 47:1-12
2:8	Isa. 44:6; 48:12
2:8-9	Dan. 1; 3
2:10	Gen. 24:55; 31:7, 41; Num. 14:22; Job 19:2-3; Dan. 1:12-15, 19; 5:3-4; 7
2:12	Isa. 49:2
2:12-13	Ps. 89:37; Isa. 43:10-12
2:13	Ps. 89:37
2:14	Num. 22:1–25:3; 31:8, 16; Deut. 23:4; Josh. 13:21-22; 1 Kgs. 16:31-32; 2 Kgs. 9:22; Neh. 13:2; Ps. 106:39; Isa. 47:10; Nah. 3:1-4
2:16	Isa. 49:2

Revelation	OT Allusion
2:17	Exod. 16:13-15, 31ff.; 28:9-12; Num. 11:7; Ps. 78(77):24;Isa. 11; 49; 62:2; 63; 65:15
2:18	Ps. 2; Dan. 3:24-25; 7:9-13; 10:6
2:19-20	1 Kgs. 16:31; 19:1; 21:5, 7, 25; 21:25; 2 Kgs. 8:18; 9:22
2:20	Num. 25:1-2; 1 Kgs. 16:31; 18:19; 21:25; 2 Kgs. 9:22, 30
2:21	1 Kgs. 16:31; 21:25; 2 Kgs. 9:22; Num. 25:1ff.; 31:16
2:21-23	1 Sam. 16:7; 1 Kgs. 8:39; 21:17-29; 2 Kgs. 9:30-37; 10:1-11; Ps. 7:8-11; Prov. 24:12; Jer. 11:10-17, 20; 17:3, 10-11; 20:12; 39:17-19; Ezek. 18:30; 24:14
2:23	1 Sam. 16:7; 2 Kgs. 10:7; Pss. 7:9, 10; 26:2; 62(61):12; Prov. 17:3; 21:2; 24:12; Jer. 11:20; 17:10; 20:12
2:24-25	Dan. 3:15-22
2:26	Ps. 2:8-9
2:26-27	Ps. 2:8-9
2:28	Num. 24:14-20; Ps. 2:7-8; Isa. 14:12

Revelation	OT Allusion
2:29	Pss. 115:4-8; 135:15-18; Isa. 6:9-10; Ezek. 3:27; 12:2-16
3:1	Isa. 11:2; Zech. 3:9; 4:10
3:4-5	Dan. 11–12; Zech. 3:5-6
3:5	Exod. 32:32-33; Pss. 69(68):28; 139(138):16; Isa. 4:3; Ezek. 13:9; Dan. 7:10; 12:1-2; Mal. 3:16
3:7	Job 12:14; Isa. 22:22
3:8	Isa. 45:1
3:9	Ps. 86:9; Isa. 43:4; 45:14; 49:23; 60:14; 66:23
3:9-10	Pss. 24:1; 33:8; 49:1; 72:9; Isa. 24:17; 43:4; 45:14; 49:23; 60:14; Hos. 4:1; Joel 2:1
3:12	Isa. 56:5; 62:2; 65:15; Ezek. 48:35
3:14	Gen. 1:1; Ps. 89(88):28, 37; Prov. 8:22; 14:25; Isa. 43:10-12; 65:15-16
3:17	Hos. 12:8ff.; Zech. 11:5; 12:5
3:18	Exod. 20:26; Job 23:10; Prov. 27:21; Ezek. 16:36; 23:29; Nah. 3:5; Zech. 13:9; Mal. 3:2-3
3:19	Prov. 3:12
3:20	S. of S. 5:2
4:1	Exod. 19:16-20, 24; Num. 10:1-3; Josh. 6; Judg. 7; Isa. 27:12ff.; Ezek. 1:4; 2:9; 8:2, 4, 10; 10:1, 9; Dan. 2:28-29, 45; 7:2, 6-7, 9; Jer. 4:23-26; Zech. 2:1; 4:2; 5:1, 9; 6:1
4:1–5:14	Ezek. 1–2; Dan. 7
4:2	1 Kgs. 22:19ff.; 2 Chr. 18:18; Pss. 11:4; 47(46):8, 9; 103:19; Isa. 6:1ff.; Ezek. 1:26-28; 10:1; Dan. 7:9
4:3	Gen. 9:13; Exod. 24:10; 28:17-20; Ps. 104:2; Ezek. 1:26-28; 28:13; Dan. 7:9c
4:4	Num. 11:16-17; 1 Kgs. 8:1; 2 Kgs. 23:1; 1 Chr. 24:3-19; 25:6-31; 26:17-19; Ezra 5:5, 9; 6:7, 14; 10:8; Isa. 6; 24:23; Ezek. 1; 14:1; 20:1; Dan. 7:10b
4:5	Exod. 19:16-20; Deut. 5:22; Pss. 18:7-15; 29:3-9; 77:18ff.; Ezek. 1:4-28; Dan. 7:9d-10a; Zech. 4:2-3, 6, 10

APPENDIX A

Revelation	OT Allusion
4:6	Gen. 1:8; Exod. 14:16; Ps. 74:12-15; Isa. 6:1ff.; 51:9-11; Ezek. 1:5, 18, 22, 26, 28; 10:1; 32:2; Dan. 7:2-3
4:6-7	Ezek. 1:5-10; 10:14
4:6-8	Exod. 25:17-22; 37:6-9; 1 Kgs. 6:24ff.; 2 Chr. 3:13; Isa. 6:1ff.; Jer. 3:16-17; Ezek. 1; 10:12-15, 20-22
4:7	Ezek. 1:10; 10:14
4:8	Exod. 3:14; Ezek. 1:18; 10:12; Isa. 6:1-4; 41:4; Hos. 12:6; Amos 3:13(LXX); 4:13(LXX); 5:14-16; 9:5-6; Nah. 3:5; Zech. 10:3; Mal. 2:16
4:9	1 Kgs. 22:19ff.; 2 Chr. 18:18; Ps. 47(46):8; Isa. 6:1ff.; Ezek. 1:26-27;Dan. 4:34; 6:26; 7:9; 12:7
4:10	1 Kgs. 22:19ff.; 2 Chr. 18:18; Ps. 47:8; Isa. 6:1ff.; Ezek. 1:26-27; Dan. 4:34; 6:26; 12:7
4:11	1 Chr. 29:11, 12
5:1	1 Kgs. 22:19; 2 Chr. 18:18; Ps. 47(46):8; Isa. 6:1; 29:11; Ezek. 1:26-27; 2:9-10; 3; Dan. 7; 12:4, 9
5:2	Dan 4:13-14, 23; 7:10
5:3	Exod. 20:4; Ps. 146:6; Isa. 29:11-12, 18; Ezek. 2:9ff.; Dan. 7:10; 8:26; 12:4
5:4	Isa. 29; Dan. 7
5:5	Gen. 49:9-10; Isa. 11:1, 10; 29; Jer. 11:19; 23:5; 33:15; Dan. 7:10; 12:4, 9; Zech 3:8; 6:12
5:6	Gen. 22:10; Exod. 12:3, 5-6; Lev. 1:10ff.; 17:5; Deut. 33:17; 1 Kgs. 22:11; Ps. 89:17; Isa. 11; 53:7-9; Jer. 11:19; Dan. 7:7–8:24; Zech. 3:9; 4:2, 10; 6:5
5:7	1 Kgs. 22:19; 2 Chr. 18:18; Ps. 47(46):8; Isa. 6:1; Ezek. 1:26-27; Dan 7:9ff., 13
5:8	1 Chr. 25:6-31; Ps. 141(140):2
5:9	Pss. 33:3; 40:3; 96:1; 98:1; 144(143):9; 149:1; Isa. 42:10; Dan. 3:4, 7; 5:19; 6:26; 7:10, 14; 12:4, 9
5:10	Exod. 19:5-6; Isa. 61:6; Dan. 7:22b, 27a
5:11	Num. 10:36; Dan. 7:10

Revelation	OT Allusion
5:12	1 Chr. 29:11-12; Isa. 53:7; Dan. 2:20, 37; 4:30-31
5:13	Exod. 20:11; 1 Kgs. 22:19; 2 Chr. 18:18; Neh. 9:6; Pss. 47(46):8; 146:6; Isa. 6:1; Ezek. 1:26-27; Dan. 2:38; 4:37
6:1-8	Exod. 7–11; Deut. 32:24-25; Pss. 77:18; 144:6; Isa. 5:28; Jer. 4:29; 6:23; 50:14, 29; Ezek. 5:16-17; 14:12-23; Dan. 7–12; Hab. 3:8-11; Zech. 1:8-15; 6:5-8
6:2	Ps. 45:3-5; Jer. 15:2; Ezek. 5:16ff; Zech. 1:8; 6:1-6, 7-8a
6:4	Isa. 27:1; Jer. 32:24; Ezek. 14:17, 21; 21:9-15, 21; 38:21; Zech. 1:8; 6:2
6:5	Zech. 6:2, 6
6:6	Lev. 26:26; 2 Kgs. 6:25; 7:1; Jer. 12:12-13; Ezek. 4:10, 16; Joel 1:10-11
6:6-8	Ezek. 5:1-2, 12, 16-17
6:7	Zech. 6:4-5, 8
6:7-8	Ezek. 14:21; Dan. 2; 7; Zech. 6
6:8	Deut. 32:23-27; Lev. 26:18-29; Job 17:13-16; 33:22; Pss. 6:5; 49:14-15; Prov. 2:18; 5:5; S. of S. 8:6; Isa. 28:15; Jer. 14:12-19; 15:3; 16:4-5; 21:7, 9; 24:10; 29:17-28; 42:17; 43:11; Ezek. 5:12, 17; 6:11-12; 7:15; 12:16; 14:19-21; 29:5; 33:27; 34:28; Dan. 7; Hos. 13:8, 14
6:9	Exod. 29:12; 30:1-10; Lev. 4:7, 18, 30, 34; 5:9; 8:15; 17:11
6:9-11	Isa. 49:9-10, 19
6:10	Gen. 4:10; Deut. 32:43; 2 Kgs. 9:7; Pss. 6:3; 13:2; 74:10; 79:5, 10; 80:4; 89:46; 90:13; 94:3; Dan. 8:13; 12:3-6; Zech. 1:12; 6:1-8
6:11	Gen. 15:6; Lev. 17:11
6:12	Isa. 13:10; 50:3; Ezek. 32:7, 8; Joel 2:10, 31; 3:15; Amos 8:8; Hag. 2:6
6:12-13	2 Sam. 22:8-16; Eccl. 12:1ff.; Pss. 18:7-15; 102:25-26; Isa. 2:19-21; 5:25, 30; 13:10-13; 24:1-6, 19-23; 34:4; 51:6; 64:1; Jer. 4:23-28; Ezek. 30:3-4, 18; 32:6-8; 38:19-20; Joel 2:10, 30-31; 3:15; Amos 8:7-10; Micah 1:4-6; Hab. 3:6-11; Hag. 2:6-7

Revelation	OT Allusion
6:12-14	Deut. 4:19; 17:1-4; 2 Kgs. 23:4-5; Ps. 68:7-8; Isa. 13:10-13; 24:1-6, 19-23; 34:4-6; Jer. 4:23-28; 8:2; 31:35-36; 33:20-21, 25-26; Ezek. 8:16; 32:6-8; Joel 2:10, 30-31; 3:15-16; Amos 8:8-9; Hab. 3:6-11
6:13	Deut. 4:19; Judg. 5:20; Isa. 14:12; 24:21; 34:4; 47:13; Jer. 8:2; Dan. 8:10
6:13-14	Isa. 13:10; 34:4
6:14	Pss. 46:2-3; 72:10; 97:1; Isa. 34:4; 41:1; 49:1; 51:5; 60:9; Jer. 51:25; Ezek. 26:18; Zech. 4:7
6:15	Pss. 2:2; 48(47):4 (LXX); Isa. 2:10, 19, 21; 24:21; 33; 34:12; 35:1-4; Jer. 4:29
6:15-16	Isa. 2:10, 18-21; Jer. 4:23-29; Hos. 10:8
6:16	1 Kgs. 22:19; 2 Chr. 18:18; Ps. 47 (46):8; Isa. 6:1; Ezek. 1:26-27; Hos. 10:8
6:17	Ps. 76(75):8; 130:3; Isa. 2:10, 18-21; 13:9; Joel 2:10, 11, 31; Nah. 1:4-6; Zeph. 1:14ff., 18; 2:2-3; Mal. 3:2; 4:5

Revelation	OT Allusion
7:1	Pss. 18:10; 104:3-4; Isa. 11:12; 19:1; 66:15; Jer. 4:11-12; 23:19; 49:36; Ezek. 7:2; 37:9; Dan. 7:2; 8:8; 11:4; Hos. 13:15-16; Zech. 2:6; 6:1-8
7:2	Exod. 12:23; Ezek. 9:4f
7:2-3	Gen. 2:8; Exod. 12:7, 13, 22-28; 19:6; 28:11-21, 36-38; Isa. 42:6-7; 49:6; 51:4-8; Ezek. 9; 14:12-23; 43:2-4; Dan. 3–7
7:3	Ezek. 9:4
7:4-8	Gen. 39:10; 49:8-11, 17; Exod. 19:6; 24:4-9; 28:11-21; Num. 1:3, 18-21, 23, 44; 2:3ff., 32; 26:2, 4; 34:19; Josh. 4:3-24; 21:4; Judg. 1:2ff; 2 Sam. 24:1-9; 1 Kgs. 12:28-30; 1 Chr. 5:2; 12:23-37; 27:23; Ps. 87; Isa. 11:10-14; 14:2; 27:12-13; 43:4; 45:19; 49:23; 60:14; 66:19-21; Jer. 8:16-17; 31:7-9; Ezek. 37:15-25; 40–48; Dan. 7:18, 22; Hos. 4:17–14:8; Micah 5:1-4, 7-8; Zech. 2:11; 8:23; 9:7; 14:16-19
7:9	Gen. 1:26-28; 12:2; 13:16; 15:5; 16:10;

Revelation	OT Allusion
	17:2-19; 18:18; 22:17-18; 24:60; 26:4; 32:12; 35:11-12; 46:3; 48:3-4, 19; Exod. 1:7; 19:6; Lev. 23:40, 43; Deut. 1:10; 10:22; 1 Chr. 27:23; Neh. 8:15; Dan. 7:22, 27; Hos. 1:10; Micah 5:6-9
7:9-17	Isa. 11; Micah 5
7:10	1 Kgs. 22:19; 2 Chr. 18:18; Ps. 47(46):8; Isa. 6:1; Ezek. 1:26-27; Jonah 2:9-10
7:11-12	Dan. 7:9; 12:1
7:13-14	Gen. 49:1-9, 11; Exod. 19:10, 14; 24:8; Lev. 13:58-59; Isa. 1:18; 4:4-6; 64:6; Ezek. 37; Dan. 12:1-2, 10; Zech. 3:3-5
7:14	Gen. 49:11; Exod. 19:10, 14; Dan. 12:1
7:15	Exod. 19:6, 10, 14; 24:4-8; 29:10-21; Lev. 8:30; 23:34; 26:11; Deut. 16:13; 1 Kgs. 22:19; 2 Chr. 18:18; Pss. 47(46):8; 68:17; Isa. 4:5; 6:1; Ezek. 1:26-27; 37:26-28; 43:7; Hos. 1:9-10; 2:23; Zech. 2:10-11, 13; 8:3, 20-23; 14:16-21
7:16	Ps. 121:6; Isa. 49:10; Jer. 2:13
7:16-17	Pss. 23:1-2; 36:8-9; 46:4-5; Prov. 14:27;

Revelation	OT Allusion
	Isa. 12:3; 25:8-9; 33:21; 49:6, 9-13; 55:1-3; Jer. 2:13; 31:16; Ezek. 34:23-25; 37:24-28; Joel 3:18
7:17	Pss. 23:1-2; 126:5-6; Isa. 25:8; 49:10; Jer. 2:13; 31:16; Ezek. 34:23; 37:24
8:1	1 Sam. 2:9-10; Pss. 31:17; 76:8; 115:17; Isa. 23:2; 41:1-5; 47:5; Lam. 2:10-11; Ezek. 27:32; Dan. 7:25; 12:7; Amos 8:2-3; Hab. 2:20; Zeph. 1:7; Zech. 2:13
8:2	Exod. 12:23
8:3	Exod. 30:1-3; Ps. 141(140):2; Isa. 63:9; Amos 9:1
8:3-5	Exod. 3:7-9
8:4	Exod. 29:18, 25; 30:8-10; Lev. 2:1-2; 16:12-13; Ps. 141:1-2; Dan. 9:20ff.; 10:10ff.
8:5	Exod. 19:16-19; Lev. 16:12; Pss. 18:7-13; 68:8; 77:18-19; Isa. 29:6; Ezek. 10:1-7; Hab. 2:20–3:15
8:7	Exod. 9:18-26, 31-32; 19:16-19; Isa. 10:16-20; 28:2; Ezek. 5:2, 12; 38:22; Joel 2:30; Zech. 13:8-9

Revelation	OT Allusion
8:8	Exod. 7:17-21; Ps. 78:44; Jer. 51:25; Hos. 4:3
8:8-9	Gen. 1:20; Exod. 7:18-24; Isa. 41:15; 42:15; Jer. 51:25, 63-64; Ezek. 29:3-5; Hab. 1:14; Zech. 4:7
8:8-11	Exod. 7:20-25
8:10	Deut. 29:17-18; Isa. 14:12; Dan. 8:10
8:10-11	Exod. 7:15-24; Deut. 29:17-18; Ps. 78:44; Prov. 5:4; Isa. 14:12-15; 24:21; Jer. 8:13-14; 9:15; 23:15; Lam. 3:15, 19; Hos. 10:4; Amos 5:7; 6:12; Zech. 9:14
8:11	Jer. 9:15; Amos 5:7; 6:12
8:12	Exod. 10:21-23; 12:12; Isa. 13:10; Ezek. 32:7-8; Joel 2:10; 3:15; Amos 5:18, 20; 8:9
8:13	Exod. 19:4, 16; Deut. 28:26, 49; 32:11; Isa. 24:16-18; Jer. 4:13; 7:33-34; 16:3-4; 19:7; 34:18-20; 49:22; Job 9:26; Lam. 4:19; Ezek. 17:3; 39:17-20; Hos. 4:1-3; 8:1; Hab. 1:8
9:1	Exod. 15:5; Job 38:16; 41:10, 23-24; Pss. 71 (70):20; 74:12-13; 77(76):16; Isa. 14:12; 24:21-22; 27:1; 51:10; 63:13; Ezek. 31:15; Dan. 8:10; Jonah 2:6; Amos 9:3
9:2	Gen. 19:28; Exod. 10:15; 19:18; Isa. 13:10; Joel 2:10, 31; 3:15
9:3	Exod. 10:4-15; Deut. 8:15; 1 Kgs. 12:11; 2 Chr. 10:11, 14; Isa. 14:31
9:4	Exod. 8:22-24; 9:4-7, 26; Ps. 105:33-35; Ezek. 9:4
9:5	Deut. 4:30; 8:15; 28:14,27-29, 34, 60-61, 65-67; 29
9:6	Exod. 9:27-28; 10:16-17; 1 Kgs. 19:1-4; Job 3:1-26; 6:8-9; 7:15-16; Jer. 8:3; 20:14-18; Hos. 10:8; Jonah 4:3, 8
9:7	Exod. 10:1-20; Joel 1:1-20; 2:1-32
9:8	Joel 1:6
9:9	Job 39:19-25; Isa. 33:1-4; Jer. 51:14, 27; Joel 2:4-5
9:11	Exod. 12:12-29; Job 18:14; 26:6; 28:22; 31:12; Pss. 78(77):49; 88:11; Prov. 15:11; 27:20; 30:27;

Revelation	OT Allusion
	Ezek. 38–39; Hos. 13:13-14;Amos 7:1
9:13	Exod. 27:2; 30:1-3; 1 Kgs. 1:50-51; 2:28-34; Zech. 4
9:14	Gen. 15:18; Deut. 1:7; Josh. 1:4; Isa. 7:20; 8:7-8; Jer. 1:14-15; 4:6-13; 6:1, 22; 10:22; 13:20; 25:9, 26; 46:6, 10, 22-23; 47; 50:41-42; Ezek. 26:7-11; 38:6, 15; 39:2; Dan. 10:13, 20-21; Joel 2:1-11, 20-25
9:15	Ezek. 5:2; Zech. 13:8-9
9:16	Gen. 24:60; Lev. 26:8; Deut. 32:30; 33:2, 17; Judg. 6:3, 5; 7:12; Ps. 91(90):7; Jer. 46:2-10, 22-23; Dan. 7:10; Micah 6:7
9:17	Gen. 19:24, 28; 2 Sam. 22:9; Isa. 34:9-10; Ezek. 38:22
9:18	Gen. 19:24, 28; Lev. 26:21, 25; Deut. 29:22-23; Ezek. 9
9:19	Num. 21:6; Deut. 32:24; Jer. 8:17
9:20	Exod. 14:4-8, 17; 20:4-5, 13-15; Deut. 4:28; 31:29; 32:17 (LXX); Pss. 95:5 (LXX); 105:36-37; 106:37; 115:4-8; 135:15-18; Isa. 6:9-10; 17:8; 43:7, 9; Dan. 5:3-4, 23ff.; Micah 5:12
9:21	2 Kgs. 9:22; Isa. 47:9-10; 48:5; Jer. 7:5-11; Hos. 3:1–4:2; Micah 5:12–6:8; Nah. 1:14; 3:1-4
10:1	Gen. 16:10; 22:11-18; 24:7; 31:11-13; Exod. 3:2-12; 14:19; Judg. 2:1; 6:22; 13:20-22; Ezek. 1:26-28; Dan 3:25; 7:13; Zech 3:1-3
10:3	Hos. 11:10
10:4	Dan. 8:26; 12:4, 7, 9; Hab. 2:3
10:5	Deut. 32:40; Dan. 12:7
10:5-11	Gen. 14:19, 22; Exod. 20:11; Deut. 32:40; Neh. 9:6; Ps. 146(145):6; Dan. 12:7
10:5-6	Deut. 32:40; Dan. 12:7
10:6	Gen. 14:19, 22; Exod. 20:11; Neh. 9:6; Ps. 146:6
10:7	Isa. 27:13; Dan. 2:19, 27-30, 47; 9:6, 10; 11:29–12:13; Amos 3:6-7; Zech. 1:6
10:8	Exod. 19:16-19; Ezek. 1–3; Dan. 12:4, 9

Revelation	OT Allusion
10:9	Isa. 3:14; Jer. 15:16ff.; Ezek. 2:8ff.; 3:1-3; Zech. 5:2
10:9-10	Deut. 8:3; Pss. 19:7-11; 119:97-104; Prov. 5:4; 16:21-24; Jer. 6:10-11; 15:16-17; 23:15; Lam. 3:15, 19; Ezek. 2:8; 3:1-3; Dan. 12:4, 9
10:10	Ezek. 3:1, 3
10:11	Jer. 1:10; 25:30; Ezek. 2–3; Dan. 3:4; 7:14
11:1	2 Sam. 8:2; 2 Kgs. 21:13; Ps. 2:9; Isa. 34:11; Jer. 31:39; Ezek. 40:3ff., 47; 41:13; Amos 7:7ff.; Zech. 2:1-2
11:1-2	Exod. 19:6; 2 Sam. 8:2; Pss. 2; 80:6; Isa. 28:16-17; 63:18; Jer. 31:38-40; Ezek. 29:6; 40–48; Dan. 7:25; 8:11, 13; 9:27; 12:7, 11-12; Micah 2:5; Zech. 1:16; 4:7; 6:12-13; 12:3; 14:1-11
11:2	Ps. 79(78):1; Isa. 63:18; Dan. 7:21, 25; 8:13; 9:27; Zech. 12:3 (LXX)
11:3	Num. 35:30; Deut. 17:6; 19:15
11:4	Exod. 25:30-31; Num. 8:1-4; 1 Kgs. 7:48-49; Zech 4:2-3, 7, 10-14, 25
11:5	2 Sam. 22:9; 2 Kgs. 1:10ff.; Ps. 97(96):3; Jer. 5:14
11:5-6	Lev. 24:17-21; 26:19; Num. 35:30; Deut. 11:16-17; 19:15; 1 Sam. 4:8; 2 Sam. 22:9; 1 Kgs. 17:1; 2 Kgs. 1:10-17; Pss. 18:8; 97:3; Mal. 3:1-5; 4:1-6
11:6	Exod. 7:17, 19-20, 7:27–11:10; 1 Sam. 4:8; 1 Kgs. 17:1
11:7	Exod. 12:23; 14:19-28; 1 Sam. 17:44, 46; Ps. 79:1-5; Dan. 7:3, 7-8(LXX), 21
11:7-10	Deut. 29:22-26; 32:28-33; Isa. 1:9-15; 3:9; 14:19-20; 24:6; 26:21; Jer. 6:12; 8:1-2; 9:22; 16:4-6; 22:8, 19; 23:14-15; Ezek. 16:26, 44-57; Dan. 5:9; Hos. 4:1; Joel 1:2, 14; 2:1; 3:19; Amos 4:10-11
11:8	Isa. 1:9-10; 3:9; Ezek. 16:48; 23:3-27
11:10	Ps. 105(104):38
11:11	Exod. 15:16; 1 Kgs. 22:1; Ps. 105:38; Ezek. 37:5-14
11:12	2 Kgs. 2:11

Revelation	OT Allusion
11:13	Gen. 24:7; 2 Chr. 36:23; Ezra 1:2; 6:9-10; 7:23; Neh. 1:4-5; 2:20; Ps. 136:26; Isa. 6:1; Jer. 10:22; Ezek. 3:12; 38:19-20; Dan. 2:18-19, 37, 44; Jonah 1:9
11:15	Exod. 15:18; Pss. 2:2; 10:16; 22(21):28; Dan. 2:44; 7:14, 27; Obad. 21; Zech. 14:9
11:17	Exod. 3:14; Pss. 46:9; 96:1; 98:1; Amos 3:13(LXX); 4:13 (LXX)
11:18	Pss. 2:1, 5, 12; 46:6; 92:1; 95:10; 99(98):1; 110:5; 115:13; Isa. 40:10; Dan. 12:2; Joel 2:28-32; Isa. 40:10; Dan. 9:6, 10; 12:2; Joel 2:28-32; Amos 3:7; Zech. 1:6
11:19	Exod. 9:24; 15:13-18; 19:16; 1 Kgs. 8:1-6; 1 Chr. 15:24; 2 Chr. 5:7; Neh. 12:41; Jer. 3:16-17; Ezek. 1:13
12:1	Gen. 37:9; Ps. 104:2; S. of S. 6:4, 10; Isa. 7:14; 26:17–27:1; 54:5; 60:19-20; 61:10; 62:3, 5; Jer. 3:6-10; Ezek. 16:8; Hos. 2:21ff.
12:2	Gen. 3:15-16; Isa. 26:17; 62:1-5; 66:6-7; Hos. 13:13; Micah 4:10
12:2, 5	Isa. 66:6ff.
12:3	Ps. 91:13; Isa. 27:1; Ezek. 29:3; Dan. 7:7, 24
12:4	Jer. 4:31; Dan. 8:10
12:5	Pss. 2:7-9; 110:1; Isa. 7:14; 66:7; Jer. 20:15
12:6	Exod. 19:4; Deut. 2:7; 29:5; Neh. 9:19, 21; Ps. 91:4; Dan. 7:25; 12:7; Hos. 13:5
12:7	Dan. 10:13, 20-21; 12:1
12:8	Ps. 2; Dan. 2:35
12:9	Gen. 3:1, 13-16; Job 1:6ff.; Isa. 14:12; Dan. 2:35; Zech. 3:1ff.
12:10	Job 1:6-11; 2:1-6; Ps. 2:2; Zech. 3:1-2
12:12	Deut. 32:43; 1 Chr. 16:31; Ps. 96:11; Isa.5:8-22; 44:23; 49:13; Jer. 51:48
12:14	Exod. 19:4, 14; Deut. 1:31; 32:11; Isa. 40:31; Ezek. 17:3, 7; Dan. 7:4, 25; 12:7
12:15	Exod. 1:22; 14; Pss. 18:4; 74:15; Isa. 59:19; Ezek. 29:3; 32:2
12:16	Exod. 14; Num. 16; Deut. 11:4-6; Ps. 106:17

Revelation	OT Allusion
12:17	Gen. 3:15; Isa. 61:8-9; 65:9; Dan. 7:7, 21
13:1	Job 40; 41; Isa. 27:1; Dan. 7:1-8, 11, 20, 25
13:1-2	Isa. 11:6ff.; Jer. 5:6; Dan. 7:2-7, 20, 24; Hos. 13:7ff.
13:1-7	Dan. 7
13:2	Dan. 7:4-6, 8, 16
13:3	Gen. 3:15; Ps. 74:13; Isa. 27:1; Hab. 3:8-15
13:4	Exod. 8:10; 15:11; Deut. 3:24; Pss. 35(34):10; 71(70):19; 86:8; 89:8; 113:5; Isa. 14:4; 40:18, 25; 44:7; 46:5; Micah 7:18
13:5	Dan. 7:6, 8, 11, 20, 25; 8:10-12, 23-25; 11:30ff., 36
13:6	Dan. 7:25; 8:10-13; 11:36
13:7	Dan. 7:7-8, 21
13:7-18	Dan. 7:14
13:8	Exod. 32:32-33; Ps. 69(68):28; Isa. 53:7; Ezek. 13:9; Dan. 7:10; 12:1-2
13:9	Isa. 6:9-10
13:10	Jer. 15:2; 43:11; Ezek. 14:12-23
13:11	Dan. 7:17; 8:3
13:13	Exod. 4:17, 30; 7:11; 10:2; 11:10; Deut. 13:1-5; 1 Kgs. 18:24-39; 2 Kgs. 1:10-14
13:14	Deut. 13:1-5; Isa. 24:17; Dan. 3; 7:4b, 6b; 8:25; 11:32; Hos. 4:1
13:15	Dan. 3:5-6
13:16-17	Exod. 13:9; Isa. 44:5
13:17	Isa. 44:5; Ezek. 9:4; Dan. 3:5ff.
13:18	1 Kgs. 10:14; Dan. 3:1; 12:10
14:1	2 Kgs. 19:31; Pss. 2:6-12; 48:2, 10-11; 74:2, 7; 125:1; Isa. 4:2-3; 10:12, 20; 24:23; 33:16; 37:30-32; 42:6-7; 49:6; 51:4-8; 62; Jer. 3:17; Ezek. 9:4; 48:35; Joel 2:32; 3:16-17; Obad. 17, 21; Micah 4:5-8; Zeph. 3:9-20; Zech. 8:2-7; 14
14:2	Pss. 81:3; 149:3; 150:3; Ezek. 1:24; 43:2; Dan. 10:6
14:2-3	Pss. 2:6-12; 33:3; 40:3; 92:4; 96:1; 98:1; 144:9; 149:1; Isa. 42:10; Ezek. 1:5, 24
14:3	Pss. 33:3; 40:3; 96:1; 98:1; 144(143):9; 149:1; Isa. 42:10

Revelation	OT Allusion
14:4	Exod. 4:22; 19:15; Lev. 15:16-18; Deut. 23:9-10; 1 Sam. 21:5; 2 Kgs. 19:21, 30-31; Isa. 37:22; 53:7; 65:4; Jer. 2:2-3; 3:1-10; 14:17; 18:13; 23:14; 31:4, 7-8, 13, 21; Lam. 1:15; 2:13; Ezek. 23; 48:8; Hos. 1:2; 11:1; Amos 5:2
14:5	Ps. 32:2; Isa. 44:20; 53:9; 57:4-5; Jer. 3:23; 13:25; 23:14; Zeph. 3:13
14:6	Isa. 40:9; 52:7; 60:6-14; 61:1
14:7	Exod. 20:11; Josh. 7:19; Neh. 8:6; Pss. 22:23; 115:1; 146(145):6; Isa. 24:15; 42:12; Jer. 13:16; Ezek. 7:7; 22:3; Dan. 4:34; 5:21; Mal. 2:2
14:8	Gen. 41:32; Ps. 75:8ff.; Isa. 13:19-22; 21:9; 23:15-18; 29:9; 51:17-23; Jer. 25:15-16; 28:8; 50:2, 39-40; 51:7-8, 24-26, 62-64; Dan. 4:27, 30; Hos. 4:11-12; Nah. 3:4; Hab. 2:15-16
14:10	Gen. 19:24, 28; Deut. 29:23; 2 Sam. 22:9; Job 21:20; Pss. 11:6; 60:3; 75(74):8; Isa. 1:22; 30:27-33; 51:17, 21-23; 63:6; Jer. 25:15-18; 51:7; Ezek. 38:22; Obad. 16
14:11	Isa. 34:9-10; 60:11, 15; 62:6; Jer. 14:17; Lam. 2:18; Ezek. 37:26-28
14:13	Isa. 57:1-2; Dan. 12:13
14:14	Dan. 7:13; 10:16
14:15	Gen. 15:16; Ps. 68:24; Isa. 17:5; 63:2ff.; Jer. 51:33; Joel 3:13
14:15, 18	Joel 3:13
14:17-20	Gen. 15:16; Exod. 23:16; 34:22; Num. 18:12; 19:3; Isa. 27:12; 63; Jer. 2:3; 51:33; Hos. 6:11; Zech. 14:2-5, 12-16
14:18	Joel 3:13
14:19	Isa. 63:1-6; Lam. 1:15; Joel 3:14
14:20	Isa. 63:3; Lam. 1:15; Joel 3:13
15:1	Lev. 26:21; Deut. 4:30
15:2	1 Kgs. 7:23, 44; 2 Kgs. 16:17; 2 Chr. 4:2, 15; Ps. 74:12-15; Ezek. 32:2
15:3	Exod. 15:1ff., 11; 34:10; Deut. 31:30; 32:3-4; Josh. 14:7;

Revelation	OT Allusion
	22:5; Pss. 86:9; 92:5; 110; 111(110):2; 139(138):14; 145:17; Jer. 10:6-7, 10; Hos. 14:9; Amos 3:13(LXX); 4:13(LXX); Mal. 1:11
15:4	Deut. 32:4; Pss. 86(85):9-10; 98:2; 119:75; 145(144):17; Isa. 66:23; Jer. 10:6-7, 10; Mal. 1:11
15:5	Exod. 25:21-22; 38:21; 40:34; Num. 1:50
15:6	Lev. 26:1, 21, 30-31; Dan. 10:5
15:7	Exod. 38:23-26; Num. 4:14-15; 7:13-89; Ps. 75:8; Isa. 51:17, 22; Jer. 25:15
15:8	Exod. 19:18; 29:43; 40:28-29, 34ff.; Lev. 16:2; 26:21; Num. 9:15; 1 Kgs. 8:10-11; 2 Chr. 5:13-14; Isa. 6:1, 4; 66:1; Ezek. 10:2, 4; 44:4
16:1	Pss. 69(68):24; 79:6; Isa. 66:6; Jer. 10:25; Ezek. 22:31; Zeph. 3:8
16:2	Exod. 9:8-11; Deut. 28:35
16:3	Exod. 7:17-21
16:3-4	Exod. 7:17-21
16:4	Exod. 7:17-24; Pss. 78(77):44

Revelation	OT Allusion
16:5	Exod. 3:14; Deut. 32:4; 2 Chr. 19:7; Job 8:3; 34:10; Pss. 92:15; 119(118):75, 137; 145(144):17; Isa. 41:4
16:6	Ps. 79(78):3, 10, 12; Isa. 34:7; 49:26
16:7	Deut. 32:4; Pss. 19(18):9; 119(118):137; Amos 3:13(LXX); 4:13(LXX)
16:8	Exod. 10:21
16:9	Deut. 32:24; Isa. 48:9-11
16:10	Exod. 10:21-23; Isa. 8:22
16:11	Dan. 2:19
16:12	Gen. 15:18; Exod. 14:21-22; Deut. 1:7; Josh. 1:4; Isa. 11:15-16; 41:2, 25; 44:27; 46:11; 50:2; 51:10; Jer. 50:38; 51:36
16:13	Exod. 8:2-7; 1 Kgs. 22:21-23; Jer. 14:14; 27:14; 29:8ff.; Ezek. 22:28; Micah 3:5
16:14	Ps. 104:30; Amos 3:13(LXX); 4:13(LXX)
16:15	Isa. 20:4; Ezek. 16:36; 23:29; Nah. 3:5
16:16	Judg. 5:19; 2 Kgs. 9:27; 23:29ff.;

Revelation	OT Allusion
	2 Chr. 35:22; Ezek. 39:17; Zech. 12:11
16:17	Exod. 9:22; Isa. 66:6
16:18	Exod. 19:16-26; Dan. 12:1
16:19	Ps. 75:8; Isa. 51:17, 22; Jer. 25:15; Dan. 4:30; Hag. 2:6; Zech. 14:4
16:21	Exod. 9:18-34; Josh. 10:11; Ezek. 38:19-22
17:1	Jer. 28:11-13; 51:13
17:2	Isa. 1:21; 23:1-17; 29:9; Jer. 2:20; 25:15-16; 51:7; Ezek. 16:33-34; 26–28; Hos. 4:11-12; Amos 1:9; Jonah 3:5-10; Nah. 3:4
17:3	Isa. 13:21; 14:23; 21:1-10; Jer. 50:12-13; Ezek. 2:2; 3:12, 14, 24; 11:1; 20; 43:5; Dan. 7:3-7, 20, 24
17:4	Jer. 2:34; 4:30; 13:27; 51:7-8; Ezek. 16:10, 22; 28:13; Hos. 4:16-17
17:5	Jer. 27:12(LXX); Dan. 2:18-19, 27-30, 47(LXX); 4:9, 30
17:6	Isa. 34:7; 49:26; Dan. 4:17, 19(LXX); 7:15-16
17:7	Dan. 2:27; 4:19 (LXX); 7:3, 23
17:8	Exod. 32:32-33; Ps. 69:28; Dan. 7:3, 10-11(LXX), 17(LXX), 21; 11:36; 12:1-2, 10
17:9	Isa. 2:2; Jer. 51:25; Ezek. 35:3; Dan. 2:35, 45; 7:3-7, 17, 23; 11:33; 12:10; Zech. 4:7
17:10	Dan. 7:3-7
17:11	Ps. 2:9; Eccl. 11:2; Dan. 7:11, 17, 21; Micah 5:5
17:12	Dan. 4:17 (LXX); 7:7-8, 19-24
17:14	Deut. 10:17; Dan. 2:47; 4:34, 37(LXX); 7:21-22
17:15	Ps. 18:16; Isa. 8:7; 17:12-13; 23:10; Jer. 46:7-9; 47:2; 51:13; Dan. 3–6
17:16	Lev. 21:9; 1 Kgs. 16:31; 18:4; 2 Kgs. 9:7, 22, 30-35; 10:9; 2 Chr. 21:11, 13; Ps. 27:2; Isa. 1:21; 16:37ff.; 23:15-18; 57:3; Jer. 2:20–4:30; 10:25; 50:8, 32; 51:6; Ezek. 16:15, 17, 28, 35, 37-41; 23:1-21, 25-29, 31-34, 44, 47; Hos. 2:2-5, 12; 4:12, 15, 18; 5:4; 9:1; Micah 1:7; 3:3; Nah. 3:4-5, 15; Micah 3:2ff.
17:17	Exod. 4:21; 7:3; 9:12; 10:1; 14:4, 8; 1 Kgs. 10:24; 2 Chr. 30:12;

Revelation	OT Allusion
	36:22-23; Ezra 1:1; 7:27; Neh. 2:12; 7:5; Jer. 32:40; Ezek. 16:37-41; 23:22, 29, 47; 38:21; Hag. 2:22; Zech. 14:13
17:18	Pss. 2:2; 89(88):27
18:1	Ezek. 40–48; 43:2
18:2	Isa. 13:21; 14:23; 21:9; 34:10-11, 13-14; Jer. 9:11; 50:39; 51:8; Dan. 4:30; Zeph. 2:14-15
18:3	Isa. 23:17; 51:17, 22; Jer. 25:15-16, 27; 51:7; Ezek. 26–28; 27:12, 33
18:4	Gen. 12:1; 19:13-15; Num. 16:26; Isa. 48:20; 52:11; Jer. 50:8; 51:6, 9, 45
18:5	Gen. 18:20-21; 19:13; Ezra 9:6; Ps. 109:14; Jer. 51:9; Hos. 9:9; Jonah 1:2
18:6	Pss. 75(74):8(9); 137(136):8; Isa. 40:2; Jer. 16:18; 50:15, 29; Lam. 4:21; Ezek. 23:31-35(LXX); Hab. 2:15-17
18:7	2 Sam. 22:28; Prov. 16:18; Isa. 47:8-9; Jer. 50:31-32
18:7-8	Isa. 47:7-9
18:8	Lev. 21:9; Isa. 47; Jer. 50:34; Ezek. 26–27
18:9	Gen. 19:28; Ps. 48:4-5(LXX); Isa. 23:17; 34:9-10; Jer. 50–51; Ezek. 26:16-17; 27:30-35
18:9-19	Ezek. 26; 27
18:10	Isa. 5:8-22; Ezek. 26:16-18; Dan. 4:30
18:11	Ezek. 27:30-36
18:12	Ezek. 27:12-13, 22
18:12-13	Ezek. 27:7-25
18:13	Ezek. 27:13
18:15	Ezek. 27:30-31, 36
18:16	Exod. 28; Jer. 4:30; Ezek. 16:13, 23; 27:7(LXX); 28:13; Amos 5:16(LXX); Hab. 2:6, 17
18:17	Isa. 23:14; Ezek. 27:26-30
18:17-19	Ezek. 27
18:18	Ezek. 27:32
18:19	Ezek. 26:19; 27:9, 30-34, 36
18:20	Deut. 32:43(LXX); 2 Kgs. 9:7; Pss. 48:4-7, 11; 96:11; Isa. 1:24; 44:23; 49:13; Jer. 51:48
18:20-24	Jer. 51:48

Revelation	OT Allusion
18:21	Isa. 41:12; Jer. 51:63ff.; Ezek. 26:21; 26–27
18:22	Isa. 24:8; Ezek. 26:13
18:22-23	Isa. 24:6, 8; Jer. 7:34; 16:9; 25:10; Ezek. 26:13
18:23	2 Kgs. 9:22; 2 Chr. 33:5-7; Isa. 23:8; 34:12; 47:9; Jer. 7:34; 16:9; 25:10; Ezek. 16; 28:5, 9; Micah 5:11-12; Nah. 3:4
18:24	Jer. 51:49; Ezek. 24:7; Nah. 3:1, 4
19:1	Pss. 58:10-11; 104:35; 105(104); 113:1; 113–118
19:2	Gen. 4:11(LXX); Num 31:2(LXX); Deut. 32:43; 1 Sam. 24:12; 2 Kgs. 9:7; Pss. 19:9; 79(78):10; 119(118):84, 137; Isa. 1:24; Jer. 51:25
19:3	Isa. 34:9-10
19:3-8	Ps. 104:35
19:4	1 Kgs. 22:19; 2 Chr. 18:18; Pss. 47(46):8; 106:48; Isa. 6:1; Ezek. 1:26-27
19:5	1 Chr. 16:36; 23:5; 2 Chr. 20:19; Pss. 22(21):23(24); 115:13; 134(133):1; 135(134):1, 20(LXX)
19:6	Exod. 15:1, 18; 1 Chr. 16:31; Pss. 22:28; 47(46):7(8)-8(9); 93(92):1; 96(95):10; 97(96):1; 99(98):1; 104:35; Isa. 52:7; 61:10; Ezek. 1:24; 43:2(LXX); Dan. 7:14; 10:6; Amos 3:13(LXX); 4:13(LXX); Zech. 14:9
19:7	Ps. 118:24
19:7-8	Gen. 3:21; 35:2; Exod. 25–37(LXX); Lev. 20:7-8; Deut. 22:23-24; 1 Chr. 16:28, 31; Pss. 45:14(13); 58:10-11; 118:24; 132:9, 16; Isa. 52:1; 54:5-8; 59:17; 61:10–62:5; Ezek. 16:8-10; 44:17; Hos. 2:14-20; Zech. 3:5-6(LXX)
19:8	Isa. 61:10
19:9	Isa. 25:6-7; 65:13-17
19:10	Exod. 35:31; Ezek. 39:29; Joel 2:28-32
19:11	Pss. 9:8(9); 72(71):2; 96(95):13; 98(97):9(LXX); Isa. 11:4; 49:23; 52:6; Ezek. 1:1; Zech. 1:8; 6:3, 6
19:12	Exod. 6; Isa. 62:2-3; 63:1-3; 65:11-18; Jer. 42:5; Ezek. 38:23;

Revelation	OT Allusion
	Dan. 2:45; 10:6, 14; 10:21–12:13; Zech. 9:9-10
19:13	Prov. 30:5; Isa. 61:10; 63:1-4; 65:17-19; Dan. 2:28-45
19:14	Ps. 2; Ezek. 9:2 Dan. 10:5; 12:6
19:15	Pss. 2:9; 45:3-5; 57(56):4; 80(79):1(2); Prov. 5:3-4; Isa. 11:4; 49:2; 63:2-6; Jer. 6:3; Lam. 1:15; Hos. 6:5; Joel 3:13; Amos 3:13(LXX); 4:13(LXX)
19:16	Gen. 24:2, 9; 47:29; Exod. 32:27; Deut. 10:17; Judg. 3:16, 21; Ps. 45:3; Isa. 63:1-6; Dan. 2:47
19:17	Lev. 26:29; 1 Sam. 17:44; 2 Kgs. 9:36; Isa. 34:6; Jer. 12:9; 46:10; Ezek. 39:4, 17-20
19:17-18	Ezek. 39:4, 17-20; Dan. 2; 4:35(LXX); 7:14; Zech. 14
19:19	Ps. 2:2, 9; Ezek. 38:2-9; 39:2; Dan. 7:21; Micah 4:11-12; Zeph. 3:8; Zech. 12:3; 14:2, 13-14
19:20	Gen. 19:24; Lev. 10:2; Num. 16:35; Pss. 21:10; 55:15; Isa. 30:33; 34:9ff.; Ezek. 38:22; Dan. 3; 7:9b-11; 12:2
19:21	Ps. 2:2, 9; Isa. 11:4; 49:2; Ezek. 38:2-8; 38:20-23; 39:2, 17-20
20:1-3	Gen. 2:16-17; 3:1, 4-5; Ps. 2:1-2, 9; Isa. 14:12; 24:21-22; 27:1; Dan. 6:17
20:1-6	Ps. 2:9; Isa. 1:26; 2:2; 11:4; 49:2; Jer. 30:24; 48:47; 49:6; Ezek. 38–39; 37–48; Dan. 2:28; 7:3, 10, 18, 22, 27; 10:14; Hos. 3:5; Zeph. 3; Zech. 12–14
20:2	Gen. 3:1; Isa. 24:21; Zech. 3:1ff.
20:4	Gen. 2:7; Exod. 19:6; Pss. 69(68):33; 119(118):175; Prov. 3:22; Isa. 22; 55:3; 61:6; Dan. 7:9-22, 26-27
20:4-6	Gen. 3; Exod. 19:6; Deut. 1:10-11; 32:30; Josh. 23:10; 1 Chr. 16:15-17; Job 9:3; 33:23; Pss. 2:2, 9; 16; 50:10; 68:17; 90:4; 142(141):5(6), 7(8); Eccl. 6:6; Isa. 7:23; 26:19-21; 30:17; 43:18-19; 60:22; 65:16-17(LXX); Ezek. 37:1-28, 36-48; Dan. 7:10, 27;12:2;

Revelation	OT Allusion
	Hos. 6:2; Amos 5:3; Hag. 2:6-9(LXX)
20:5-6	Exod. 19:6; Isa. 61:6; 65:16-17; 66:22; Zech. 6:13
20:6	Exod. 19:6; Isa. 61:6
20:8	Josh. 9:2; Judg. 7:12; 1 Sam. 13:5; Ps. 2; Ezek. 7:2; 37:9; 38:1- 2, 4, 9, 15; 38–39; Dan. 7:2; Zeph. 3; Zech. 12–14
20:9	Num. 5:1-4; 31:19; Deut. 23:14; 2 Kgs. 1:10-14; Pss. 31:21; 78(77):68; 87(86):1-3; 122:6; Isa. 66:10; Jer. 11:15; 12:7; Ezek. 38:11, 16, 22; 39:2, 6; Dan. 12:2(LXX); Hab. 1:6(LXX); Zeph. 3:14-17
20:10	Gen. 19:24; 2 Kgs. 1:10-12; Ps. 11:6; Isa. 30:33; Ezek. 38:22
20:11	Ps. 114(113):3, 7; Isa. 6:1; Dan. 7:9ff.
20:11-12	Dan. 7:9-10
20:11-15	2 Chr. 15:13; Pss. 28:4; 102:25-27; 115:13; Isa. 51:6; Jer. 16:6; Ezek. 1:26-28; Dan. 7:9-10; 12:1-2
20:12	Exod. 32:32-33; Ps. 69(68):28; Dan. 7:10; 12:1
20:12-13	Pss. 28(27):4; 62(61):12; Prov. 24:12; Isa. 59:18; Jer. 17:10
20:14	Isa. 22:14; 25:8; 65:14-18; 66:22-24; Jer. 51:57; Dan. 12:1-2
20:15	Exod. 32:32-33; Ps. 69(68):28; Isa. 4:3; 30:33; Dan. 12:1(LXX); Mal. 3:16
21:1	Gen. 8:22; Isa. 43:18-19; 51:10-11; 57:20; 65:16-18; 66:22
21:2	S. of S. 6; Isa. 52:1-10; 61:10; 62:1-5
21:3	Gen. 12:1-3; 17:2-8; 26:24; Exod. 6:7; 25:8; Lev. 26:11-12; Deut. 26:17-18; 28:1-14; 29:12-13; 2 Sam. 7:14, 24; 2 Chr. 6:18; Ps. 95:7; Isa. 8:8; 35:10; 51:11; Jer. 7:23; 11:4-5; 24:7; 30:22; 31:1, 33; 32:38; Ezek. 11:20; 34:30-31; 36:27-28; 37:23, 26-28; 43:7; 47:22-23; Hos. 2:23; Zech. 2:10-11; 8:8; 13:9
21:4	Isa. 25:8; 35:10; 43:18; 51:10-11; 65:17, 19-20; Jer. 31:16
21:5	1 Kgs. 22:19; 2 Chr. 18:18; Ps. 47(46):8; Isa. 6:1; 43:18-19;

Revelation	OT Allusion
	65:16-17; 66:22; Ezek. 1:26-27
21:6	Pss. 23; 36:8-9; Isa. 12:3; 41:4; 43:10; 44:6; 48:12; 49:10; 55:1; Jer. 2:13; Joel 3:18; Zech. 14:8
21:7	2 Sam. 7:14; Pss. 2:7-9; 89(88):26-29; Isa. 55:1-3
21:8	Gen. 19:24; Lev. 19:26-29; Deut. 18:9-11; Judg. 7:3(LXX); 2 Kgs. 9:22; Pss. 11:6; 106:36-38; Isa. 30:33; Jer. 3:7-10(LXX); Ezek. 38:22
21:9	Lev. 26:21
21:9-10	Ps. 48:2; Isa. 2:2-3; 4:1-5; 25:6–26:1; 40:9; Ezek. 2:2; 3:12, 14, 24; 11:1; 28:14, 16; 40:1-2; 43:5; Micah 4:1-2
21:10	Isa. 52:1; Ezek. 40:1-2
21:11	Lev. 26:11; Isa. 58:8; 60:1-3, 19-20; Ezek. 37:27; 43:2, 4-5; Dan. 12:3(LXX)
21:12	Exod. 28:21; Ezek. 48:30-35
21:12-13	Gen. 3:24; Isa. 26:1-2a; 62:2, 5-6, 10; Ezek. 40:5-6; 41:25; 42:15-19; 48:31-34; Zech. 2:5
21:12—22:5	Ezek. 40–48
21:14	Exod. 28:21; 39:14; 1 Chr. 24:3-19; 25:6-31; 26:17-19; Isa. 54:11-12; Ezek. 41:22; 44
21:15	Ezek. 40:3-5
21:16	Gen. 11:4; Exod. 27:1; 28:16; 30:2; 1 Kgs. 6:20; Ezek. 40:5; 41:21(LXX); 43:16-17 (LXX); 45:1-5; 48:8-13, 20(LXX); Zech. 1:16
21:16-17	Ezek. 48:16-17
21:17	Deut. 3:5; 28:52; Isa. 54:1-4, 11-13; Ezek. 40:3, 5; 42:20; 48:16, 35; Zech. 1:16; 2:2-5
21:18	Isa. 54:11-12
21:18-20	Exod. 28:2-30; 36:16; 39:8-14; 1 Kgs. 6:20-22; 7:9-10; Isa. 26:1-3; 52:1ff; 54:11-12; 62:1-5; Lam. 4:1-2; Ezek. 28:12-16; 48:35; Zech. 9:16
21:19	Isa. 54:11-12
21:21	2 Chr. 3:4-5, 8; 4:20-21; 9:15; Job 25:5; 28:19; Isa. 54:11-12; Dan. 2:32; Hab. 3:4(LXX)
21:22	Isa. 65:17; Jer. 3:16-17; Ezek. 40–43; Amos 3:13(LXX); 4:13(LXX); Hag. 2:9

Revelation	OT Allusion
21:23	Isa. 24:23; 30:26; 60:1, 19-20; Ezek. 43:2, 5; Mal. 4:2
21:23-26	Isa. 60:1-13, 19
21:24	Pss. 72(71):10; 89(88):27; Isa. 60:3, 5, 11b
21:24-26	Gen. 3:24; Ps. 72:10; Isa. 2:2, 5; 11:6-12; 49:6-8; 60:3, 5, 11-14; Zech. 14:7, 11, 14
21:25	Isa. 60:11; Zech. 14:7
21:26	Ps. 72:10-11
21:27	Exod. 32:32-33; Ps. 69(68):28; Isa. 4:3; 35:8; 52:1; Ezek. 44:9; Dan. 12:1
22:1	Gen. 2:10; Ps. 46:4; Ezek. 47:1; Joel 3:18; Zech. 14:8
22:1-2	Gen. 2:9-10; 3:22; Isa 35:4, 6-10; 41:18-20; 43:18-20; Jer. 2:13; Ezek. 36:25-27; 47:1-9, 12; Joel 3:18; Zech. 14:8
22:2	Gen. 2:9-10; 3:22, 24; 1 Kgs. 6:18, 29, 32, 35; Isa. 35:6-9; 41:17-20; 43:18-20; 51:3-6; Ezek. 36:26-35; 41:18-26; 47:8-9, 12, 17; Joel 3:18
22:3	Isa. 61:6; 65:22-23; Ezek. 44:15; Zech. 14:2, 11

Revelation	OT Allusion
22:4	Exod. 28:17-21, 36-38; 33:20; Num. 6:25-27; Job 19:25-27; Pss. 11:4-7; 17(16):15; 27:4; 42:2
22:5	Pss. 4:6; 8; 31:16; 67:1; 80:3, 7, 19; 119:135; Isa. 60:19-20; Dan. 7:18, 27; Zech. 14:7, 9
22:6	Isa. 43:18-19; 65:16-17; 66:22; Dan. 2:28-29, 45
22:7	Isa. 40:10; Dan. 2:28-29, 45
22:8	2 Kgs. 17:7-23; 2 Chr. 24:18-19; Neh. 9:26-27a
22:10	Dan. 2:28-29, 45; 8:27; 12:4, 8-9, 13
22:11	Isa. 6:9-10; 29:9-10; Jer. 44:25; Ezek. 3:27; 20:39; Dan. 12:4, 9, 10
22:12	Lev. 19:2; Job 41:11; Pss. 28(27):4; 62(61):12; Prov. 24:12; Isa. 40:9-10 (LXX), 13-14; 47:11; 59:18; 62:11; Jer. 6:26; 17:10; Dan. 2:28-29, 45; Mal. 3:1
22:13	Isa. 40:10; 44:6; 48:12
22:14	Gen. 2:9; 3:22; 49:11; Ps. 100:4; Isa. 26:2; 60; 62:10-11; 65:22(LXX); Ezek. 47:12

Revelation	OT Allusion
22:15	Gen. 3:23-24; Deut. 23:18, 19; Pss. 59:6, 14; 101:3, 7-8; Isa. 56:10-11; Jer. 8:10; Mal. 3:5
22:16	Num. 24:17; Isa. 11:1, 10; 53:2; 60:1-3; Mal. 3:1
22:17	Isa. 55:1; Zech. 14:8
22:18-19	Deut. 4:1-2; 12:32; 28:58-61; 29:19-21; Prov. 30:6; Jer. 25:13
22:19	Gen. 2:9; 3:22; Deut. 29:20; Ezek. 47:12
22:20	Mal. 3:1, 5

Notes

1. Several resources were used in compiling the list of allusions. See the appropriate pages in B.A. Aland, K. Aland, J. Karavidopoulos, et al., *The Greek New Testament,* 4th ed. (Stuttgart: United Bible Societies, 1994); *Nestle-Aland Novum Testamentum Graece,* 27th ed. (Stuttgart: United Bible Societies, 1994); and B.F. Westcott and F.J.A. Hort, *The New Testament in the Original Greek,* vol. 1, The Greek Text (Cambridge: Cambridge University Press, 1881). In a fresh translation of Revelation, P.S. Minear also included a compilation of allusions. See *I Saw a New Earth,* 300-365. Perhaps the best commentary with the most comprehensive analysis of the allusions is Beale's *The Book of Revelation.* Virtually every page of the commentary on the text of Revelation discusses John's use of the Old Testament.
2. See pp. 89-90 for discussion of this example.

APPENDIX B

A KEY TO SELECT SYMBOLS IN REVELATION

Symbols are a part of everyday life. We frequently understand and accept them, usually without even thinking about them. Some symbols picture what they represent, while others don't, or they may do so rather obscurely. If we hear on the news "The White House said today . . ." we do not picture a white building talking to us. Growing up in the United States, a citizen would know what was being communicated. But if a person from another country heard the report, the meaning could be missed, namely, "The President said today . . . " A visitor from another country, upon hearing the report, may get stuck on the symbol, instead of moving beyond the symbol to what it means. Why? Context is missing.

One who visits the book of Revelation can get bogged down as well. (The phrase "bogged down" is symbolic, isn't it?) We need to avoid making the mistake of getting stuck on the symbols and failing to move on to the true meanings. Many take the symbols literally: a literal beast; a literal battle of Armageddon; and a literal thousand-year period. Very few, however, would think of Jesus as a literal seven-horned and seven-eyed Lamb. They would know that symbols are being used and that those symbols point to a deeper reality.

Living nearly two thousand years after Revelation was written, we as Bible students are in a fortunate position. Scholars have been able to discover the meanings for almost all of the symbols in Revelation. As I suggested earlier, most have their roots in the Old Testament. For instance, we know that seven was a symbol of completeness and that a horn symbolized power and authority. Therefore, the image of a Jesus with seven horns emphasizes his complete authority (Rev. 5:6).[1] Some of the symbols may have even been influenced by first-century culture.[2] Regardless of the source, we must go beyond the symbol to what it really means. We do not have to think of Jesus as literally a Lamb or a Lion or a Bridegroom.

What about application? To make proper application we must understand the context. Perhaps a modern illustration will help. "The White House" in the 1950s symbolized Presidents Truman and Eisenhower; in the 1980s it represented Presidents Reagan and Bush. Over the decades the symbol always meant the current occupant of the White House—the U.S. President, often with his executive department as well—but its specific meaning changed as the administrations changed. It had a number of specific applications while preserving much in common with former meanings. This point was explored more fully in the chapter on symbols.

To attempt to assign an interpretation to every symbol is beyond the scope of this appendix. Furthermore, since this is a book on principles, there is much to be said for your doing a personal study of the symbols. I give here a partial list of symbols in major categories, revealing their rich and pervasive use in Revelation:

- Creatures (lion, lamb, ox, eagle, horses, scorpions, locusts, a dragon, a serpent, two beasts, a leopard, a bear, frogs, birds, cattle, sheep, and so forth);
- Pieces of furniture and household and agricultural items (thrones, lamps, lampstands, keys, altars, a censer, a sickle, a winepress, bowls, a millstone, articles made of citron wood, ivory, costly wood, bronze, iron, marble, and so forth);
- Precious minerals and jewels as well as metals (jasper, carnelian, bronze, iron, brass, copper, silver, gold, pearls, sapphire, chalcedony, emerald, sardonyx, beryl, topaz, chrysoprase, jacinth, amethyst, and so forth);

- Clothing items (robes, garments, sackcloth, fine linen, silk and scarlet cloth, crowns, and so forth);
- Parts of the human body (heads and foreheads, mouths, hands, feet, eyes, ears, and so forth);
- Food and beverages (wine, manna, bread, water, oil, wheat, barley, and so forth);
- Musical instruments (harps, flutes, trumpets, and so forth);
- Inanimate objects (sun, moon, stars, morning star, hills, islands, mountains, desert, and so forth); and
- Cities and countries (Babylon, Rome, Egypt, New Jerusalem, Sodom, and so forth).

Consulting the appendix on the Old Testament allusions is a good starting point for exploring the symbols listed above and below. When coupled with your analysis of the best commentaries, you can reach a degree of certainty in identifying what the majority of the symbols represented. For example, many Christians would see the connection of the following symbols with appropriate Old Testament passages: the tree of life, the hidden manna, the rod of iron, the temple, pillars in the temple, the morning star, the key of David, the four living creatures, the two beasts, and so forth).

Finally, the key presented below for two major categories of symbols is offered as an example of what you can discover when you follow the principles presented in this book:

1. *The Meaning of Some of the Numbers*[3]

a. Two is associated with witness or testimony (Rev. 11:1ff.) and probably derived from its use in the Old Testament (Deut. 17:6; 19:15; Zech. 4:2-3, 11-14).

b. Three is often associated with the divine (God, Christ, and the Holy Spirit in Rev. 1:4ff.) or even unholy forces (the dragon and the two beasts as a gang of three in Revelation 12–13; the three plagues of fire in 9:18; or the three unclean spirits like frogs in 16:13). Three and a half years; 1260 days; time, times, and half a time; and forty-two months are associated with a period of calamity and suffering on the part of God's people and probably have their roots in Daniel 7:25 (see also Rev. 11:2-3, 9, 11; 12:6ff.; 13:5).

c. Four emphasizes totality and possibly derives from the image of the four points of a compass (Rev. 4:6, 7, 8, 9; 5:8, 11, 14; 6:1, 3, 5, 6, 7; 7:1, 11; 9:14; and so forth). The number is even represented in the description "from every tribe and language and people and nation" (Rev. 5:9).

d. Ten and multiples of ten (1,000 and thousands and thousands) are found, often in association with evil (2:10; 12:3; 17:3, 12, 16; 20:1ff.). The reference to the saints reigning 1,000 years is the one place where the number is used in connection with Christ and his people (Rev. 20:4f.). Thousands and thousands of angels worship Christ (Rev. 5:11). Perhaps the symbolism of the number goes back to the Old Testament in such passages as the ten plagues in Exodus 7–12, the ten commandments in Exodus 20, and so forth.

e. Twelve and its multiples (24 and 12,000) are linked with God and the people of God on earth (Rev. 4:4 [perhaps the 24 elders are representatives of the chosen people under both the old and the new covenants]; 7:1ff.; 12:1; 21:12, 14, 20, 21; see also James 1:1). It is well known from the Gospels (the twelve apostles, Matt. 10:1ff.; 19:28), as well as the Old Testament (the twelve tribes, Gen. 35:22; 49:28; Exod. 24:4; 39:14; Josh. 4:1-9). Essentially, twelve and its multiples are the number for the people of God.

f. The number 666 in Revelation 13:18 has received considerable attention. Some see a reference to a specific emperor (e.g., Nero or Domitian), while others see the number in contrast with seven, falling one short of completeness. Perhaps the threefold six emphasizes how completely evil the beast is. What matters is not the precise identification but the ability of Christians to discern evil, no matter what form it takes.

2. *The Meaning of Some of the Colors.*

a. White usually refers to purity (Rev. 1:14; 2:17; 3:4-5; 6:11; 7:9, 13; 14:14; 19:14), but sometimes it is a parody of purity (6:2).

b. Black signals judgment, distress, or disaster (Rev. 6:5, 12).

c. Red reminds the reader of violence, doom, and blood (Rev. 6:4; 8:7, 8; 9:17; 11:6; 12:3; see also 1:5; 5:9; 6:10, 12; 7:14; 8:7, 8; 11:6; 12:11; 14:20; 16:3, 4, 6; 17:6; 18:24; 19:2, 13 for references to blood).

d. Green (or pale) is associated with death (6:8).

e. Purple and scarlet are associated with the splendor of evil in all its debauchery (Rev. 17:3-4; 18:12, 16).

Notes

1. Beale observes about the use of Daniel 7: "In Rev. 5:6 ironic parody is used in the portrayal of the Messiah in his defeat of the enemy by means of the imagery of Daniel 7, where it is used of the beast's defeat of the saints." See *The Book of Revelation,* 354.

2. See Hemer, *The Letters to the Seven Churches of Asia in Their Local Setting,* for examples.

3. See p. 109 for a discussion of the number seven.

APPENDIX C

RECOMMENDED COMMENTARIES

What are the best commentaries for specific books of the Bible? This is one of the questions I am most frequently asked as a seminary professor. For commentaries that focus primarily on how Revelation would have been understood by the first-century recipients, I recommend the following categories. The first level lists works that are helpful for those without knowledge of the biblical languages. The second level includes works that require little if any such language awareness, but are more advanced with regard to discussion of major exegetical issues. The third level requires knowledge of the biblical languages.

Level One:

Gregg, S., ed. *Revelation: Four Views, A Parallel Commentary.* Nashville: Thomas Nelson, 1997.

Hendriksen, W. *More Than Conquerors: An Interpretation of the Book of Revelation*. Grand Rapids: Baker, 1939.

Hicks, P. *Revelation: Crossway Bible Guide*. Leicester, England: Crossway Books, 2004.

Wilcock, M. *The Message of Revelation.* The Bible Speaks Today. Downers Grove, IL: InterVarsity, 1975.

Level Two:

Beasley-Murray, G.R. *The Book of Revelation,* rev. ed. The New Century Bible. Greenwood, SC: Attic Press, 1978.

Caird, G.B. *The Revelation of St. John*. Black's New Testament Commentary. Peabody, MA: Hendrickson, 1966.

Keener, C.S. *Revelation*. The NIV Application Commentary. Grand Rapids: Zondervan, 2000.

Koester, C.R. *Revelation and the End of All Things*. Grand Rapids: Eerdmans, 2001.

Mounce, R.H. *The Book of Revelation*, rev. ed. New International Commentary on the New Testament. Grand Rapids: Eerdmans, 1998.

Level Three:

Aune, D.E. *Revelation*. 3 vols. Word Biblical Commentary. Dallas: Word, 1997–1999.

Beale, G.K. *The Book of Revelation*. The New International Greek Testament Commentary. Grand Rapids: Eerdmans, 1999.

Beckwith, I.T. *The Apocalypse of John*. Grand Rapids: Baker, 1979.

Witherington III, B. *Revelation*. The New Cambridge Bible Commentary. Cambridge: Cambridge University Press, 2003.

Swete, H.B. *The Apocalypse of St. John*. Grand Rapids: Eerdmans, 1908.

GLOSSARY OF TERMS

1. **Allusions** – An allusion is an indirect reference without a formal, direct quotation. *Revelation has numerous Old Testament allusions, but there are no formal quotations from the Old Testament.*
2. **Antagonist** – The antagonist is the principle adversary or opponent of the principle hero or good character in a narrative. The hero is called the protagonist. *While God is the protagonist in Revelation, Satan is the antagonist.*
3. **Antitype** – An antitype is a person, event, or thing that is prefigured or foreshadowed by an earlier similar person, event, or thing. Often a New Testament reality is prefigured by an Old Testament counterpart reality, called the "type." *The Old Testament plagues inflicted on Egypt are the type; the similarly described seven bowls of God's wrath (Rev. 16:1ff.) are the antitype.*
4. **Apocalypse** – The term "apocalypse" is often used to refer directly to the book of Revelation, whose opening word in the original Greek text is *apokalypsis*, which means "revelation" or "disclosure." It may also refer to literature of the apocalyptic genre, defined below. *The Apocalypse was written by the apostle John in an apocalyptic style.*
5. **Apocalyptic** – Apocalyptic is a specific type or genre of literature, popular from 200 B.C. to A.D. 200, which is characterized by fantastic visions, otherworldly messengers, and overt reliance on symbolic/metaphoric language. Apocalyptic was used with the intention of encouraging and exhorting the reading audience in the present, by "revealing" otherworldly truths and giving glimpses of a promised future deliverance from evil,

which some have linked to instilling hope and perseverance in light of present dangers and/or oppressions. *Both Daniel and Revelation use the apocalyptic genre to reveal God's message of encouragement and exhortation to their audiences.*

6. **Beatitudes** – While "beatitude" is commonly used to designate the opening sayings of Jesus in the Sermon on the Mount ("Blessed is . . ."), it can simply refer to the pronouncement of a promised blessing found in any given text. John delivered a beatitude when he wrote, *"Blessed are those who hear it [this prophecy] and take to heart what is written in it"* (Rev. 1:3).

7. **Canon** – Canon, originally meaning "measuring rod" or "standard," refers to the group of books that are accepted as the authoritative Word of God, commonly referred to as the Holy Scripture, or Bible. They are the inspired standard for belief and behavior. For Christians this is the sixty-six books of the Old and New Testaments (with Catholics adding books of the Apocrypha). Judaism recognizes only the Old Testament books. *By adopting Revelation as part of the canon of Scripture, the early fathers of our faith witnessed to its authoritative and inspired status.*

8. **Canonical Exegesis** – Canonical exegesis studies how a biblical passage or book fits into its entire biblical or canonical context. *We are practicing canonical exegesis when we discover that Revelation's emphasis on living faithfully now in these last days puts it squarely in the context of New Testament teaching.*

9. **Chiasm** – A chiasm is a literary device, popular in ancient writings, in which ideas were presented and then restated in reverse order (A-B-C-B´-A´). The middle element(s) of a chiastic structure is often the one the author is most emphasizing. *An example of a chiasm from Revelation 2–3 follows: (A) Jesus chides the church at Ephesus for diminishing commitment, (B) Jesus encourages Smyrna, (C) Jesus roundly criticizes three churches for idolatry and immorality, (B´) Jesus encourages Philadelphia, (A´) Jesus chides Laodicea for diminishing commitment. Note similarities in (A) and (A´), (B) and (B´).*

10. **Concordance** – A concordance lists in alphabetical order words of a given Bible version with their location and context.

There are three kinds of concordances: exhaustive, complete, and analytical. An exhaustive concordance lists all words in a given translation, giving under each word its occurrences in context, except for words like articles ("the"), conjunctions ("and"), and so forth. A complete concordance lists all words in a given translation, giving under each word representative (and for some words, all) occurrences in context. An analytical concordance goes further by grouping word occurrences under the original language source word (Hebrew, Aramaic, and Greek), showing one or more ways the original-language word is translated in that version. Lately, publishers have blurred some of these distinctions by adding original language material to exhaustive concordances, to aid the reader. *Looking in a concordance, we are able to examine all occurrences of the word "door" in Revelation.*

11. **Critic** — A critic is one who analyzes, evaluates, and expresses informed opinions and judgments on a matter. In the context of biblical studies, the critic examines Scripture using the best principles and methods, so that God's voice is clearly heard. *When critics probe the date, purpose, audience, and even the grammar of Revelation, they develop a clearer perspective on the author's intended meaning.*

12. **Doxology** — A doxology is a form of praise offered to God in the context of worship. It is commonly indicated in Scripture by its concluding "Amen." *The doxology in Rev 1:4-8 offers praise and also introduces some of Revelation's themes: the work of God, Christ, and Holy Spirit; living as priests in the kingdom between Jesus' first and final comings; and Christ's ultimate triumph.*

13. **Epistle/Epistolary** — The word "epistle" simply means "letter," referring to the correspondence between an author and his selected audience. Epistolary refers to a specific literary genre characterized by having the form of a letter. *Revelation's classification as an epistle is supported by its introductory greeting (1:4-6), its closing (22:21), and its messages expressly for the seven churches (chs. 2–3).*

14. **Eschatology** — Eschatology means literally the study of last things, coming from the Greek word *eschatos*, meaning "last."

The term, which does not appear in the Bible, is used by Christian theologians to mean beliefs about the closing events of world history: final cataclysmic events, death, resurrection, God's intervention in history with Christ's return, Final Judgment, triumph of good over evil, mankind's destiny—punishment or reward, new heaven and earth or hell, afterlife in a totally new order. Notwithstanding theologians' future emphasis, eschatology has really more to do with Jesus Christ, who is the First and the Last (Rev. 1:17) and with our Christian living and hope in what are already the last days, the days between Christ's first and final comings. *The book of Revelation reshapes our notions of eschatology by exhorting and encouraging Christians to live responsible hope-filled lives between Christ's first and final comings.*

15. **Exegesis** — Exegesis literally means "to lead out" or "to draw out." Accordingly, exegesis is the science and art of drawing out the meaning of a text, with the purpose of understanding and explaining the original author's intended meaning. The means employed include word study, grammar study, form and structure, the historical and biblical contexts, and so forth. *Exegesis of the book of Revelation must include studying various symbols in their original contexts.*

16. **Foretelling** — Foretelling is predicting or telling beforehand (events, situations, and so forth). When applied to prophecy, it stresses the predictive nature of prophecy as opposed to the forth-telling aspect (see below). *Rather than focusing on Revelation as a guide to foretelling, or predicting, the future, we should see it as a guide for proper Christian living between Christ's first and final comings.*

17. **Forth-telling** — Forth-telling stresses the prophet's goal to set forth the Word and will of God. It focuses on God's Word and will for the audience in the present, more so than the future. However, forth-telling may be emphasized by foretelling good or bad consequences of current choices. *John's emphasis in Revelation is forth-telling God's Word and will for His people; Christian character, conduct, and call to witness are highlighted again and again.*

18. **Genre** — Genre is the kind, form, or style of a class of literary works. The Bible has numerous genres: narrative, law, history, poetry, wisdom, prophecy, gospel, epistle, apocalypse, and so forth. Genres communicate in unique ways and must be interpreted with principles appropriate to each genre. *Unlike historical narrative, the apocalypse genre is characterized by fantastic visions, revelations, otherworldly messengers, symbolic language, and both exhortation and encouragement.*

19. **Hermeneutics** — Hermeneutics is the science and art of understanding and interpreting Scripture. It refers to the principles followed in order to interpret correctly what a given text meant to the original recipients so that we may know what it means for us today. Hermeneutical principles include, among others: interpret Scripture with Scripture; interpret obscure texts by clear ones; and interpret in light of the original historical, cultural, and literary contexts. *Among the sound hermeneutical principles we must employ to correctly interpret Revelation is seeing it on its own terms. We do this by studying six key elements: 1. Scriptural Stage (scriptural contexts), 2. Storied Setting (historical-cultural context), 3. Style, 4. Sources, 5. Symbolism, and 6. Structure.*

20. **Historical Setting** — The historical setting is the time period, culture, situation, atmosphere, customs, lifestyle, and general living of both the biblical author and his audience. The interpretive task attempts to reconstruct as closely as possible the historical setting to better understand the author's original intent and meaning. *The historical setting for Revelation's first Christian audiences included Roman Empire domination and Jewish oppression.*

21. **Imperial Cult** — The imperial cult was the worship phenomenon in which Roman emperors were exalted as gods. Emperor worship expressed itself in temples to emperors, sacrifices to the emperors, and addressing emperors as a god. Christians who refused such emperor worship were persecuted and even killed. *Revelation's message to Christians who were being asked to participate in the idolatry of the Roman imperial cult was to be faithful and persevere because God would ultimately triumph.*

22. **Inclusio** – An inclusio is a literary device, also called bracketing or framing, which occurs when similar key concepts are found at both the beginning and end of a unit of Scripture. The key concepts stand like bookends around the text. The purpose of an inclusio is to reinforce the importance of the repeated material. *The calls to obedience and faithfulness, found at the beginning and end of the book of Revelation, form an inclusio.*

23. **Libretto** – A libretto is "the text of a work (such as an opera) for the musical theater" (*Merriam-Webster's*, 11th ed.). It can also refer to sacred musical works. *Handel composed "The Messiah" using a libretto containing rich scriptural passages about Jesus.*

24. **Literal** – The word "literal" is derived from the Latin word "littera" which means "letter." When the literal interpretation of a text is demanded, then, the natural meaning of a passage is to be interpreted according to the rules of grammar, speech, context, and the genre of the writing. In common usage we use "literal" for a word's normal, straightforward meaning, as opposed to a symbolic or figurative meaning. *When studying Revelation, which is filled with symbolism, we need to discover whether to interpret something in a literal or a symbolic way.*

25. **Metaphor** – A metaphor is a symbolic, direct comparison or representation that identifies one subject with another, thereby implicitly associating the attributes as well. *Rev. 1:20 identifies a metaphor used earlier: "the seven lampstands are the seven churches."*

26. **Millennial** – Millennial refers to a thousand years. The term is often used in reference to the thousand-year reign of Christ (millennium) mentioned in Revelation 20:4. Theologians interpret this variously: Christ will return before the millennium (premillennialists); Christ will return after the millennium (postmillennialists); and, in a symbolic interpretation of the millennium, Christians are reigning with Christ now, either on earth or in heaven (amillennialists). *Sincere Christians hold differing views of the millennial kingdom.*

27. **LXX.** See Septuagint.

28. **Muse** – In the world of the arts, a muse is "a source of inspiration . . . a guiding genius," deriving from Greek mythology where muses presided over the arts (*Merriam-Webster's,* 11th ed.). *When John wrote Revelation his inspiration was no ordinary muse; he was inspired by the God of heaven.*

29. **Nonliteral** – Nonliteral refers to a symbolic or figurative meaning for a specific term or phrase. *Revelation 12:3 uses the nonliteral, symbolic imagery of a red dragon to refer to the devil, interpreted plainly in Revelation 12:9.*

30. **Parallelism** – Parallelism is a literary device, especially prevalent in Hebrew poetry, where successive lines have a thematic correspondence, by actual repetition, similarity, contrast, or expansion. The correspondence may be in words, phrases, symbols, and so forth, in order to emphasize the particular aspect being paralleled. Chiasm is a specialized form of parallelism. *Parallelism is evident in the opposing lines of Proverbs 10:1 – "A wise son brings joy to his father, / but a foolish son grief to his mother."*

31. **Parody** – A parody is a literary device which uses feeble or ridiculous imitation to emphasize a comparison or to ridicule that which is being compared. *The beast out of the sea in Revelation 13:1ff. is a parody of the Lamb; he has horns, heads, crowns, a fatal wound that was healed, universal authority, and he is worshiped.*

32. **Parousia** – The word parousia literally means "coming," "arrival," or "presence," and is often used by theologians to refer to the final coming of Christ. *The parousia of Christ will mark the time of the Final Judgment.*

33. **Pentateuch** – The Pentateuch is the first five books of the Old Testament (Genesis, Exodus, Leviticus, Numbers, and Deuteronomy). *In the Pentateuch there is repetition in the two accounts of creation (Genesis 1–3) and the two accounts of giving the Ten Commandments (Exod. 20 and Deut. 5).*

34. **Prophecy/Prophetic** – Prophecy is proclamation, or forthtelling the Word and will of God, coupled with a command to obey. Prophecy's focus, then, is not primarily on predicting the

future, but on obedience to God's Word and will in the present. "Prophetic" refers to the literary genre that consists of prophecy. *Like Old Testament prophetic books, Revelation contains prophecy, delivered by a prophet, proclaiming God's Word and will for His people, with calls to obedience.*

35. **Protology** – The word protology refers to the study of the "first things" or the origins. Oftentimes, this is associated with God's primary purposes for all of humanity. *Just as Revelation informs eschatology (study of last things), so the opening chapters of Genesis inform protology (study of first things).*

36. **Recapitulation** – Recapitulation, is repetition with intentional progression. It is a strategy of describing the same events in different ways and with ever-increasing intensity. *The triad of the seven seals, seven trumpets, and seven bowls in Revelation is an example of recapitulation, showing progressive intensification.*

37. **Recitatives** – A recitative is a narrative song that describes some action, thought, or emotion. *My compact disk of Handel's Scripture-based "Messiah" includes a total of fifty-three recitatives.*

38. **Repetition** – The word "repetition" refers to the recurrence, or repeating, of a word, a phrase, a main clause, a sentence, or even an entire section with the intent of reiterating, and/or bringing attention to, an important point or idea. *Repetition is found in Revelation chapters 2–3 when Jesus addresses the seven churches with the same formula: "To the angel of the church in . . ."*

39. **Rhapsody** – Rhapsody is commonly used as a musical term to refer to an instrumental composition in which a composer yields to his imagination in regard to form and organization of the composition. Rhapsody is characterized by free, improvisatory instrumentation and dramatic mood changes. *Revelation bears resemblance to a rhapsody with its imaginative form, evocative scenes, and dramatic mood shifts.*

40. **Septuagint** – The Septuagint is a Greek translation of the Hebrew Bible (our Old Testament), completed by Greek-speaking Jews in Alexandria, Egypt, from the third to the second century B.C. It is often abbreviated "LXX" since one tradition held that there were seventy translators. *Some of Revelation's*

Old Testament allusions appear closer to the Septuagint wording than the Hebrew Bible wording.

41. **Simile** – A simile is a literary device in which two dissimilar things are compared using the words "like" and/or "as" in order to communicate a deeper meaning. *Revelation uses simile in 1:14 when it says that Jesus' "eyes were like blazing fire."*

42. **Storied Setting** – The word "storied" is used in the sense of having an interesting history, and the story of John and the disciples at the end of the first century is just that, interesting. Therefore, the storied setting refers to the interesting history behind the text which deals with its atmosphere, environment, culture, and so forth. *To better understand what Revelation may have meant to its first hearers, we need to look at the storied setting of the book.*

43. **Symbols/Symbolism** – A symbol is a literary device characterized by one thing representing another. The symbol both points beyond itself and participates in what it symbolizes. Symbolism refers to the collection or system of symbols used. Symbols are commonly used to communicate abstract ideas in concrete ways. *Revelation's symbols represent spiritual realities; thus the double-edged sword in Jesus' mouth (Rev. 1:16) represents power and truth, not an actual sword in his mouth.*

44. **Synoptic** – The word "synoptic" means "to have a common view" or "taking a similar or same point of view." *The Synoptic Gospels of Matthew, Mark, and Luke present much of the same material from the life of Jesus."*

45. **Synoptic Gospels** – The Synoptic Gospels are the first three books of the New Testament, the Gospels of Matthew, Mark, and Luke. They are referred to as the Synoptic Gospels due to similar information or principal parts within their accounts, a makeup that differs widely from John's Gospel. *The Synoptic Gospels were written before John's Gospel.*

46. **Type** – A type is a person, event, or thing that prefigures or foreshadows a later similar person, event, or thing. Often an Old Testament reality prefigures a New Testament counterpart reality, called the "antitype." *Destruction of Old Testament*

Babylon, which seduced and opposed God's people, is the type; Revelation's predicted destruction of New Testament Babylon (Rome and the like), which seduces and opposes God's people, is the antitype.

47. **Typology** — In biblical studies, typology is a method of interpretation that connects events, persons, or things in one text (usually in the Old Testament) to similar counterparts in a later text (usually in the New Testament) through strong parallelism, similar to a foreshadowing and the culmination of the foreshadowing. Typology is expressed through the past reality (type) and the new reality (antitype). *The Exodus affords an example of typology: The Old Testament Exodus – deliverance from Egypt's earthly powers – is the type; Revelation's depicted final Exodus – deliverance from all of Satan's powers – is the antitype.*

BIBLIOGRAPHY OF WORKS CITED

Aland, B.A., K. Aland, J. Karavidopoulos, et al. *The Greek New Testament*, 4th ed. Stuttgart: United Bible Societies, 1994.

________. *Nestle-Aland Novum Testamentum Graece*, 27th ed. Stuttgart: United Bible Societies, 1994.

Aune, D.E. "St. John's Portrait of the Church in the Apocalypse." *The Evangelical Quarterly* 38 (1966): 131-149.

Beale, G.K. *The Book of Revelation*. The New International Greek Testament Commentary. Grand Rapids: Eerdmans, 1999.

Beasley-Murray, G.R. *The Book of Revelation*, rev. ed. The New Century Bible. Greenwood, SC: The Attic Press, 1978.

Bell, J.S., and S. Campbell. *The Complete Idiot's Guide to the Book of Revelation*. New York: Alpha, 2001.

Blevins, J.L. *Revelation as Drama*. Nashville: Broadman Press, 1984.

Block, D.I. *The Book of Ezekiel*. The New International Commentary on the Old Testament. Grand Rapids: Eerdmans, 1997.

Boxall, I. *Revelation: Vision and Insight*. London: SPCK, 2002.

Bruce, F.F. *New Testament History*. Grand Rapids: Eerdmans, 1969.

________. *Peter, Stephen, James, and John*. Grand Rapids: Eerdmans, 1979.

Caird, G.B. *The Revelation of St. John*. Black's New Testament Commentary. Peabody, MA: Hendrickson, 1966.

Card, Michael. *Unveiled Hope*. Franklin, TN: Word Entertainment, 1997.

Chesterton, G.K. *Orthodoxy*. New York: Lane, 1908.

________. *Varied Types*. New York: Dodd, Mead, 1908.

Coleman, R. *Singing with the Angels*. Grand Rapids: Baker, 1998.

Conyer, A.J. *The Eclipse of Heaven*. Downers Grove, IL: InterVarsity, 1992.

Cullmann, Oscar. *Christ in Time*. Trans. by F.V. Filson. Philadelphia: Westminster, 1950.

________. *Salvation in History*. Trans. by S.G. Sowers. New York: Herder & Herder, 1967.

DeMoss, M.S. *Pocket Dictionary for the Study of New Testament Greek*. Downers Grove, IL: InterVarsity, 2001.

Di Lella, A.A. *The Book of Daniel*. The Anchor Bible. Garden City, NY: Doubleday, 1978.

Doty, W.G. *Letters in Primitive Christianity*. Guides to Biblical Scholarship. Philadelphia: Fortress Press, 1973.

Eco, U. *The Name of the Rose*. Trans. by W. Weaver. San Diego: Harcourt, 1994.

Ellis, P.F. "*Inclusio*, Chiasm, and the Division of the Fourth Gospel." *St. Vladimir's Theological Quarterly* 43 (1999): 269-309.

Fee, G.D. *Listening to the Spirit in the Text*. Grand Rapids: Eerdmans, 2000.

Fee, G.D., and D. Stuart. *How to Read the Bible for All Its Worth*, 3rd ed. Grand Rapids: Zondervan, 2003.

Frend, W.C. *Martyrdom and Persecution in the Early Church: A Study of a Conflict from the Maccabees to Donatus*. New York: Anchor Books, 1967.

Friesen, S.J. *Imperial Cults and the Apocalypse of John*. Oxford: Oxford University Press, 2001.

Goldingay, J.E. *Daniel*. Word Biblical Commentary. Dallas: Word Books, 1989.

Goodrick, E.W., and J.R. Kohlenberger, ed. *The Strongest NIV Exhaustive Concordance*. Grand Rapids: Zondervan, 2004.

Grant, R.M. "The Martyrdom of Polycarp." In *The Apostolic Writings: A New Translation and Commentary*, 6 vols. Camden, NJ: Thomas Nelson, 1967.

Gregg, S., ed. *Revelation: Four Views, A Parallel Commentary*. Nashville: Thomas Nelson, 1997.

Greidanus, Sidney. *The Modern Preacher and the Ancient Text: Interpreting and Preaching Biblical Literature*. Grand Rapids: Eerdmans, 1988.

Guthrie, D. *New Testament Introduction*, 4th ed. Downers Grove, IL: InterVarsity, 1990.

Hemer, Colin. *The Letters to the Seven Churches of Asia in Their Local Setting*. Grand Rapids: Eerdmans, 2001.

Hendriksen, William. *More Than Conquerors: An Interpretation of the Book of Revelation*. Grand Rapids: Baker, 1939.

Johnson, B.D. "The Disciple Who Follows: An *Inclusio* of John 1 and 21," Unpublished paper delivered at the Midwest Regional Evangelical Theological Society 49th Annual Meeting, Lincoln, Illinois, 19 March 2004.

Johnson, J.W. *The Books of the American Negro Spirituals*. Cambridge, MA: De Capo Press, 2002.

Käsemann, Ernst. *Jesus Means Freedom*. Trans. by F. Clarke. Philadelphia: Fortress Press, 1970.

Koester, C.R. *Revelation and the End of All Things*. Grand Rapids: Eerdmans, 2001.

König, A. *The Eclipse of Christ in Eschatology: Toward a Christ-Centered Approach*. Grand Rapids: Eerdmans, 1989.

Kyle, R. *The Last Days Are Here Again: A History of the End Times*. Grand Rapids: Baker, 1998.

Lewis, D.J. *3 Crucial Questions about the Last Days*. Grand Rapids: Baker, 1998.

Lewis, N., and M. Reinhold, eds. *Roman Civilization Sourcebook II: The Empire*. New York: Harper & Row, 1955.

Lightfoot, J.B. *The Apostolic Fathers*. London: Macmillan, 1890.

Lilje, Hanns. *The Last Book of the Bible*, 4th ed. Trans. by O. Wyon. Philadelphia: Muhlenberg Press, 1957.

Lowery, R. "Christmas on Patmos." *The Christian Standard* (19 December 2004): 14-15.

________. "Study Notes on Revelation." *The Quest Study Bible*, fully rev. Grand Rapids: Zondervan, 2003.

Martin, R.P. *Worship in the Early Church*. Grand Rapids: Eerdmans, 1974.

Metzger, Bruce. *Breaking the Code: Understanding the Book of Revelation*. Nashville: Abingdon, 1993.

Minear, P.S. *I Saw a New Earth: An Introduction to the Visions of the Apocalypse*. Washington, DC: Corpus Books, 1968.

Moffatt, J. "The Revelation of St. John the Divine." In *The Expositor's Greek Testament*, vol. 5. Grand Rapids: Eerdmans, 1951.

Morris, L. *The Revelation of St. John*. Tyndale New Testament Commentaries. Grand Rapids: Eerdmans, 1969.

Mounce, R.H. *The Book of Revelation*, rev. ed. New International Commentary on the New Testament. Grand Rapids: Eerdmans, 1998.

Niles, D.T. *As Seeing the Invisible: A Study of the Book of Revelation*. New York: Harper and Brothers, 1961.

The Oxford English Dictionary, Vol. III. Oxford: Clarendon Press, 1933.

Page, T.E., et al., eds. *Suetonius*. Loeb Classical Library, vol. 2. Trans. by J.C. Rolfe.

Peterson, Eugene. *Reversed Thunder: The Revelation of John and the Praying Imagination*. San Francisco: Harper & Row, 1988.

Phillips, J.B. *The Book of Revelation: A New Translation of the Apocalypse*. London: Geoffrey Bles, 1957.

Ramsay, W. *The Letters to the Seven Churches of Asia*. London: Hodder and Stoughton, 1904.

Rossetti, C.G. *The Face of the Deep: A Devotional Commentary on the Apocalypse*. New York: E. & J.B. Young & Co., 1895.

Rossing, B.R. *The Rapture Exposed: The Message of Hope in the Book of Revelation*. Boulder, CO: Westview Press, 2004.

Rowley, H.H. *The Relevance of Apocalyptic*. Greenwood, SC: Attic Press, 1980.

Russell, D.S. *The Method and Message of Jewish Apocalyptic*. Philadelphia: Westminster, 1964.

Ryken, L., ed. *Dictionary of Biblical Imagery*. Downers Grove, IL: InterVarsity, 1998.

Ryrie, C.C. *The Ryrie Study Bible: The New American Standard Bible Translation*. Chicago: Moody Press, 1976.

Sandy, D.B. *Plowshares and Pruning Hooks: Rethinking the Language of Biblical Prophecy and Apocalyptic*. Downers Grove, IL: InterVarsity, 2002.

Sandy, D.B., and R.L. Giese, Jr. *Cracking Old Testament Codes: A Guide to Interpreting the Literary Genres of the Old Testament*. Nashville: Broadman & Holman, 1995.

Scofield, C.I. *The Scofield Reference Bible*. New York: Oxford University Press, 1945.

Scott, E.F. *The Book of Revelation*. New York: Charles Scribner's Sons, 1940.

Smith, G.V. *The Prophets as Preachers: An Introduction to the Hebrew Prophets*. Nashville: Broadman and Holman, 1994.

Smith, S., and M. Card. *Unveiled Hope: Eternal Encouragement from the Book of Revelation*. Nashville: Thomas Nelson, 1997.

Stibbe, M.W.G. *John's Gospel*. London and New York: Routledge Press, 1994.

Stott, J.R.W. *What Christ Thinks of the Church*. Wheaton, IL: Harold Shaw, 1990.

Strom, M. *The Symphony of Scripture*. Downers Grove, IL: InterVarsity, 2001.

Sweet, J.P.M. *Revelation*, rev. ed. TPI New Testament Commentaries. Philadelphia: Trinity Press International, 1990.

Swete, H.B. *The Apocalypse of St. John*. Grand Rapids: Eerdmans, 1908.

Theissen, G. *The Shadow of the Galilean: The Quest of the Historical Jesus in Narrative Form*. Trans. by J. Bowden. Philadelphia: Fortress Press, 1987.

Walvoord, J. *The Revelation of Jesus Christ*. Chicago: Moody, 1966.

Weber, T.P. *On the Road to Armageddon: How Evangelicals Become Israel's Best Friend*. Grand Rapids: Baker Academic, 2004.

Weinrich, W.C., ed. *Revelation*. New Testament XII. Ancient Christian Commentary on Scripture. Downers Grove, IL: InterVarsity, 2005.

Westcott, B.F., and F.J.A. Hort. *The New Testament in the Original Greek*, vol. 1. The Greek Text. Cambridge: Cambridge University Press, 1881.

Westermann, C. *Basic Forms of Prophetic Speech*. Trans. by H. White. Louisville, KY: John Knox/Westminster, 1991.

Wevers, J.W. *Ezekiel*. The New Century Bible Commentary. Grand Rapids: Eerdmans, 1982.

Wilcock, M. *The Message of Revelation*. The Bible Speaks Today. Downers Grove, IL: InterVarsity, 1975.

Wilson, D. *Armageddon Now*. Grand Rapids: Baker, 1977.

Witherington III, B. *Revelation*. The New Cambridge Bible Commentary. Cambridge: Cambridge University Press, 2003.